the memory collector

the memory collector

by DOC GREENE

with an introduction by
BOB CONSIDINE

DOUBLEDAY & COMPANY, INC.

GARDEN CITY, NEW YORK 1970

for my mother-in-law
VIRGINIA ELLEN HALLETT

Introduction

Doc Greene of the Detroit *News* and the book world was my
friend. I realize that's not enough of a recommendation to transfix
the reader of his assorted recollections and his thought-provoking
outlook on man, woman, and their respective follies. But that's the
best thing I can say about him. Friends are tough to come by. The
older you live the fewer you have, and in the reflective quiet of the
night you realize you didn't have many to start with, really.

Doc's best friend, I suppose, was his father. I have an indelible
memory of the two of them—both nationally known sportswriters
by that time—having what seemed to the rest of us a wonderfully
confidential talk in the clutter and cacophony of the baseball writers' free-load suite at an otherwise forgotten World Series. It must
have been a year or two before Sam Greene died. He must have
died happy, knowing that the son he loved so much had finally
gotten over the nonsense of not wanting to work in the same town
with the old man. I miss Sam Greene. He had a lot of Grantland
Rice in him. He'd take a stranger in the Navin Field or Briggs Sta-
dium press box, introduce him around to the likes of, say, H. G.
Salsinger, the local Pope of baseball writers, and make him feel
that he was One of the Boys. That's a great joy for a newcomer.
I'm glad Sam left a pup around. Doc, that is.

Doc was a lucky bum in many ways. Take his newspaper
training: He has better bloodlines than the winner of the last Kentucky Derby. His grandfather enriched Virginia journalism by
founding papers in Staunton, Stewart, and Clifton Forge, where
Doc went to work as a printer's devil at thirteen or fourteen.

These papers were planted in the course of a running argument with Doc's grandmother, who believed that it was wicked and probably punishable by law to live anywhere other than Richmond. Her husband wanted to live and die in Texas. He didn't make it.

But his boy Sam, who begot Doc, made good in Detroit. Most sons would have been happy to fall into a soft spot under the wing of his father. Not Doc. When he was old enough, if he was, he went to work for Hearst's Chicago paper, whatever it was called at the time. He worked for two of the most remarkable characters that never played *Front Page* on stage. They played it only in the City Room. Their names were Walter Howey and Ray Helgesen. Helgesen was the most romantic figure I've ever known in the newspaper business: long, lean, alternately sympathetic and mean as hell, ready at all times to leap for the jugular vein of a circulation-building story. Howey was a more complex soul. He held many jobs under the benign tolerance of W. R. Hearst, and usually had something going on the side. For example, he invented a hearing aid which would retail for fifty cents. It was a button that fitted into the ear of the victim of deafness. A wire extended from the button to the lapel of the victim's coat, where it was fastened by a hook.

"That's a fraud," a friend told Howey. "You'll get locked up if you put that on the market. It's not a hearing aid."

Walter was offended.

"Of course it's a hearing aid," he said indignantly. "When somebody sees somebody else wearing it, he'll talk louder."

In time, Doc made good his escape from that wonderful world and wound up in Detroit, of all places. The year was 1956. The only reason he made his move was something he heard a guy say in the press box during a game between the White Sox and the Tigers. The guy was introducing the great Sam Greene to somebody. The way he did it was, "You know Doc Greene's father, don't you?"

That did it.

Doc stayed with the Detroit *News* from then on. He was to the *News* what Herb Caen is to the San Francisco *Chronicle*, let's say, or Dan Parker was to the New York *Mirror*, or Bill Cunningham was to the Boston *Post* and later the *Herald*. Not many newsmen command a following of that devotion.

Doc was lucky in other ways. He had Marilyn, for example. She was Miss Florida one year, and Florida never had it better. They were introduced by George Preston Marshall, the owner of the Washington Redskins, at Maxim's—the one in Miami, not Paris. They were married on the island of Elba, the *real* Elba, by the mayor of Pimobino. Doc's only memory of the occasion was that the mayor wore a sash.

I got Doc in trouble during his honeymoon in Rome during the 1960 Olympics. He had been resisting his beautiful wife's suggestions that they visit St. Peter's. Doc said something like, "To hell with it," which upset his bride, a product of St. Mary's Convent, Miami.

But then, after a talk I had with him at the Games, he repented. Yes, he said to his wife, he would go to the Basilica. And he did. As they approached the great Bernini altar, Doc took a sharp left turn through a door marked "Treasury" in several languages. He led his bewildered beauty through several splendid suites until he came upon a salon which features a gold bust. Then he turned right, then right again, and led the dear girl into a saloon.

Alas, I, a Papal Knight, had given him the instructions.

"She forgave the Church, forgave you, but never forgave me," he once wrote me.

Doc was a thin one. He never had a weight problem. The Japanese arranged that. They shot him up pretty badly when he and some other guys were taking Okinawa. Nobody quite knows how many of them Doc shot up. But the Navy had enough information to award him the Navy Cross, a couple of Purple Hearts and a Presidential Unit Citation. He was shipped home on a hospital scow named the *Relief*.

It seemed appropriate, both for Doc and the enemy.

Anyway, here's Doc. Don't eat an apple while reading this book. Nobody in his right senses would want to keep the Doc away.

BOB CONSIDINE

1. memory

I am a memory collector.

This is to distinguish me from a numismatist, a philatelist, an art collector or other such baggage that people seem to want to collect. I knew a guy once who collected matchboxes and he had one from some saloon in Chicago with the inscription A. Capone on it. It was very valuable to him and he mistakenly loaned it to me, thinking I might find it in my heart to say something about it or *him* subsequently which I never did. Although when my cigarettes needed lighting I used up all the matches in the packet and then tossed away the empty folder.

He never quite forgave me for it and since then no one can press any part of a collection of anything upon me except memories.

I have left three record collections with various friends in one part of the world or another rather than encumber myself with them. And occasionally when I wish I had a record of Fats Waller's record of the Duke Ellington tune, "Ring Dem Bells," or Pee Wee Russell's "Clarinet Marmalade," or Anita O'Day's "Let Me Off Uptown" with Roy Eldridge blowing the horn, or Jimmie Lunceford's "Margie," I am saddened.

On the other hand I would have been hump-backed by now.

Like what I mean is that one morning at the Masters Golf Tournament in Augusta, Georgia, I wandered out to the first tee where Dr. Cary Middlecoff, then in his heyday, was preparing to tee off.

He accepted his no. 1 wood from his caddie and politely asked his name, since they were about to spend four days together.

"Poe," answered the youngster. "P-O-E."

Middlecoff teed up his ball and stepped back to take a practice swing. "You're not any relation to that famous writer, Edgar Allan Poe, are you?"

"Suh, ah is Edgar Allan Poe," he replied with some dignity.

Cary flubbed his tee shot.

See what I mean.

I am not just one of your run of the mill, fly-by-night memory collectors. To me a memory must have some pith to it.

Another happened to me not long after I made my first trip to Vietnam to cover the war. I ran into a youngster in Tan-Son-Hut Airport one afternoon where we were both waiting for planes.

He told me about where he was stationed, a little artillery base down in the Mekong Delta where he was shipping over for another six months. Six was then a normal tour of duty there but he liked it.

He went quite a ways toward explaining how the war was working over there, which was useful to know.

His name was Nathaniel Armstrong and he was from Hyde Park, a suburb of Chicago.

The name of the place where he was stationed was Cha La, which I have never heard of before or since. It had two 155 mm. howitzers in an enclosure about fifty yards around. There was a wall about eight feet high surrounding the two guns, whose function it was to fire ground support for any infantry units moving in that area.

There was a garrison of three Americans, a captain and two staff sergeants at the post and mainly what they did was play a South Vietnamese bridge game called *cati*.

One day they ran out of beer, than which nothing more calamitous can happen to an outpost.

The captain mulled this over for an afternoon and then radioed up the river to Cam Au, their chief supply depot, and asked them to send some beer down river to the camp.

The message was received and the order filled and dispatched.

Down the river it came, was met by the Viet Cong inspector, who duly authorized its delivery, after which it was delivered to the camp and life resumed normalcy.

It was no more than a couple of months later that they encountered a serious shortage . . . fuel oil. So the captain radioed up again asking for a fifty-gallon drum of oil so that his refrigerators, or reefers as they are called out there, would not cease to operate and their canned food would be chilled and their fresh food left unspoiled.

The same thing happened to this request, it was promptly filled and dispatched but this time when it reached the Viet Cong inspector, duty was levied again, and so overcome was the inspector by the munificence of the load, that he issued a receipt for it.

"One fifty-gallon drum . . . fuel oil, accepted and passed through Viet Cong post number 11."

He signed it with a flourish.

The fifty-gallon drum was eventually received at the base and the captain dourly examined the receipt for a few minutes after which he had it framed and placed over his desk.

I can think honestly of nothing that so thoroughly explained to me what was going on in the war.

Or then there was a fellow named Mark who made his living, as you will see, somewhat precariously, by selling things to museums.

On this particular day, he walked into the Metropolitan Art Museum in New York and rather shyly approached the clerk at the desk.

"Yes," said the clerk, somewhat aloofly.

"Well," said Mark, extracting a bit of lace from his pocket. "I have here a bit of Queen Victoria's wedding train. And you people being in the museum business, it occurred to me that you might be interested in purchasing it."

Just as aloofly, the clerk inspected the scrap of cloth and finally announced, "Well, young fellow," he said patronizingly. "You'll have to wait a few moments while I go and get Mr. Witherspoon, our curator, who must verify the authenticity of the Queen's train before we could possibly make any decision about the purchase thereof."

"Okay," said Mark.

He settled himself on a bench and waited.

Pretty soon a roly-poly little guy with tufts of hair sprouting out around the sides of his head came bobbing down the stairs.

Mark rose to meet him.

"This really is an authentic piece of the Queen's wedding train. I'd ask you how you happened to come by it. But it doesn't really have any consequence to me. You see we have an entire bolt of the Queen's train upstairs in the vault so obviously we are not interested in this fragment."

Somewhat dejected, Mark departed.

Two or three weeks later he returned.

He was greeted equally superciliously by the clerk, who wondered what the object of his visit was this time.

Then Mark extracted a piece of wood from his pocket.

"I have here a piece of Noah's Ark and you people being in the museum business I thought I might interest you in the purchase of the same."

"Oh," replied the clerk. "Noah's Ark, eh."

He examined the piece and then said:

"Well, same as last time, I'm going to have to go and get Mr. Witherspoon again to verify the authenticity of your piece of wood."

So Mark ensconced himself on the bench again until in just a few minutes Mr. Witherspoon came again and examined the wood.

"This is remarkable that twice you have been here and both of your samples are thoroughly authentic. However, I have a cord of wood from the Ark and so naturally we wouldn't be interested in buying this splinter, which is I believe a stern piece."

Further dejected, Mark left again.

This time he was gone six weeks before he finally returned again.

This time his manner was different, he had a lilt to his walk and a little skip in it as he walked across the room to the clerk.

Before the clerk could say anything, he reached in his pocket and said grandly, "I have here, my young friend, in my possession, one of King Tut's balls. I know you'll be interested in buying it and before you trouble to go upstairs and get Witherspoon again, here's the other one."

This takes me back to the summer of 1946, when I showed up in Chicago, to work for the *Herald-American*. I had a job in Detroit on the Hearst paper there but in one of those summit meetings they were always having out in San Simeon, Hearst was still with us in those days, Bill Anderman of the *Times* took to bragging about how he had two young sports writers who were so brilliant that they couldn't be contained.

He got to bragging so much that eventually Bob Wylie took up the matter with the old man and demanded to know, since they were all working for the same organization, why he didn't have one or two gifted men from Detroit. So with the chief presiding it was decided that Anderman would send me or E. A. Batchelor, Jr., to Chicago.

Promptly upon his return to Detroit.

So I journeyed to Chicago after we compared notes. Batchelor was married and I wasn't. I wanted to go, since I was just beginning to learn that changing jobs was one way you could get raises in this ridiculous profession so for $100 per week I left.

I discovered happily, and on dull days, unhappily, that my assignment was to write about anything, as long as it had to do with sports.

Also the word was passed down from Bob Wylie that my copy was not to be touched. It took me about six months to live that down with the rest of the staff.

Anyway, on the first day I went to work on the *Herald-American*, I wrote my piece, submitted it to the hostile but unprotected desk and went across the street to a saloon called the Press Row.

There I encountered a man named Charles O'Shaughessy, an assistant city editor, and a fellow named John L. Sullivan who looked like a caricature of Clark Gable, complete with moustache.

A few drinks later it turned out we were able to rent a hansom cab complete with a horse named Dimples and a driver named Cuthbert, and we took off for the near north side with the final stop designed for the Chez Paree at which one Joe E. Lewis was performing.

He told about checking in that morning at a new and wondrous hotel called the Welcome Arms . . . on a clear day you can see the dresser. I looked at the room clerk and he looked at me as if I had no money. I looked at him as if I did. My room had not only indirect but intermittent lighting from the neon sign across the way.

He was wonderful and after the last show was over he began to gravitate toward the tables where there was whiskey left. We not only had whiskey at our table, to which he was welcome, but champagne as well.

"I'll just take a little whiskey," he said. "No point in mixing my drinks at this stage of my life."

We thereafter descended to the hansom cab, which had the top down on it since we had been picking up various entertainers and itinerants during our foray around Rush Street.

We'd collected many people on this pilgrimage in the cab, and now with the show over we halted at the Singapore to collect chicken and ribs and then we were off in the dawn to awaken Bushman, a very prominent citizen gorilla of the community.

When he died a few years later the *Tribune* ran a banner: BUSHMAN DEAD. Nothing else was necessary.

Bushman lived in a zoo on the lakefront and it was the first time I'd ever heard the remark, "doesn't everybody" which is the story of Joe E.'s life . . . the pilfered line.

His answer has always been:

"Forget it. I'll think of another one."

It was a year ago that we walked out of Bernard Shor's restaurant in New York and he gave the doorman a dollar not to get him a cab, "because I need both the air and the exercise."

Always there's the fear when you haven't seen Joe for a while that he won't be fresh again.

It's a foolish fear.

He did a parody on "Strangers in the Night."

> "Stranger in the night,
> What do they talk about,
> The Dempsey-Firpo fight."

To the point that when you examine an old friend you look for the tarnish . . . to see how young he's remained.

He's had a stroke now and doesn't locomote as well as he did. It's put him out of the night club business.

But watch him the next time you can . . . on TV.

He still toddles.

Sometimes, you pick them up with just a tiny bit of eavesdropping, forgivable sometimes in a newspaper guy.

Like this day when a marriage was in the process of breaking up at the next table.

It was in one of those restaurants where the tables are located for the owner's convenience rather than the customer's, so you can't help but overhear.

The guy was impeccably tailored and distinguished, the girl was handsome . . . fortyish for him . . . thirtyish for her. He had a highball in front of him and she, one of those sticky looking things in a stemmed glass.

"I've used you up," he was saying. "That's all of it really. I don't mean that you're used up for somebody else. Just for me, you're used up. It happens to people all the time."

"What do you mean?" she said grimly. "You've got another girl."

He shrugged and laughed in resignation.

"No. That's the way you want it. Black and white. Something dramatic. Something you can get sore about. I'm trying to be open so you'll understand and not get sore. We've used each other up."

The girl twisted the glass by the stem, drawing a damp circle in the table cloth.

"Maybe if you came home more . . ." she said.

"That's one of the things right there," he answered. "I don't want to come home now. There was a time when I was eager to get home, eager to meet you, looked forward to the time I would be through with work and I would see you. I'd think about what I would say and what you would say, and now I don't think about you at all.

"It's the way that it is. Think back at all the friends you've . . . I've . . . we've used up in our lifetimes. Remember the friends you had in high school. How'd the joke go. 'Who's your new best friend?' You use them up. You look forward to being with them for a while. You party together and enjoy one another and then gradually it all wears out. Nobody's fault."

"A marriage is supposed to be different," she said. "That's what marriage is. Something that doesn't wear out. You've got yourself another girl. I didn't think you would. I thought you were different."

He shook his head again slowly.

"You've got it all wrong. Look at the Fishers. We used to see them all the time. We'd go away weekends together. Back and forth to each other's houses for dinner. Golf. Movies together. How often do we see one another now?"

"We don't."

"That's what I mean. We used them up. Or they used us up or we both did. I'm not mad at Harry. You're not mad at Gladys. Nothing happened. We just wore it out. That's what happened to us."

The waiter came and brought new drinks and dumped the ashtrays and took away the tired glasses.

"What precisely do you want, Dick? A divorce? Is that it?"

He waited a moment and then said:

"Ugly word, isn't it? Divorce. Yes. That's the only way. We're both young enough to discover somebody else.

"I remember how it used to be with me . . . Every day when I got up I went out as if something wonderful were going to befall me on that day. Not corny. I don't mean big things. I just mean that every day when I went out I waited for some fun to happen. Now I don't. And I never think about you all day long and then I come home."

"Maybe," she said, "if we'd had children."

"Maybe. Maybe. But we didn't. I don't even know why we didn't."

"Why couldn't we try for some now. It might help things."

"I don't think you can use kids as cement for a marriage. A kid ought to be more than a piece of mortar."

She gulped her drink all the way down.

"You're not kidding me any. It's that Mary Downing. She's had her eye on you for a long time."

"Look, you're wrong. It's not a question of somebody else."

She signaled for another drink.

"Don't give me that. I've seen her. The other night at Lafferty's she couldn't keep her hands off you. I'm going to call her up and straighten her out."

"Cripes. That'd be all we'd need. Look there's nobody. No Mary Downing . . . especially not Mary Downing. I'm trying to say we've just used each other up. I'm working out all the financial arrangements so everything will be all right. It's just over. That's all. Look

at most of the married people we know. Numb. Dead and numb
and bored."

She gulped her new drink, murmured "excuse me" and departed to the ladies' room with its telephone. She was gone a long
time. When she returned her face was flushed.

"I told that Mary Downing off . . . that creep. Boy didn't I
ever let her have it."

The guy groaned.

"You didn't. You really didn't. Say you didn't."

"She tried to deny it. Then she started to laugh. Boy, did I ever
tell her off. I told her I was going to call her boss. That sure shut
her up. Waiter, bring me another drink."

The guy shut his eyes as if to blot it all out and shook his head
as if in great pain.

"What's the matter with you?" she demanded.

"Nothing," he said. "I've just never been so ashamed."

"You shouldn't have fooled around with her."

"I didn't. Now I've got to go in the office and see her and Ralph
. . . her 'boss' as you call him. I've never been so embarrassed or
so ashamed."

She seemed to sober a moment.

"Honey," she said, speaking like a child, "I'm sure if we try we
can put us all back together again."

He looked at her as if she were an object.

"I'm sure we never can," he said and got up and walked out,
handing a bill to the waiter.

After a while the girl began to cry.

I once ran into a guy named Elmer Finucan, who was staying
at the Racquet Club in Florida, and had a story to tell about split-
ting his upper plate and the trouble he was having locating a
dentist.

He began by telling how he went first to Dr. Uriah Sliplait's
office, having selected the name at random from the phone book.

He presented his upper plate, which was now in two parts and
inquired politely on what precisely Dr. Sliplait could do about it
and how much, if he pleased, would he charge for it.

"What you need is a new plate. I can make one up for you in
no time. And I'll charge you $50."

Well, now Finucan was no great expert on dental prices but $50 seemed awfully cheap to him and he was suspicious.

"Doctor, that sounds a little cheap to me. How do I know this plate you propose manufacturing for me will be any good. Begging your pardon, sir?"

Dr. Sliplait riled up a little at this.

"Look. I've been a dentist for thirty years and during that time I've never had any complaints from my customers. As a matter of fact I keep a file on all my patients. Won't you take a name from my file and call up one of my customers and listen to what he tells you. Here's a list of patients I've made plates for."

Elmer considered this notion for a moment.

Then he selected a card—Mr. Ivan Flipfarb—and dialed Union 7-6777.

"Mr. Flipfarb," he addressed the "hello" on the line, and receiving a "yes." "I'm over at Dr. Sliplait's office and you had some teeth made by him a couple of years ago and I'm interested in the kind of work he does. Could you tell me . . ."

The voice interrupted promptly.

"Let me tell you about it. I'm a great baseball fan. I'm a Tiger fan mainly and have been for years. I'd about given up on us after 1967. Wasn't last year great though? But never mind that you want to know about the teeth."

"Yes," said Finucan. "I want to know about the teeth."

"Well, last fall, I was working very hard and I couldn't get there until the seventh game. You remember the one . . . when Mickey Lolich beat the Cards for the championship in St. Louis . . . well, I got there for that game. I finally managed to dig up a ticket in the bleachers from a bellhop at the Chase Hotel."

"About the teeth," murmured Finucan gently.

"Right, about the teeth," continued Flipfarb. "Well, you remember how in the eighth inning, Mike Shannon came up for the Cards and hit a home run off Lolich, right into those bleachers in left field. Those were the bleachers I was in, all surrounded by mad St. Louisans.

"There I was rooting for the Tigers and all wedged in between those St. Louisans and I'm rooting for the Tigers and Shannon gets hold of that Lolich pitch and whammo. And there I am wedged in to the point where I can't move and here comes that line drive heading for me. I can't move, you understand and here comes that ball . . ."

"It hit you in the teeth," burst out Finucan.

"No," said Flipfarb, "in the belly and it's the first time in two years my teeth didn't hurt."

2. christmas

The day Wally decided to propose to the prostitute he came over to an apartment I was occupying at what was then the Salle de Tuscan Fencing School on East Jefferson.

"I know how much affection and respect you have for Shirley and I've got a funny idea I want to discuss. Funny like odd," he said.

"Have you asked her yet?"

"No," he said, "and that's what I wanted to talk about. I'm worried that she'll be afraid of it because of her background, maybe even afraid I don't have character enough. You know how she is."

He was walking up and down and eating cigarettes. This is a Christmas story and all of it began on Christmas Day of 1954. It was because of a peculiar set of circumstances that I happened to be present at one of the "lonely" parties that Shirley used to give on that day, when they met.

If you're alone in a city on Christmas, this can be the very edge of emptiness. I've spent it in a diner. The restaurants are all closed and the night clubs have folded. If you have a family you're with it, grateful, and unconcerned about the out of town or single people who have no place to go after the office party.

Shirley combatted the problem simply.

She gave a party, had given one every year for two or three at that time, for the people who had no families around. Judging from the one I attended, when Wally's and her romance began, they were as good as bread.

The girls collaborated on the dinner and the fellows paid for the booze. Presents costing less than $5 were in order although flowers and things general like that were permitted as extras, things sort of for everybody. She had an apartment out on Second Boulevard.

The only qualification that was necessary was that you had no one to be with on Christmas Day.

I qualified because it was the year 1954 and my father was West at the Michigan State-UCLA Rose Bowl game and my mother had taken advantage of his absence to drive out to see her mother in New Mexico. I was aware of the party through my friendship for Shirley and some of the regulars who went to it every year. One year I'd sent a copy of H. L. Mencken's A Christmas Story for reading—as in Dickens' A Christmas Carol—aloud for the holiday.

This is the one in which a benevolent cynic gives a party for skid row in Baltimore, the purpose being to have a wing-ding of a brawl where the unfortunates were not required to repent and pray and such to earn it. At the very end, they repent, confess and pray anyway, voluntarily. If you haven't read it, you should.

"What I thought I'd do," said Wally, "is to make up a background for myself that I'll tell her in the proposal. I'm going to tell her I've been in jail and I want her to know and forgive me. It may sound silly but I want her to have something she's going to have to accept about me, too. Does this make any sense?"

"I wouldn't presume to advise you," I replied. "I suppose there is such a thing as a white lie and I guess that's what you mean it to be. Personally, I've never seen falsehood be particularly useful to anybody but then I can be wrong without startling anybody. You obviously are in love. You must have some notion how she feels. Why complicate it?"

"I've thought about that," he said. "And naturally I know her a lot better than you. She's got a kind of pride-shame. She was married when she was fifteen and it didn't work and she ended up with a son, Jerry, who's six now. She's got him away in boarding school. Did you know that?"

"No. I'm not much of a prier into other people's affairs. She's smart and she's nice and asks no quarter and I admire her. She reads a lot and we've exchanged books a few times, that's all. When I met her she was a waitress and somewhere she changed her mind. I guess it was because of the kid, now that you bring that into the open. Money."

Mainly he just wanted to talk about it. Like most people who seek advice, he didn't really want it. The only other thing I remember about the afternoon is asking a question of which I remain ashamed.

"Are you sure you're just not trying to be noble?" I asked him. "If there's one thing I can't stand it's pseudo-nobility."

I knew immediately by his expression that I shouldn't have asked it, and apologized.

Anyway, he proposed and he told the lie with it and subsequently they were married. It's all fresh now because I recently met them in a downtown saloon. They were wearing happiness that made you warm all over.

Jerry is sixteen now and is coming home from military school for the holidays. They've got two of their own, a boy seven and a girl eight and the pictures show them handsome and strong. They bought ski things for the kids. The family plans to spend the winter learning it.

One thing, when Shirley left for a moment I had a chance to ask: "Did she ever find out you were lying about that jail term?"

Wally laughed and ordered another highball.

"You would remember. About a year and a half after we were married, I decided I didn't even want a white lie between us and I started to tell her but I never got to do it."

"Why not?"

"She interrupted me," he said. "She told me that she knew all along it wasn't true. But she said not to explain anything about it. Her eyes were glistening I remember and she looked at me and her exact words were:

"You were lying and it was the nicest thing anybody ever did for me in my whole life."

When Richard Burton first began to be impressed on this consciousness, it was because of what was then apparently an affair with Elizabeth Taylor. At least that's what it sounded like in the public prints.

This was not the sort of thing that would tend to make you regard a man loftily. Prudery has nothing to do with this attitude.

Richard had merely placed himself among a rather large number of people who had had truck with Elizabeth.

He was placing himself with Mike Todd, Nicky Hilton, Michael Wilding, and Eddie Fisher, a singer who almost made me physically ill several times through his rendition of some sentimental guff called "Oh Mein Papa."

Seeing him on this basis is not exactly like having a man introduced to you as, say "Ponsonby, here. He was with the Coldstream Guards at Dunkirk," or "W. C. Handy. He wrote 'St. Louis Blues,'" or "Byron White, Supreme Court Justice."

See what I mean?

He was achieving distinction in a rather nondistinguished fraternity.

But impressed upon this consciousness he was. Since then I have become aware of his great talent, first observing him in odd bits and pieces of motion pictures and finally when he portrayed Hamlet.

Although a disparity in our ages precluded my seeing John Barrymore at this chore, I did manage to witness Leslie Howard, Walter Hampden, John Gielgud, and Maurice Evans at it so I was not like Toots Shor, who after the second act with Evans, remarked: "I'll bet I'm the only one here who doesn't know how it comes out."

Actors, like bullfighters, live only in the memory of those who have seen them and Burton was—going away—the finest.

I had stupidly formed a hasty conclusion about him, dismissing him lightly. I lay this on my profession, which ladled up a personal life to the public appetite to a nauseating degree but then that's the sort of profession it can be. I knew a picture caption writer, who, every time he saw a picture of the late Aly Khan with a new girl, tried to write "Aly Khan and Alley Cat" under it, a prank that never got by his editors.

Then Burton wrote a book.

I'd heard somewhere that Burton had remarked that he'd rather be a writer than an actor and I discovered it's not a question of rather being, Burton is.

It is a brief book published by William Morrow and Company and it is called A Christmas Story. It is written autobiographically, although of its literalness I cannot vouch, through the eyes of an eight year old boy in a Welsh mining town of the sort Richard Burton comes from.

It begins:

"There were not many white Christmases in our part of Wales in my childhood—perhaps only one or two—but Christmas cards and Dickens and Dylan Thomas and wishful memory have turned them all into white.

"I don't know why there should have been so few in such a cold wet land—the nearness of the sea, perhaps. The Atlantic, by way of the Bristol Channel, endlessly harried us with gale and tempest.

"Perhaps our winds were too wild and salty for the snow to get a grip. Perhaps they blew the snow over us to the Black Mountains and Snowdonia and England."

Burton's little boy remembers a Christmas Eve when his sister, who has been mother to him since the death of his true one, is having a child and he is taken away from the house by his uncle, "Mad Dan," while the birth takes place.

He has a childish fear that—he doesn't know what he will receive from Santa—his gift will be Tommy Elliot's farm which has been Tommy's toy for two years.

He fears it will be refurbished and passed along to him.

"It would be shameful to have a secondhand present. Everybody would know."

Mad Dan takes him to the meeting ground of their part of the village, where he stands around the fire listening to his uncle rant and to the talk of the other miners. Uneasy because he is not at home awaiting Santa, he demands to go home.

"Can I go home, Mad Dan?"

"Shut your bloody trap and listen," he said, "or I'll have you apprenticed to a haberdasher."

He sets to wondering about why his aunts are at the house and a lady named Mrs. Tabor T.B. who had eight children die of tuberculosis in their teens.

Suddenly he knows his sister is dying.

His phrase is, "I dimly guessed what time in mist confounds."

He is kept there by the fire.

"The crag-faced miners sang with astonishing sweetness a song about a little engine.

> "Crawshaw Bailey had an engine;
> It was full of mighty power.
> He was pull a little lever;
> It was go five miles an hour."

Eventually the word comes: "Nine pounds a wench."

His present is "A furious, red-faced, bald, wrinkled old woman, sixty minutes old."

The little boy's conclusion is: "Well, at least, it isn't Tommy Elliot's farm."

He wrote it with tenderness and restraint and makes you remember it's a Child's birthday we're celebrating.

This is as close as Christmas will get to a nod from me.

However, there was a time a few years back when I had an apartment in the Lafayette Plaisance on the fifteenth floor and I was able to partially express my real feelings about the Yuletide.

The girl I live with and I plotted it out just before I had to duck to New York on something and she accomplished it while I was gone.

I flew in at about eight in the evening and she met me at the plane in a high degree of excitement, "It's done, it's done," she gasped at me. "The sign is up."

"How does it look?"

"Just great. I had an awful time with it but I got some of the girls to help me. I bought some spotlights to put behind it. I painted the windows solid around the letters that I drew on first. So what you have is an inverse silhouette."

"I'll drive down Lafayette when we go home. I've got it lit up now so, well, you'll see when we get there."

With the expressways, it's about twenty-five minutes from the airport. I could hardly wait.

As we drove up Lafayette, there it was, fifteen floors up: the two words emblazoned across the 40 foot long windows of our apartment.

It read *BAH! HUMBUG!*

Cars were slowing down as people noticed it.

"There was an accident last night. A car ran into another parked car," she said. "It's great to watch from the apartment . . . the way the buses slow down and everything. You'll just love it."

I found it so engrossing to watch the reactions of the vehicles on the road that I stayed up until 5 A.M. nursing my scotch and soda and feeling very much like the King of the Hill.

The next day trouble began.

The manager of the apartment called and inquired:

"What are you trying to pull?" he said.

"Whaddaya mean? Trying to pull? What?"

"Look I want to tell you that sign has got to come down," he stated flatly.

"What's the matter with it. It's my Christmas message!"

"Don't give me that. That sign is an insult to everybody. What do you think of the people in this apartment that have kids. How do you think that makes them feel?"

"Frankly I haven't given that a nickel's worth of thought. How does it make them feel?"

"They don't like it. That's what."

Seeing that we were getting nowhere, I told him:

"Look that's my Christmas decoration. Has anybody asked me how I feel about all those windows with Christmas trees in them, and scenes of the Nativity and all that? No. They haven't. Let me volunteer the information that 'Every time I see an artificial Christmas tree, I up and shed a plastic tear.' I'll take down my message when the other people take down theirs. That's a deal I'll make with you. Let everybody clean up their windows of all this Yule nonsense and I'll clean mine."

"You. You're crazy," he screamed into the phone.

"Name calling will get us nowhere," I answered as politely as possible and then gently put the phone on its cradle.

Within five minutes he was back on the phone. I could feel him holding his breath over the phone.

"Look. I've found you in violation of your lease."

"Just a minute till I find my copy."

I keep tax papers, leases, and canceled checks all in a pile in my desk, so there was no trouble with the hunt.

I got back on the phone.

"What paragraph are you talking about?" I asked.

"Paragraph 13 where it forbids you to put up any advertising in your window."

"What the hell am I advertising? Pizza? Chop suey? What?"

By now I was beginning to thoroughly enjoy the man's discomfiture. Man what a success I was having with two little pilfered words from Charles Dickens.

I finally told him that the sign had two weeks until Christmas, after which I would take it down.

I hung up on him again.

He didn't phone back, at least, for a couple of days.

That night the parade started. It lasted until after Christmas and it consisted of a number of people, most of them taken in drink, who would stand outside the apartment and count up the floors to No. 15, set the apartment location in their minds and then up in the elevator they came.

Most of them were relatively reasonable, after they'd gotten off a few pithy remarks like "What do you think you're doing?"

I would explain what it was I didn't care for about Christmas. About this same time a man in Birmingham, Michigan, put up a dollar sign on his lawn to commemorate the holidays.

I never found out how he fared.

But I did explain about the Thanksgiving Parade and how it bored me, how the music on all the radios turned me off, "Do you remember any longer whether you ever liked 'White Christmas' or not?" I'd inquire. Then I'd get into the bills. That girl insists on buying Christmas cards in May. The way they run . . . they're from some fancy place in Chicago. A nice old lady sells them to us each year. Besides going for anywhere from seventy-five cents to a dollar, they were now, with postage rates going up all the time, getting so it cost a quarter to mail the damned things.

All right, so whose fault is that? Mine, okay. And I suppose that my honoring of my wife's charge accounts at Bergdorf Goodman, Bonwit Teller, Henri Bendel, Tiffany's and all the rest of it is my fault, too. But one thing that isn't my fault is all the mewling and puking that goes on at this time each year, if you'll pardon the Shakespearean phrase "mewling and puking."

Then one night, a guy came to the door and when I opened it whammo, he belted me on the chin. It was a sucker punch but a dandy.

I later remarked to that girl, "Maybe we've had the decoration up long enough. This business of all these do-gooders is getting about enough."

But mostly it was fun.

It took about five years before I came up with another beautiful idea. We had subsequently moved from the apartment into a one story town house on Chateaufort Place and though we had picture windows on both sides of the house, you wouldn't get any range with a sign.

It was along about the fifteenth of December when Christmas is usually really getting to grind me that I produced this idea.

I rigged four spotlights on each corner of my roof, pointing toward its center where I erected a gallows from which I hung an effigy of Santa Claus.

I always claimed great credit when the trouble started with my neighbors that I hadn't made it a trio and hung Jesus and Mary along with Santa.

The night that someone threw a rock through the living room window it wasn't very funny either. And though I armed myself with my duck gun and some rock salt shells, I could never find the heaver of that brick.

He was sneaky, the creep, not outspoken and open as I had been with my decorations.

Right after that broken window, my wife got me a record by Kenny Burrell entitled "Have Yourself A Soulful Little Christmas" which had a jazz version of all the Christmas carols on it.

So I would sit and listen to "Away in a Manger," "Silent Night" and such in a manner in which they were barely recognizable.

It was, all in all, the best Christmas I ever had.

3. the dead

Walt Disney decided once to make a motion picture based on leprechauns.

The fact that his father Elias was of Irish-Canadian extraction probably didn't have anything to do with it. It was an obvious notion for an imagination that flowed the Disney vein.

It was shortly after World War II that Disney went to Ireland, to browse the country, get the feel of his people and their feel about leprechauns.

Snow White had appeared in 1937 and become an international classic. Walt Disney had become a legend of his own before that.

He held what amounted to a rendezvous with his old friends of the Abbey Theatre in Dublin, with Sean O'Casey, Paul Vincent Carroll and those, and after a few days they urged him to go to Galway on the Irish Sea where he would find the real Irish.

Here then was the Ireland of the leprechaun.

"You'll find Irishmen down there that speak nothing but Gaelic. You should take an interpreter. Spend some time with the Gaels. Many of them really believe in leprechauns and you'll come away understanding more. Watch the sun go down on the bay."

This was his advice.

The first thing that happened to Disney in Galway was that no one knew who he was, outside the Galway Hotel, where the management had been prompted. The car he hired for the trip over was being driven back by a native, who not only didn't know him but didn't know him after it was explained who he was.

As any visitor there can testify, there is no place where a stranger can exist less.

The only advice he got was at the hotel where they warned him to beware that the tinkers didn't set upon him and rob him, the way he was dressed and all. The tinker, as you know, is an Irish gypsy, with no great reputation at honesty.

The way the *Irish Digest* reported the story afterward, Mr. Disney wandered about Galway for three or four days, hanging about the pubs and probably not since he was going broke back in Missouri with his pen and a borrowed camera, had he encountered such a frost.

Not only was he a stranger, and not noticeably Irish, at that with his tailored clothes but he wanted to discuss leprechauns, no less.

Shurr, and the divil take 'im!

But he was in pocket at the pubs and after a day, he was able to purchase a few rounds. He was accepted thus far. And then one elderly white-haired granddaddy, pin whiskers and all, and an eternal thirst adopted him and followed him from pub to pub.

By the time he was ready to leave, the old man had come to be a nuisance. He smoked his pipe and nodded and agreed with whatever Disney wanted to discuss, and kept drinking his pints.

The day before he left, he finally confronted the old man.

"Please join me in another pint," he offered with a trace of sarcasm.

The old man agreed again and then Disney said:

"Tell me something, old man. Do you believe in leprechauns?"

The old man was somewhat abashed at this direct approach but allowed that he did.

"Well, have you, you personally ever had any dealings with a leprechaun?"

The old man fussed and finished his pint and had another, but never really answered.

In the *Digest* story it was carefully pointed out that the old man wouldn't lie.

A freeloader perhaps, but a liar never.

Finally Disney laid it to him cold.

"Look, what I want to know . . . yes or no . . . did you ever actually see a leprechaun?"

The old man could see the source dwindling away. He coughed and scuffed and ordered another, perhaps the last, but he wouldn't lie.

"Did you? Did you ever see one?"

"Well," said the old man slowly and confidentially. "No. But I've seen their tracks."

So Disney returned to Dublin.

It was some time later in New York and Disney was accepting another award for one of his films, a nature film if I recall and an editor friend had an invitation to a subsequent cocktail party and could take a friend.

He knew Disney, of course, and on the way over there was a wonder here whether there was any truth to the story or not.

There was some.

"I remember seeing that piece in the *Digest* and it wasn't quite as unfriendly as all that," said Disney. "And there was this old man who said, "No. But I've seen their tracks."

"The same thing has happened to me lots of times in the desert, in Lapland once. And every time it ever happened to me I thought it was good for me. It's a good thing to remember that you basically always remain a nobody . . . not really important."

When he died a couple years ago in a Burbank hospital of cancer, it reminded me of what we've known for so long. That Walt Disney was important . . . to all people everywhere.

Some of his friends had begun a campaign to nominate him for a Nobel Peace Prize.

Is it possible, posthumously?

But then, his work is the prize.

It was during the theatrical season of 1939–40 and Robert E. Sherwood had written a play called *There Shall Be No Night* which concerned itself with Russia's invasion of Finland and its effects on a prominent Finnish scientist and his family and thereby the world.

Alfred Lunt and Lynn Fontanne were cast as the doctor and his wife and Montgomery Clift played the role of their son Eric, who against the family wishes, goes off to fight in the Mannerheim Line midway through the second act.

The critics gave up kudoes to the cast and to Mr. Sherwood

although to the latter with some reservations, since the play was accused of having most of its success due to the timeliness of the work, rather than any basic dramatic quality.

Timely it certainly was.

Americans, particularly war age Americans, could suddenly see themselves in the same position as these Finns. There had been Czechoslovakia and Poland and it was apparent that the world was being caught up.

In the scene when Eric shows up at the family home to bid his farewells to unaccepting and disapproving parents, he uttered a final line . . . he has been unable to explain his point of view . . . so he adds:

". . . But if it's any consolation to you—I hope you'll remember —you have a son who at least obeys the Fourth Commandment . . . honor thy father and thy mother."

A couple of weeks earlier, I had made the decision to quit the university I was attending, a matter that was greeted by my parents with the muted enthusiasm they reserve for such occasions.

The day before I had made arrangements to take a drive-away auto train south as far as Oklahoma City, where I planned to hitchhike to Galveston and hopefully to land a job on a United Fruit boat bound for South America.

I wished to spend whatever time was left, before the war would require my presence, outside of the classroom and the library.

Later that evening, following the performance, a friend introduced some of us to the members of the cast and mentioned this line of Clift's to Clift and joked that he had put me wondering about whether I was "honoring my mother and father" or not.

Within a couple of months, we were the same age and my defection seemed to interest him. As I recall now, we were both very earnest about everything.

"What you're doing is good. The important thing is to do something," he remarked.

I agreed.

Sounds like a couple of serious nineteen-year-olds doesn't it?

He talked about his acting career, which was, of course, just beginning then. And when I read about his untimely death, he was not yet forty-six, I noted that it said that his only purpose had always been to be an actor and keep improving himself at his profession.

But that night, I remember him saying, "Acting is a substitute for being and if I can ever be, I'll forget about it. That's what's important . . . to be."

They were the only two times I ever saw him in the flesh, on stage in the play and afterward that evening.

But I always followed his work thereafter with great interest and he really did develop into a fine artist.

His performance in *From Here to Eternity* and *Raintree County* moved me very much and it wasn't too long ago that he appeared on the late show one evening as the lovelorn columnist in *Miss Lonelyhearts,* which somehow I'd missed although the book has long been a favorite.

I was reminded again then of the long ago evening. There'd been more rioting around the country that day and I wondered, as I often do, whether "Honoring thy father and thy mother" works to the good with everybody or whether it behooves mothers and fathers to work harder at being worth honoring.

I wonder now whether he ever got to "be."

For himself, that is.

I know I never did.

And he no longer has further chance at it.

The greatest sack artist I ever knew was a wonderful photographer in Chicago named Max Shirkel. When Max sat down, even his teeth relaxed. If he walked by a showroom with a bedroom suite displayed he became limber.

Rip Van Winkle was an insomniac by comparison. When he managed to get prone, which was as frequently as possible, he sort of disintegrated into the area.

We called him "Zzzzz." You could lean him against door casings without disturbing him. He would fold into a bathtub or other cramping receptacle like a business graph without disrupting the regularity of his breathing.

Zzzzz worked quickly when necessary.

"Let's get this over with," he'd say and there would be a great barrage of flash bulbs exploding and plates changing and then Zzzzz would be back in the car asleep.

Inventions like the steam engine, the telephone and the electric lamp did not move Zzzzz.

He thought man's finest artifact was the hammock.

After a late assignment one evening, he stayed downtown at the La Salle Hotel at the paper's expense rather than take the Illinois Central out to suburbia.

It was the night of the big fire in which some forty people, a figure I would not trust after all these years, died from leaps and suffocation. Zzzzz slept through it all and emerged not only unscathed but refreshed.

There are two reasons why he stands silhouetted in the mind now.

One is that a catalog arrived from the Norman Dine Sleep Center in New York.

Norman, generally referred to as the Sandman, has made a rather huge business success of the theory that people can be put to sleep by gadget.

If everyone were temperamentally equipped as Max, Norman would have to seek another field of endeavor.

A stall walker, as you undoubtedly know, is a horse that walks up and down in his stall, all night. Being the human equivalent, I am always beguiled by Norman's gadgets.

He has a sleep machine that looks like a small bedside radio and operates similarly. You press buttons and get four sounds—surf, rain on the roof, and two varieties of what he calls white sound.

White sound is supposed to neutralize the other noises in the area so if someone is operating a trip hammer it won't disturb you. I find that if you're exhausted enough, this will help you.

He also has a brain-lulling sleep conditioner but this is redundant in my case since nature anticipated Norman.

If you don't want to get so fancy, Dine will sell you earplugs or you can get a stereo pillow and have violins whacking at your subconscious.

He's got a gimmick called Nautilus which purifies the air in the room, removing, as he says, smoke, odors, pollen, dust with germicidal foam and activated charcoal although he doesn't say whether it's coconut charcoal or not.

This is apparently the way they purify air in a submarine which is where it gets its name.

There's a strap thing that you can put over a bald head and English sleep socks you can put over chilled tootsies and an electric gadget that will toast them, too. Securing you into sleep, no doubt.

The second reason mentioned, is that in the same mail came a letter from a friend informing that Max had passed away and there was a comment that "we all lament that it was cancer as for so many years we hoped that if Max ever had an illness it would be sleeping sickness."

If my correspondent's observation seems a bit inappropriate to you . . . forgive . . . since Chicago newspapermen come of a very rough tradition dating back to the Capone era.

When I first went to work in that town they suggested I put up a buck for the "Lottery." The number I drew was 818 which meant 8 o'clock and 18 seconds.

They were dismissing a murderer in the electric chair that evening, presumably at 8 o'clock, although these things never come off precisely on time.

The lottery was for the precise second the executioner pulled the switch and I won the $22.

Afterward I said:

"My luck is running better. The last lottery I was in was when they were voting for Pope and were sealed into the Vatican. I drew a ninety-three-year-old Spanish cardinal."

They decided I was welcome in Chicago.

I don't suppose his next-of-kin will go through with it and maybe he mellowed away from the outrageously spectacular man he was then but one day Zzzzz and I were going someplace on assignment and I sold him an idea.

"You're the most comfortable man I ever saw," I told him. "And someday, unless they improve things, you're going to die. It will be hard to tell when you do but people ferret around and discover these things.

"And when you do, you're the only guy ever made with a ready-made epitaph."

"What is that?" he asked.

"Zzzzz. Just that, in there with all the RIP's and things. Just Zzzzz."

His eyes went adance.

"Think of it. Maybe one of those steeplelike stones . . . a sort of five-foot Washington Monument. No dates. Nothing. Zzzzz."

Nothing ever works out the way you want it but isn't it pretty to think so. My gallant somnambulist—his nose athumb to the world forever.

Don Quixote was perhaps his real name and Henry Agard Wallace a pseudonym.

He passes for the last time, a victim of lateral sclerosis, a word or two should be mentioned perhaps about the role that a fool sometimes plays in history.

For his contemporaries in politics regarded Henry Wallace as one of those.

Henry was not a "fool" in that he was stupid. Far from that.

He knew as much about farming as any man and he was a great Secretary of Agriculture during the depression, so great that FDR took him along as Vice-President.

As men like John Swainson, to take a close example, have discovered, if you are to survive in politics, you must sometimes hide your principles. John, other opinions around here to the contrary, was unable to sign the Bowman bill, which in his own words "would allow a man working next to another at Chrysler to pay city taxes while his fellow-worker didn't because they lived a mile apart."

It cost him the governorship of Michigan or at least, was a factor.

But John is a "fool" in politics.

Woodrow Wilson was a "fool" over the League of Nations.

He lost, didn't he?

The last time I was in Lansing, I ended up with some senators who were surprised because I didn't consider "survival" the most important thing in this grisly business, "survival" meaning re-election.

The notion sounds pretty. What good are you if you are not in office? I must believe that the "fools" contribute more than the run-of-the-mine stayers. Who are they? Who remembers?

Anyway, Henry, as Orson Welles insisted we all must . . . how did he say . . . "Death as it must to all men?"

But he was a political "fool."

When he ran for President in 1948 on the Progressive ticket and drew about as many votes as you will find on a normal evening in the Anchor Bar he did these foolish things.

When he campaigned in the South, he refused to eat in a segregated restaurant.

Can you imagine?

He could have eaten the groceries he was pelted with.

Jousting at windmills.

I discover more and more that the toughest thing a man of genuine character must do is curtail the showing of that character if he is to succeed.

If he stands along with his principles, as the Bible says, he may "inherit the wind."

It was my privilege back in '40 or '41 to observe Henry Wallace visit Mexico City.

Franklin Roosevelt had inaugurated what turned out . . . judged by execution . . . to be merely a phrase. It was called the "Good Neighbor Policy," which meant that the United States was suddenly going to be truly concerned over our Latin American neighbors.

Henry Wallace was given the nod to represent the policy.

The first thing he did was hire a tutor in Spanish.

He really cared about Latin America. Who else has since?

Henry was naive and thought that if an American Vice-President actually took the trouble to learn another language so that he might go and speak to another people, that it would be a plus for the country.

So he studied his lessons.

Then he came to Mexico.

The Mexicans had of course heard about his language studies and were curious. Avila Camacho was President then and introduced Mr. Wallace who tendered them a speech in farmer-Spanish.

His audience tittered some, but Henry knew it was an affectionate titter.

Americans living in the American colony never troubled to learn Spanish or talk to the Mexicans. Their wives did, because they had maids. But that was all.

The people . . . just people . . . loved him.

There was the Mexican comedian-genius Cantinflas, before

he came out of Mexico to turn international actor, who at the time had a weekly stage show. Cantinflas originated the Week-That-Was.

As Henry left, Cantinflas opened with a show entitled *Adios, Mr. Wallace.*

He did takeoffs on Henry. He imitated his mannerisms, his dubious accent, everything but the things Henry said. The Mexicans loved the show and the whole city laughed, but the thing that never came through to Josephus Daniels, our former Secretary of the Navy and then semi-senile ambassador, was that the laughter was affectionate.

Daniels protested. The U.S. press lampooned Wallace.

He had been a "fool" again.

Nobody in Mexico thought so. But they did here.

Wallace never learned about what politicians, tough politicians, call the "reality of politics."

Nothing much counts except "how much you are rich" or "how many votes" so Wallace was wrong, but a "fool" counts.

He wouldn't eat at a segregated restaurant.

This kind of "fool" is the guy who hollers "charge" and gets himself killed.

I like to think that even the politicians who clobber against them are still affected by their passage.

I hope.

Henry was a beautiful fool.

4. safari

It was Henry M. Stanley who wrote this in his autobiography about safaris and it is still true, as nearly as I was able to tell.

"One of the first sweet and novel pleasures a man can experience in the wilds of Africa is the almost perfect independence; the next, is the almost perfect indifference to all earthly things outside his camp, and that, let people talk as they may, is one of the most exquisite, soul-lulling pleasures a mortal may enjoy."

There is a part of the safari these days that is not exactly soul-lulling and that's the expense and if you go on one, which I recommend to everyone, there is no point in stinting on the money.

Mert Wertheimer, an old Detroit gambler, taught me at a tender age that "it only costs a few cents more to go first class" and this knowledge has helped me over many ordeals since and it did in the case of the safari.

The safari began in a tiny joint called the Anchor Bar, which is located on Fourth Street in Detroit between Fort and Lafayette. The reason for its existence is that the Detroit *News* is located one block away and in it one evening, considerably in his cups, was located a young man named Charles Lord.

Charley was a hunter of some repute. He was always wandering about Alaska or Mexico or South America in search of big horn sheep. Once he shot one and brought the mounted head down to WWJ-TV the television station where he worked and dragged me out of the Anchor to look at it.

I happened to own a set of long-horn cuff links at the time, made of gold, so I gave them to Charley to commemorate his sheep, which made me, in his eyes, a hunting nut also.

It was shortly thereafter that Charley, whose money comes from his family, decided to take a year off and go round the world plunking away at various animals. During this time he arranged an African safari and this night in the Anchor he asked me if the girl I live with, Mickey, and I would like to come along. In my condition, I thought it a splendid idea.

Along about November, I received a letter from Safari Outfitters, Inc., a Chicago firm conducted by an ex-judge from Poland named Roman Hupalowski.

This missive explained that the cost of a hunting safari was $3600 for twenty-one days and the cost of a camera safari was $630. This did not include transportation to and from Beira, Mozambique.

This also does not include the booze you drink while you're in camp nor the mounting of your trophies afterward, nor license or export taxes.

The group that Safari Outfitters hooked us up with is known as "Safrique." It has leases for both four and ten year periods on six plots of ground in Mozambique, the plots ranging between 40 and 85 kilometers in size.

When we got to Nhamacala, which was the name of the camp, I suddenly understood what Hupalowski had meant when he said to me on the phone call in which I confirmed our reservations, "You can tell Mrs. Greene that she will be elaborately comfortable while she is in the bush."

The camp had its own air strip, a garage that housed a series of four wheel drive trucks, a dining room for the hunters, one for the white hunters, another for the native gunbearers, trackers, etc. and living quarters that included twin beds, electricity, hot and cold running water, and showers in tiny native type cottages . . . native in that they were round and had a machese type roof of clay and grass. There was also a butcher's shop and a tannery, for the preservation of trophies.

I permitted my wife to buy the tickets so we ended up with a three and a half month trip round the world which made the safari sort of incidental.

She had discovered somewhere that your air travel ticket

couldn't cost more than $1200 if you traveled tourist and never went backwards. You could go from side to side though, which we did, landing in Lisbon first, then Rome, then Tel Aviv, then Athens, then Johannesburg, then Beira, then Salisbury, Rhodesia, then Johannesburg again, then Nairobi, then Addis Ababa, then Bombay, then New Delhi, then Calcutta, then Bangkok, then Singapore, then Saigon, then Hong Kong, Taiwan, then Tokyo, then Honolulu, then San Francisco.

She had neglected to figure the cost for stopping in each place, however suffice it to say that a combination Diners' Club, American Express, and Carte Blanche cards make it all feasible, if impractical.

We arrived about 4:30 in the afternoon at Nhamacala where a tiny Portuguese named Francisco Coimbra, whom it developed was my white hunter, promptly took us out to zero in my weapons.

These were a 7 mm. rifle and a .375 magnum both equipped with Redfield scopes and a 12-gauge over and under shotgun.

I might add that the two rifles cost about one thousand dollars, so you see what you're getting into when you start on a safari. A friend of mine offered me the moral that I shouldn't hang around the Anchor Bar, but then where else are you going to hang around where you have a built-in bookmaker and credit when you are tapped out.

Anyway, we had an excellent dinner upon arrival, finished off the dinner by demolishing a bottle of Johnny Walker Black Label.

Charley brought a friend with him, George Black III, whose friendship was to become very dear to Mickey and me during the course of the hunting trip.

We all retired about 9 P.M. against the 5:30 A.M. arisal time.

After so many packings and unpackings, checking the guns in and out of customs wherever we landed, and all of the rest of the nuisances of travel, the high point of this was that we were unpacked and would stay that way for three whole weeks. Reliefsville.

One thing about a safari, there is no poising for the launching. You are either in one or not.

The next day I executed the first two of fifteen animals I would perform this on during the three weeks.

First let me tell you my reactions to the idea of hunting which may explain a little of why I went. And let me also say that up until the time of the safari, I had never even shot a deer and I come from a state where if you don't hunt deer, you're considered a little odd. Most of the strikes we have around the state, I mean labor strikes, occur in the fall of the year so that the workers can go deer-hunting and not worry about their jobs.

The few ducks I've shot with my friend Fritz Beiermeister were more in the interest of fellowship than anything else. Fritz is just a guy I like to be with.

Not only have I never declared war on deer, but a deer is the last animal in the world I've ever had the slightest yen to shoot.

Not only that but I have always been suspicious of hunters, particularly big game hunters.

It's when they start dealing out the danger that they turn me off.

This goes back to Teddy Roosevelt, Ernest Hemingway, Bob Ruark, and the lot of them.

Hemingway accomplished more about the danger and manliness of shooting than did anyone else because he was a better writer than most everybody else.

What he did in one short story called "The Short Happy Life of Francis Macomber" would make you come up writhing. The whole point to the story was that Macomber wounded a lion and then as a point of honor he had to go in and finish him off so that the animal wouldn't suffer unnecessarily. The first time he couldn't do it, threw down his gun and ran, while his white hunter finished off the lion. Then the second time he screwed up his nerve and did it, after which his wife, who had married him for his dough, accidentally on purpose shot him, since the new Francis, the nervy one, had become insufferable for her to live with any further. That was the Short Happy Life of Francis, between the time he had become a real man and the time she shot him.

Have you ever heard of such guff in your life?

But that was old Ernest for you.

Charley Lord used to talk a lot about that sort of thing on this safari, drawing out the three white hunters we had on the subject of cowardly clients until I thought one day I would scream.

Then you hear stories about Cape buffalo and elephants and how impregnable they are when they charge.

Well, an elephant can't charge you because he can't run, really. All he can do is walk at you. He walks incredibly fast, so you can ceremoniously call it a charge, but what he's really doing is walking at you very fast. If he had to jump over a ditch on his way he couldn't do it. An elephant can't leap at all.

He is not physically prepared to perform in any other manner. He's too heavy.

They also have a rumor around that Cape buffalo will charge you.

You wound him.

He charges you.

I don't believe this sort of nonsense at all. With a .375 magnum in my hand—and I intend to have one in my hand—I think I will deter any charging monster. If he attacks me first, it'll be the first animal that ever did. That goes for underwater, too, where the barracuda and moray eels have proved easy enough to get along with. Neither has ever made the slightest aggressive gesture at me and it's not because I'm a great skin diver either, just fair. It's just the way they are.

One of the things Charley got me a license to shoot was a zebra.

But really, now, shooting a zebra must be sort of like slaughtering a milk wagon horse, right?

To you hunters, who deserve this trip much more than I, I make you all one promise . . . that is, to tell the truth about this one African safari.

If I shoot an elephant in one of his walks toward me, and he turns like a normal wounded animal, I'll report that. I won't try to con you about how my heart was in my throat.

The real reason I am here is in an interest in facts.

I am certain I will not be romanced into anything.

This is my promise and all of the great white hunters in Africa will not talk me out of it.

As you know in any African hunting trip, there is a good deal of conversation about the Big Five, which are constituted of the elephant, the lion, the Cape buffalo, the leopard and the rhino.

These are the animals which, dating back to Teddy Roosevelt's time, are considered the most difficult and, certainly the most dangerous game to hunt.

Around this camp at Nhamacala, Mozambique, the rhino is

easily forgotten since it is protected by law from being hunted. That leaves us with a Big Four not a Big Five.

The day on which I killed a Cape buffalo, it was along about 4 o'clock in the afternoon when my white hunter, Francisco Coimbra, tapped on the cab of the truck, summoning it to halt.

"Buffalo," he exclaimed. "Get out of the truck. We stalk them on foot."

This was a switch. Except for one other time, when we hunted elephant, it was the first time I had descended from the truck. It was a tiny bit unsettling since I discovered I had come to regard the truck as a bastion in which no horns could touch me.

Fombe, the chief tracker, descended and shouldered a gun. Francisco, for the second time, the other time being when we had hunted elephant, took his open sighted .475. Alficio, the tracker I distinguished from the other because he had three wives, came along bearing my own .375 magnum. He would hand it to me loaded and with the safety off when the correct time presented itself.

We trudged about half a mile into some woods. Then as we approached the other side of the woods, suddenly there loomed in front of us a herd of perhaps a hundred buffalo.

We were approximately 100 yards from the herd, but we were downwind of them so they remained unperturbed and ignorant of our presence. What downwind means is that the wind was blowing over the herd down toward us, so that our scent remained protected. Had the wind been blowing the other way, they would have caught our scent long before and would have taken off through the tall grass.

"Can't we get any closer to them," I wanted to know.

They were in buffalo high grass and I didn't want to be casting about for a shot at that range where all you see were the massive horns of the animals. It would be a shot, like many I'd taken from the truck where you were guessing at where the game's left shoulder was.

"I guess so," said Francis. "But you'll have to crouch down while we cross that open space. There's a chance they might see us and be spooked, you told me you didn't like to walk."

"I've walked a mile already. I don't like to walk but let's go on and have at them."

With a couple of restful pauses we made it about 70 yards to the second really thick clump of grass.

"Are you all right," inquired Francis.

I was breathing hard.

"Cripes, yes. I'm fine," I gasped. "Which one should I shoot?"

"See that bull on the extreme left of the herd? Do you? Well, shoot him."

He stood up and offered me his shoulder as a rest for my gun.

He being a foot shorter than I, required some physical adjustment on my part, but I finally got the gun in place, put the crosshairs in the scope on the left shoulder of the bull and squeezed a shot off.

The bull leapt a few feet into the air and ran about 25 yards into the herd, which spooked at the shot and began to amble away.

"Shoot him again, quick, now. Shoot him anywhere but get some holes into him. You hit him pretty good that first time."

I lined up on him again and got off another shot. This time I hit him just back of the shoulder, in his side. He jumped again the way an animal will when hit by a high powered rifle. Shucks the way a man will, too, I know. One morning a couple of decades ago some Japanese shot me three different times one morning and I jumped, involuntarily, in the same way.

The herd had now disappeared. I often wondered later what would have happened if when they spooked, they had stampeded toward where we were standing rather than at right angles from us. I suppose it would all have been a mess then. But they didn't.

There isn't very much that could have been done with a hundred buffalo.

My wounded buffalo was now dragging himself away from us. He staggered a couple of hundred yards and I was having a rough time in the tall grass, with my limited pegs, keeping up.

Francisco and Fombe had plunged on ahead.

Then I saw Coimbra take a shot at him, which didn't slow him any, though I assume he must have hit him.

"Shoot him again," Francisco hollered back at me.

So, tall grass and all, I threw up my rifle and taking careful aim, broke his back. He went down for good.

As I panted up to where Fombe and Coimbra waited, Francisco said: "We'll wait a minute now. We now get the truck up before we go in any further. He is badly wounded now and extremely dangerous. How do you feel?"

"I can stand to wait for the truck. I'm exhausted." One of the chief things that makes hunting hunting is that you must meet an animal on his own ground. Anyone who has ever tried for big horn sheep will tell you about the near exhaustion that overcomes you as you trail a sheep that is a couple of ridges away.

I sat down in the tall grass and waited the half an hour it took for the truck with my wife and the other trackers in it to come up. Then we climbed aboard and from the height the truck afforded us, we maneuvered to the point where the Cape buffalo was down and suffering in the weeds.

"See that hole in his chest," asked Francisco. "Put another about a foot lower and he'll be out of his misery."

I did and he was.

I must give him tribute. He died as tough as an animal can die, still twisting his head and horns until the final coup de grace.

And when we first appeared in the truck, he managed to get his forelegs into the turf and raised his head and shoulders off the ground, onto two feet and eyed us for a charge, broken back and all.

He was the toughest animal I ever saw. Although when I first shot him and up until the final resurrection onto two feet, he never came in my direction.

In the final analysis I had merely executed another animal.

The next day I arose at 5:30 A.M. which is normally my bedtime and after a breakfast of orange juice, bacon, eggs, biscuits, milk and coffee, we set off hunting.

I executed two wild animals that day, a hartebeest, an animal I'd never seen before, and a zebra, "my milk wagon horse."

When we left camp in our Austin truck, there were five natives —my hunting crew and Francisco Coimbra, whom everyone called Chico, because of his diminutive stature.

Three of the natives sit behind you—Fombe, the chief tracker who always wore an overcoat in the chill of the mornings and the damnedest veteran fedora I've ever seen, who sat at my right rear, Alicia, the chief gunbearer and Ringse, another tracker.

In the cab of the truck were the guides, Bill, the driver and

Manuel. Seated in the action seats were my wife and her camera gear, me in the middle and the white hunter on my right.

It was sort of like driving through a natural park. Fombe immediately began spotting game. We saw impala, wart hog, baboon in great numbers, the first two of which I had never seen before but they were all too small to shoot. Coimbra was completely straight arrow on size of game. If it wasn't big enough you couldn't shoot it. He was his own game warden.

Then Chico put his hand on my shoulder, "Hartebeest," he murmured. "Take the one in the middle."

There were five or six of these animals and I got my gun, the 7 mm. up but I was too slow and while I was trying to sight in on them, they moved away until they were about at a range of 200 yards. The grass was all as high as they since it was the first blush of summer in Africa at the time. Chico told me that the easiest time to hunt was fall when all the grass was dead and there weren't leaves on the trees.

"You can see the game much better in fall," said Chico.

I sighted in on the biggest of the lot, who had fortunately stopped on an anthill which gave him some silhouette, I sighted down into the grass about where I thought his left shoulder would be and fired. By the time the recoil allowed the scope to bounce back to where it had been, the hartebeests were gone.

Had I missed? I didn't know. I've never fired a rifle really since World War II which was so long ago the memory remains somewhat indistinct.

Francisco took a little swagger stick he carries and pointed the driver and we crept up to where the hartebeest had been.

"I think he went down about here," said Francisco.

As we approached the spot, the hartebeest got up again, in sort of a reflex action and then tumbled down.

"What am I supposed to do," asked I over the womanly whimpers of my bride, "shoot him again."

Francisco got down from the truck and walked over to him.

"It is not necessary. He is quite dead."

In the afternoon, after we had returned to camp for lunch, I executed a zebra. This was accomplished in exactly the same way with Francisco telling me which one to shoot and me shooting it at a range of about 175 yards.

Except that when we got to where he should have gone down, he wasn't there. Instead there were streaks of blood on the tall grass.

"Cripes," I thought. "I've wounded him."

The same feeling returned that I'd had in the morning when the hartebeest got up after I'd shot him. I didn't think I could shoot him wounded and right now I didn't think I could shoot a wounded, helpless zebra.

However, the trackers tracked him and discovered him about fifty yards away, deader than anything.

Francisco wanted a picture of me with the zebra. Charley Lord, who is the real hunting nut on this safari, maintains that it is a real help to the taxidermist to have a picture of the animal taken immediately after the kill. So I permitted this mild embarrassment.

We have a rug for the front room now anyway.

We talked a little about the right and wrong of hunting that night and finally took Hemingway's easy way out of everything, "If you feel good about what you've done, it's all right."

We decided the rug was good and the act of shooting was good, and so there you were.

When we got back to camp that night it was to be warned that a pet lion belonging to Charley's white hunter, Mariano Ferriera was loose in camp so be careful going from building to building.

The natives were all holed up in the kitchen. A lion is the native's nemesis. There had been an unwary native killed two weeks before.

I was glad Mariano's leopard hadn't gotten loose also.

Which brought me to inquiring the next day, how a naturalist got to be a professional hunter.

5. novice hunter

The word that Corica was loose presented a real problem around the camp since Mariano was still out hunting with Charley Lord.

Corica is a lion that is one year old and is tethered to a clothes line, which gives her the length of the line to roam about in. What happened was Corica simply broke the chain and took off.

It caused considerable commotion in Mariano's zoo. It made the five-year-old leopard pace up and down his cage growling. The bush pig, Juliano, began doing turns around his pen.

The five baboons became more eccentric than usual and the little baby nyala, Safrique, refused to come out and be stroked, which is something she dearly loves.

We were all warned to be very careful as Corica was obviously in a bad mood otherwise why had she broken the chain. She was not expected to journey far from camp. She has spent eight months on her chain and is accustomed to the camp, but then in her uncertain mood who could determine what she would do?

In my tour of the zoo this morning with Mariano, Corica had been tremendously affectionate with him, kissing him, batting him around jovially, keeping the claws carefully sheathed, like any pussycat toying with its master, only much bigger, of course.

She must weigh a hundred and fifty pounds.

The leopard, Pintada, he trapped a year and a half ago when the cat was three years old. Mariano had been trapping for lion but had miscued and got the leopard. Pintada is king in Mariano's little jungle, although she is kept caged.

Each of the baboons has a pole to which it is chained, and they spend most of their time running up and down the poles and generally ignoring all the people about. Although one of them, who is nameless, accepted several cigarettes from me. He doesn't smoke them, he eats them.

The rest of the menagerie consists of a herd of goats, two sunis, five monkeys, an eagle which is extremely fierce and an owl which is extremely friendly. George Black III immediately developed a thing with the owl.

"I don't know," said George. "He blinks at me and hoots every now and then. He kind of gets to me . . . that old owl."

Anyway I had a long talk with Mariano about his proclivity for keeping animals and why he wanted to be a professional white hunter, and weren't the two things incongruous.

"I don't think so," he said. "I think the love I have for these animals makes me a better white hunter than I would otherwise be. For instance, no client of mine is going to shoot anything but trophy class animals. A lot of hunters permit their clients to shoot smaller animals just to fill their quotas. I wouldn't permit that."

Mariano is an extremely handsome man who wears a beard the way the kids in my country wished they looked. He was sort of made for a beard. Hearing that his lion was loose, he was immediately very concerned that Corica might be lost and in some kind of trouble somewhere. It was rather touching to see him head out of camp calling "Corica . . . here Corica . . . oh Corica" as a man might shout "here kitty, kitty, kitty."

For a half an hour anyway, you could hear his voice out in the bush summoning the wayward cat and then he was successful.

Here he came, dragging Corica back with one hand on her collar. Corica looked very happy at having been found and made no motion at all when she was tethered to the clothes line again. She didn't even run up and down the clothes line's length, not even once, but Mariano and she did play together for a time before she rolled over and went to sleep.

The whole camp breathed a little easier.

And Mariano went back to the bush pig, Juliano, and did his sleep trick with a stick with the pig. He puts him to sleep by caressing him with a stick, caressing him around his snout.

There was some tragedy about the day though. George's owl friend died during the afternoon. They hadn't noticed it until Corica was found.

It shook George a little.

At this point it may be well to tell you that the lion, all rumor to the contrary, is not the king of beasts, the elephant is.

There is a majesty about an elephant that nearly defies description. When an elephant wanders through the woodlands here in darkest Africa, he wanders with all the adjuncts that accrue to him because of his size.

He regards a human as the nonentity he can be. No other animal ever attacks him, although the pretender after his title, the lion, will occasionally attack a baby elephant, that is, if momma and daddy are not about.

We have encountered them three times thus far and the third time we hunted them. They turned out to be too small for shooting, in the tastes of Francisco Coimbra, my white hunter.

Too small!

They were two-story houses on legs.

The first time we saw a small herd of six. They were in the brush at roadside and we stopped the little Austin Gypsy as they crossed the road. The bull in the crowd uprooted a small tree with his trunk and flung it across the road, just out of plain perversity. They mark the civilized part of the world in this manner. All roads, railroad tracks, and other signs of man's trekking through the bush are similarly awarded these mementoes of the elephant.

The arrogance with which they moved gave you a lot of pause.

"Where do you shoot them?" I asked Francisco.

"The best place is to get a side shot at them and then aim about 12 inches behind their earhole. Or you can, if you're shooting them from the front, shoot for the left shoulder like you would any game, or you can shoot them just slightly above and between the eyes.

"The head is the best place to shoot them, because you rock them pretty good with a high caliber. You use your .375 magnum for elephant and Cape buffalo . . . and you stun them with the shot. Although if you hit them about twelve inches behind the earhole, you'll pierce their brain and they'll go down."

The second time we saw them was just before dusk one day and there were five of them this time, apparently a family, the bull, the mother and three baby elephants.

The mother came first into the road, sniffing out the roadbed with her trunk, then placing her forefeet extremely delicately in the road and then her hind feet in the precise spots the forefeet had been. When you track an elephant it is like tracking a two-legged animal because of this fetish of theirs, the business of placing the hind feet in the tracks of the forefeet.

The third time . . . the hunting time . . . began about four o'clock one afternoon when two of the trackers and finally the white hunter himself climbed a tree to look for game and a thousand yards away they observed the backs of five elephants.

"Elephants," said Francisco. "Come on. We track them."

At which point we left the Austin and set out on foot down the road. A half mile farther on, Francisco climbed another tree to check the whereabouts of our elephants.

They were grazing and moving through the 12-foot tall grass and would hit the road eventually approximately where we were standing in a few minutes, he reported.

At this point the girl I live with approached Manuel, one of the trackers and announced, "Me. Go back to jeep."

This was done mostly in sign language.

In sign language, he told her, "No," shaking his head wildly from side to side.

About then the first elephant hit the road and began sniffing at it. The elephant who was second raised his trunk in the air and sniffed about. We were downwind of the lot of them and so therefore they were protected from our scent.

"Too small," said Francisco. "Forget them."

The elephants looked huge to me but he carefully explained that their ivory wasn't long enough, and how an elephant can become full grown in about twenty years and then his ivory began to grow to catch up with him. It was ivory that was your trophy here, not the elephant's head.

A moment later, he asked, "Where is your wife?"

"Down the road a ways, I think."

"Ask her to come up here."

I motioned to her but she had backed off the road and was

sitting down in the grass. I finally managed to get through to Manuel and he got her up on her feet and pushed her toward us. I motioned her forward and rather gingerly she came.

"Francisco wants you."

"What does he want me for. I'm scared," she said tremulously.

Francisco, with a careless wave of his hand, said, "We are not going to shoot them. I thought you would like to take pictures of these elephants," he explained. "And what are you frightened of. You are now up with the big guns."

This didn't reassure her much. However she got her camera set and took a few snapshots of the elephants crossing the road.

Then the truck came and gathered up all of us dauntless hunters. The pachyderms had halted just around a bend in the road.

As we went by them, the bull elephant flexed his mammoth ears and trumpeted noisily.

I had my arm around the girl at the time, trying in some small way to make everything all right for her, and I could feel her trembling.

"You really are scared, aren't you?"

"Yes I am. Those big things give me the willies. Why don't you let them alone."

I'd been a little fearsome of them too, but men are not supposed to show it.

"We haven't done anything to any elephants . . . yet. But I can see you subscribe to my theory that these are the real king of the beasts, then."

"Yes," she said slowly, "except for men, they are."

I had never been sure how I felt about killing elephants. But the final day of my safari I learned how much I wanted to have one down and to figuratively put my foot on his chest and declare to the world, "This is my elephant. I killed him."

See what happens to you in the hunt. When I shot my first animal . . . a hartebeest . . . the first day and he involuntarily got up again as we drove up, I asked plaintively, "What am I supposed to do now. Shoot the poor thing again."

Since then I had dropped impala, an oribi over which I made such a fool of myself, and seen both of them gutted by the bearers before they were actually dead and had felt no emotion whatsoever.

I found myself joining Charley Lord, whom people back home had upbraided because he just didn't take pictures of animals, thereby precluding shooting them. "An animal isn't yours until he's dead," rejoined Charley to all of his do-gooder friends.

During the last days of the safari, mainly I hunted elephant. I got to feeling terribly sorry for the trackers, since Francisco knew how badly I wanted one by then, and he ran those trackers all over the bush. We would find elephant signs early in the morning, a tree thrown across the road or elephant droppings which he would pick up and examine in order to see how fresh they were, and then the trackers would start tracking.

At the end of each fruitless day, the trackers would be exhausted and we'd still be hunting for elephant.

Until the last day, when in late afternoon, Francisco called upon me to walk a half mile into the bush, where there stood a dozen elephants.

We were downwind of them and so managed to close the distance to about forty yards.

I was a little nervous. There was one giant in the crowd and he was turned in such a manner that I could get in the side shot behind the ear very easily, using a tree as a rest for the gun.

I lined up the shot several times while we waited for the big fellow to move so we could see his tusks.

He was bigger than most houses I've seen.

Mickey was all nerves again.

I had a slight premonition that I would kill him the first shot but I had failed so miserably on some occasions I couldn't be sure.

We waited for him to move. Would this be another full grown elephant who was too short in the ivory for killing?

We waited what seemed an interminable length of time. They were all huddled together. The babies were the only ones moving as they played about their fathers.

Finally he moved, backing his head from between the rumps of the two elephants that had obscured our view.

"He's too young," chirped Francisco. "You can't shoot him. Sorry."

I took down my rifle from its sighting and shrugged.

Those elephants never did move. They may be standing there today, nuzzling one another.

I remember a white hunter I once interviewed, who was touring the states with a travelogue movie film which he showed on George Pierrot's TV show one night.

"If I'm ever hurt in Africa, it will be by an elephant. They're the most dangerous of all the animals."

I believed him now, which was why the elephant was so important to me.

However, you do what a white hunter says, and the ivory tusks were not very impressive.

I've got to go back for my elephant though, and a rhino, and a leopard.

6. competition

The interplay of personalities in a hunting camp is rife enough for a novel, in fact several have been written about it, *Gilligan's Last Elephant* to name one, and later the interplay between Charles Lord and George Black has become slightly acrimonious.

Remember I declared originally as how George and Charley, lifelong buddies, had set out to tour the world on a hunting and skiing trip. They are now about three quarters done with it. They still have South America left.

Charley is the master hunter.

George is the skier and neophyte.

Except off results, which are beginning to gravel Charley somewhat.

When the safari began, George flew up early in the morning and went hunting. He got no game that morning but on his afternoon trip, just as the rest of us were arriving in camp, George wheeled in with a zebra, a reed buck and a nyala crammed into his truck.

At the end of five days, George had bagged ten animals, including a greater kudu, which was one of the reasons that Charley selected this part of the world in which to hunt, so that he could bring down a kudu. He had wounded one in the first five days but was unable to track it down.

One day Charley shot a Cape buffalo along with a zebra and he was chortling about the camp over his "very large zebra" and his buffalo head that "wasn't the largest ever taken but was a perfectly proportioned buffalo."

As we were culminating the day with a little gin, Charley was holding forth about a kudu he had seen that day but rejected. "It was not a trophy class kudu," he said.

Then he made reference to George and his "immature little kudu," which teed George off some. The next thing he was picking on Charley's buffalo.

Charley had downed his buff after three or four shots as they pursued a herd of buffalo in the jeep. This was one of those "bwana" rides, which are as dangerous as the buffalo itself.

"I'll bet you five dollars," said George finally, "that I shoot a bigger buffalo than you did."

"It's a wager," responded Charley calmly.

They didn't shake hands over it but then there you were.

Normally everybody gets up at about 5:30 A.M.

The next day Charley arose and departed camp at 5:30. George slept until 7:00, then after lingering over breakfast until 7:30, he and his white hunter, Vargilio Garcia, departed for gaming.

I had taken the morning off to catch up on some correspondence when George turned up about 4 P.M. in the afternoon with the biggest buffalo I'd ever seen.

"Here you see my five dollar buffalo," he declaimed jubilantly.

"Furthermore I shot it with one shot, which was with my 7 mm. rifle and not the .375 magnum, which is usual with this animal."

He had also shot a trophy class gray duiker and a guinea hen with his shotgun on the return trip.

Eventually, after dark, into camp stumbled Charley.

A few moments later, we were all sitting around the veranda of the hunters' dining hall, punishing the gin, as usual.

"How're things?" asked Charley of me. "What did you get today?"

I told him how I bagged a nice nyala and had a run-in with a big black sable I've been jousting with for a couple of days.

"Congratulations," he said.

He never inquired of George a thing.

So finally George, who had been burbling to tell him, exploded:

"Since you are not going to have the obvious decency to inquire about my day, I may as well tell you I slumbered until seven and then arose and leisurely breakfasted. Around 11:30 this morning I shot what Garcia refers to as my five dollar buffalo. I suggest you wander down to the tannery and check it since you put the premium of a fin on it.

"At 2:30 I shot a record gray duiker and I polished off my day with a guinea hen by way of proving my adeptness with all weapons. And, incidentally, you have failed to report what you have taken from the hills today."

It turned out that Charley had taken nothing from the hills.

He had, he explained at some length, seen and rejected another kudu.

This didn't cut any kind of ice with George.

And so the hunt goes.

Then there are the peaceful days when you can find no game.

Or rather you find it, and what with one thing and another, you can't get a shot at it or you have already taken these trophies and do not need them a second time.

You have arisen at what is beginning not to seem an ungodly hour at all, 5:30 A.M. and have breakfasted as usual on orange juice, eggs, bacon, hot rolls and coffee . . . At six o'clock you are in the truck as the sun begins to tentatively warm you.

I brought a duck jacket with me which was designed for the sleet and rain of Walpole Island in Canada and it feels wonderful at this hour.

First, you are excited by a small herd of four elephants. They rather proudly ignore you, since you are downwind of them and they do not catch your scent. They are awesome animals even though they are too small to shoot.

"Very small elephant," says Francisco Coimbra, the white hunter.

In late afternoon we discover that they are close because they have just come from ravaging the corn and cotton fields of a nearby native village.

"Why you no kill elephant? Is not too small to ruin crops. Is not too small to shoot," jabber the natives at you.

Then there is a small group of hartebeest and almost immediately there is a tiny herd of waterbuck. We do not pause for them, since I have already collected heads from both of these two animals and despite the fact that I have room for two of each on my hunting license, I have explained to Francisco that I have no desire to shoot another one.

"Impalas. Too small," says Coimbra, but halts the truck while that girl takes photographs of them. They are very young and naively stand about 10 feet from the truck. Finally, we clap our hands and they run away.

Then there are some sable antelope and the truck moves out into the tall grass to try and herd them within rifle range. They are not having any.

Overhead, a covey of buzzard is starting to follow the truck, in the hopes they will, at least, get the leavings from a gutted animal. Little do they understand that this will be a gameless day.

Since it is a Sunday, Francisco observes wryly, "The game have all gone to church today."

Then, since he tries to provide some amusement for us at all times, he has the truck halted by an ironwood tree, where he gets off and picks the six inch pods, which hold what turns out to be ironwood seed, spectacularly colored orange and black. He explains how many American girls collect these and have bracelets made out of them. That girl fills her pockets with them, smiling happily.

Then it's back to camp for lunch, me swilling a bottle of Manica beer on the way, leaving just a little in the bottle so that when I hand it back to Fombe, the chief tracker, he finishes it, without Francisco knowing. It remains our quaint little secret.

I am dragged out of my siesta by Fombe at three o'clock and off we go again on our gameless search.

There are large herds of zebra gamboling in the forest. We see some of Francisco's "Impala . . . female." Then there are wart hogs, scrambling through the brush. Then there are hundreds of baboons, good for taking pictures. Francisco borrows my rifle and shoots one to bait for leopard.

The way you hunt leopard is by placing bait, a baboon or part of a haunch of zebra, high in a tree limb. This is after the meat has begun to decompose a little. Leopards like it that way.

One comes by and feeds on it during the afternoon. The next day you go out and wait for him. At this point, he knows his dinner is where you left it and that he doesn't have to work for it. He lazes his way through the heat of the day, then comes for his highly prepared meal.

Finally sundown approaches and we round a turn. Here in the

road are perhaps fifty guinea hens. Francisco taps the cab of the truck and asks them to hand out my shotgun.

The bearer gets it clear of the case it's in, and he starts to feed a pair of shells into the chambers. At which point something spooks the guineas and they all rise in a body and disappear.

But it has been a great day, riding around the countryside and feeling close to all the game we did see, sort of like riding in a zoo without any bars.

As Alan Paton wrote about South Africa *Cry, the Beloved Country* and I'm sure this is not what he meant but I wanted to cry "You Beloved Country" all the same.

Maybe, with luck, there would be no game tomorrow either.

The next day, I had no such luck. This was the day I made a complete and utter ass of myself.

Any notion you may have nurtured that I was some sort of gallant on this trip will be immediately dispelled.

The first thing in the morning I missed a shot at a reed buck at a range of 50 yards. He was standing in some tall grass next to a tree, and Francisco said, "Reed buck, shoot him."

It is fairly difficult to miss an animal as big as a reed buck at such minuscule range, however I did it. I just missed. I didn't buck the shot or flinch it or any of the things you can do to your marksmanship. I just missed it. I had the reed buck right in the hairs of my scope and I missed.

It was about an hour later that I had a black buck sable firmly in the cross hairs again and again I missed. With a crew of six people including your white hunter, this is much more embarrassing than that time that you miss a pheasant and your dog turns back and looks at you.

All of the trackers and gunbearers and everyone look away and cough and things like that.

The girl I live with sniffed, noticeably, the second time.

And to cap it all off there is a little tiny animal, called an oribi, which is like the red and gray duiker and is considered something of a showpiece by Charles Lord, the super hunter on this trip.

It was at this point that we came upon two oribis. They were perhaps 25 yards off the road, both with their heads up in the air.

"Oribi," announced Francisco. "Shoot the one on the right."

I threw up my rifle, leveled at the oribi I thought was on the right, and fired.

"You shot the wrong one," said Francisco disgustedly.

"That was the one in my scope," I explained lamely.

"You shot the female," said Francisco. "The male is still waiting. Now you shoot him, maybe."

"You shot the girl," wailed that girl.

So I quickly got the 7 mm. rifle in position again and assuming that I had no time, since the first shot must have spooked the male oribi, I squeezed off a second shot and missed him, then squeezed off another and missed again. I heard my girl gasp in disgust and then I settled down and on my last round in my four shot magazine, I finally hit the little oribi.

"Cripes, I'm sorry. I thought he'd be spooked by that first shot and I hurried the next two because of that."

"You shot the female first and that's why the male waited. He didn't know what happened to her. So he waited for her," said Francisco.

Fombe and Alficio had run over into the brush, where they picked up the two oribi and began carrying them toward the truck.

One of the animals squealed.

"You didn't even kill him after all that," blurted the girl I live with.

"Forget it," said Francisco. "It's a reflex action. He is dead in another minute."

Then and there, while the boys gutted both of my, what do I call them . . . trophies, we came to a conclusion about the red and gray duikers and any further oribis.

"They're too little," claimed the girl. "I couldn't stand it to have them mounted around the house."

Later on she added, "I can't stand it when you don't kill something with one shot."

"Believe me when I tell you I've never been more ashamed in my entire life," I said.

7. windup

Charley Lord was clearly offended and even George Black was some miffed. I had made a totally innocuous remark, to me anyway, about the pleasant thing about the hunt being the total lack of danger in it.

"Are you serious," asked the hairbreadth Charley loftily. "What do you think that was the other day when we ran head-on into a rhino? Here he was floundering about in the bush. Mariano Ferreira thought it was a buffalo, it was making so much noise. And then there it was, a big black rhinocerous, and we couldn't even shoot it because of the game laws. We had to run and though it didn't charge, it certainly could have. And we'd've been in real trouble."

"You have just proved my point that these animals don't charge you, or anything like that, unless maybe if they're wounded. So you were in no particular danger."

This seemed to rile him further.

"And what about that big mamba snake we ran into the other day? Sure, Mariano shot it with that big cannon of his. But that mamba, baby, is the most dangerous snake in the world. What do you mean it isn't dangerous here?"

Even easygoing George dealt himself a hand.

"You know when I shot that warthog the other day, I had some trouble with it. I used up all the ammo in my 7 mm. and then I used up the rounds in my .375 and there I was on the ground in the presence of a wounded warthog. He had eleven inch tusks, the little jasper, and there I was without a gun with ammunition."

I didn't run and hide when confronted with all this evidence.

"You butchered the job on the warthog. It would have served you right, if he'd gored you," I claimed. "But he didn't because he was badly wounded," was my rejoinder.

"Tell me this," I added, pursuing my point. "Are you frightened at all. Are you scared out here in the wilds of Africa?"

"Of course not," answered Charley. "It's not a question of whether I'm scared or not. But I'm telling you there is an element of danger."

"You betcha," agreed George.

I was sitting in the dining room the next evening, fooling around with the typewriter against that day when I would surface from the hunt and have to go back to work, filing copy, when I overheard Charley telling the girl I live with how the hunt was 100 percent safe and that the reason for this was the presence of our trio of white hunters.

"He's my life insurance policy. Whatever I do and wherever I go, he's there with his big .450 magnum. He shot a snake with it just the other day. Blew its head right off," he was saying. "Be glad you've got Francisco with you and feel safe with him."

"What's all this about safety, Charley," I called to him. "You are contradicting yourself about how dangerous all this is. What I've been trying in my feeble fashion to suggest to you is that you've never been safer. You with a high-powered rifle and the king of all beasts. You're the equal of any animal you'll ever meet. That's all."

The following evening, all of us, the three professional white hunters and the three hunters, if you'll excuse the expression, were sitting around spoiling some booze when Charley asked Francisco, my own hunter, whether hunting was dangerous or not. When Francisco started to answer in the negative, Charley added, "If we don't play by the rules or we do something stupid or if we panic?"

He had the point so obscured with his qualifications that Francisco had to agree with him.

Francisco told a story about having the cook from camp out on his truck with him one day when he shot a tiny oribi buck. An oribi stands about two feet high. After he shot him, he sent the cook to pick him up. The cook went and found him and discovered he was only wounded, but picked him up anyway since he was small, when the cook returned to the truck he had the oribi's four inch horns imbedded in his stomach.

He told another about Luis Miguel Dominguin, the famous Spanish matador, who hunted with him and brought a habit from the Spanish bull ring. Each time Dominguin killed an animal he always delivered to it the Punasso, or small knife wound to the brain, to make sure it was dead. When he attempted to deliver it to a wounded warthog one day he got bitten by the warthog.

I don't know what the point to all these stories was nor how it applied to Charles' contention that big game hunting is dangerous, but Charley seemed very happy with them.

I don't know whether all this conversation about danger had anything to do with but it was the very next day, Mariano Ferreira, Charley's white hunter had something happen to him that every human on safari dreads more than anything else.

Mariano hunted all day Saturday, had a couple of cocktails after his day's work, then went off to bed.

He awakened the next morning in such agony from groin pains that he couldn't put his socks on. He just lay abed and writhed.

His wife, Maria, seeing him moaning on the bed, went off to fetch Francisco to look at him.

Francisco punched him around the groin a little and then told Maria, "I think he might have appendicitis. We should radio Beira immediately."

They tried with the radio but since it was Sunday no one was manning it at the other end.

A driver was dispatched to Maringue, a village 43 kilometers from the camp, where he was to contact the postmaster, who owned a telephone, and instruct him to call Beira.

The plan, if possible, was to get word to Beira to have a plane flown in with a doctor on it, but now the problem was how to contact Beira.

Most of the panicking was over by 6 A.M. when the plane arrived with a doctor on board. Mariano, who had been administered a 50 milligram Demerol tablet by Charles Lord, a man who thinks of everything, was loaded aboard the plane and in the hospital in Beira two hours later.

It turned out to be kidney stones and he passed a couple of them Sunday evening and was back in camp on Tuesday.

His wife, Maria, who cooks for the camp, accompanied him on his trip.

This left the camp completely in the hands of Chesini natives for two days.

The Chesini are thoroughly charming and competent in whatever they are given to do, just so they understand it.

The men marry two or more wives, depending on what they can afford—a wife costs $50 and should she prove barren during the first year—she is returned to the father who resells her for $20.

Bernice, who is the dining room attendant for guests, has a new baby, or rather his very youthful sixteen-year-old wife did, and the now eight-day-old baby has already been taken to the witch doctor and two magic bracelets have been placed on its tiny arms, and a packet of herbs around its neck for the same reason, to ward off evil.

"Don't they ever bring a baby to you for anything, or come themselves if they get sick," I asked Francisco.

"Only when the witch doctor has failed and then usually it's too late. Take your new best friend, Fombe, the tracker. He has two wives and four children. Eight of his children died within their first year. Yet he will not ask us for any help. After nine years with clients, Fombe just wants to be a tracker and preserve the status quo, and he's too old at fifty to be trying to rearrange himself now."

This was in answer to a question I'd asked on whether any of the blacks ever got to be a white hunter.

Francisco didn't particularly like the question.

"One of the first things that would happen would begin as soon as you stopped for a drink after the hunt. Fombe would try and drink it after all."

As if to prove himself, Fombe got himself so drunk on Monday since Mariano was away that he was unable to go hunting and he took Alficio and Bill, the driver guide, along with him.

"Do they have a vote in the government?"

"Oh, yes. Anyone can vote for the governor. The governor, in his turn, votes for the president. But they don't vote. Why bother is their attitude. Some of the natives in Beira vote. But most of the Chesini never get to Beira. Most of them never get to Maringue which is 43 kilometers away."

Which is my way of saying that I cannot start a civil rights movement here among the Chesini. If Stokely Carmichael feels differently, now that he has married all that money, let him come and try, although he'll discover that no television reporters and no newspapermen will follow him around here.

The problem is an educational one, just as it is in Mississippi. But with Portugal, the mother country, having the largest illiteracy rate in Western Europe, what chance is there for the Chesini.

During the last five days of the hunt three things happened to all three of us, Charley with an elephant, me with a lion and George with a leopard.

On the fifth day before the hunt closed, Charley shot an elephant. It was very strange at the time, since I was actively spending most of each day hunting elephant. One day we pulled up at headquarters for lunch and there was an elephant's tail hanging from a girder on the porch.

Francisco noticed it immediately.

"Charley has shot himself an elephant," he said.

"Congratulations, baby," I shouted. "One of us finally shot one. I'm so glad for you. That's terrific. Tell me all about it."

"There's nothing much to tell. Actually I'd rather not talk about it. It was a baby anyway. I'm sorry I shot it. It was one of those things, where I had to shoot it. But I'd really rather not say anything about it. We, Mariano and I, are disregarding this particular animal. Tomorrow we hunt elephant again."

"Yes. It was all very sad," said Mariano. "But Charley had nothing else to do. He had to shoot the elephant. The elephant did, in fact, charge him."

"Let's not discuss it any further," said Charley shortly.

"But you've got yourself an elephant anyway," I persisted.

"Let's not talk about it anymore," insisted Charley. "I would just as soon have never seen that particular animal much less have shot him. Now can we drop the subject?"

"Okay. If that's the way you want it. Okay," I said.

"That's the way I want it," said Charley while Mariano looked embarrassed.

He refused to discuss the matter at all with George when he came in a half an hour later.

Killing a lion is presumably one of the high points of any hunt. I noticed when we got back to Beira, the manager of Safrique said that the camp had radioed them that I got a lion, yet it was truly anticlimactic to me.

Despite the fact that I'd had a conversation with Herb Epstein at the Pfeiffer Brewery in which he told me, "I was never so excited as when I shot a lion," I was totally unprepared for the effect it had on everyone around me.

That girl had been waiting for a lion and even remarked to Francisco, "There aren't any lions in Africa anymore, are there?"

Francisco had not deigned to reply.

It was the second-to-the-last day of the twenty-two-day hunting trip. We started out as usual and the first animal we spotted was an impala. Which I promptly missed. I didn't see it very well, there being one bull impala mixed up with about five females. But I squeezed off a shot and there you were.

It couldn't have been more than five minutes later that we pulled around a bend in the road, and Francisco seized me by my arm.

This is unusual, normally he just grits out, "warthog" or "bush buck" or as he'd done a few moments earlier, "impala."

But now he had his hand on my arm. "Lion," he whispered as if he'd lost control of his vocal cords suddenly.

Suddenly, the entire truck seemed charged as if by a quick electric current. Fombe, the chief tracker, who stands directly behind me and a little to the right, seized me by the arm also and asked in English, this being the first time he had ever addressed me in that language, "You see him?"

I had picked out the lion's magnificent head in the tall grass, picked it out enough to see that it was huge black maned lion, not one of those littler lions which are still male and still legal to shoot. This was M-G-M's Leo done over again for me.

About that time, Francisco, who has a great respect for lions, having been charged by them and having had one bite the tire of his truck once, asked the same thing, "Do you see him?" while he reached behind our seat and got out my .375 magnum and tucked it into his shoulder.

All this business about whether I saw him or not is that often I did not really see game before I shot at it and there was a lot of focussing with the scope while I searched for it.

But "Yes," I answered both of them. "I see him."

At which point Francisco tapped on the cab roof twice and the truck skidded to a four wheel halt.

It was at a range of perhaps 175 yards and the big lion was not alone. Around behind him in the grass, a female was wandering about and another male, which was maneless.

The lion looked at me. I could see his tail twitching behind him. He just lay there, tail twitching, and stared back at me through the scope. I may have been a baboon, which lions consider a great delicacy, as far as he was concerned.

I put the cross hairs of the scope just a little below where his shoulder might be in the grass and squeezed off the shot.

For the second time in English, Fombe shouted, "Good shot" "Good shot," and clapped me on the back almost driving me onto the hood of the truck.

The lion was not a one shot kill. He got up, badly wounded through the head, and ran away from the truck a few feet. Then I shot him a second time, hitting his proper shoulder this time. Then Francisco got into the act with my .375 and by then he was down. As we approached he was still breathing and Francisco said to me, "Put one into his heart."

And I did and he died.

I sat there a little shook by the reactions of Fombe and then all the bearers and trackers descended and encircled the dead lion. They were all whooping and hollering and fussing with the carcass.

"They will gut him very quickly," explained Francisco. "He is a really beautiful lion. He may get in the record book. I'll see when we get him to camp which is right now. We have to get him cleaned up very quickly. Otherwise he will lose his hair and you don't want to lose any of that mane. It is because he eats nothing but meat that his hair falls out."

A few minutes passed and we were riding back, inside the cab, this time with Francisco driving. It was all part of shooting a lion. The natives began singing and shouting to other natives as we passed through villages.

"What are they saying and what's all this yowling about," I asked.

"You have to understand what a lion is . . . what he means to these people," explained Francisco very seriously. "This is the big animal in the minds of the natives. This is the animal who sneaks into the villages and kills off one of them. Fombe lost a brother to one two years ago. Alficio lost a cousin just a month ago. He is a no good animal to them, and today he is dead. What they are singing is improvised words about the glory that was this lion yesterday, how he walked high in the jungle yesterday but today he is no more. He is dead and you killed him. That's what they're singing about. Doesn't that make you feel great?"

"It makes me feel a little numb is all. I thought I made a much better shot on that reed buck day before yesterday or doesn't that matter anymore?"

"Believe me when I tell you, it doesn't matter at all."

I was a little touched by the fact that Francisco felt the same way. His hunter got a lion. He was as close to happiness as I'd yet seen him.

Meanwhile George Black had been hunting leopard for a week and a half. He now had ten days in in the quest for the big cat.

This is the sort of African big game hunting that appeals to me practically not at all, because you bait the trap for a leopard and then, when he comes to dine on it, you shoot him. You can see why I don't particularly care for this bit of business.

However, let me say that I've spent four days doing it, following what my white hunter says, that is, putting the bait out, and in the four days the leopard hasn't shown up.

The first three days we went out about five in the afternoon and waited until dark, but the leopard always waited until we had left before he came and took the bait.

Then we put a lantern on the bait, which presumably would spook him from eating, the theory being that the next morning you took the lantern down and by that afternoon the leopard would be so hungry, he'd come to eat and you'd shoot him.

That night we lit the lantern for my leopard and then got up at 4 A.M. to be out there at first light. The natives would take the lantern down and you would wait to shoot. When daylight finally came, it turned out the leopard had eaten by lantern light.

"That's enough," I told Francisco. "The leopard wins this one. We've tried to outsmart him and he has outsmarted us. I don't like getting up at 5:30 in the morning, if you must know. I'm a night person. And to have that damned leopard getting me up at 4 A.M., that's too much."

"Look at George," said Francisco. "This is the sixth day he's been hunting leopard. He's not discouraged."

"Let's say that I am. Let the leopard live. That's what he's going to do anyway. He's too smart for us."

In the meantime, off this tiny bit of experience, I began to watch George.

Here was a man with leopard on the brain.

About the fourth night, George saw the animal on the road after he and Vergilio Garcia, his white hunter, had left the bait and he came back to camp ecstatic.

"What a muthuh," he said. "Pintada (the leopard in the camp zoo) looks like his son. He must measure ten feet from nose to the tip of his tail. But he was going down the road after sunset when hunting has halted in Mozambique."

"Why didn't you shoot him in the road? Pretend you're still in India."

"Garcia wouldn't let me. The law's the law with him. After all it's his license at stake."

Day by day, the leopard grew on George. He got to getting up in the morning at 2:30. At dinner in the evening, it would be just that and to the sack with old George.

Charley and I sympathized with him.

Each day he began looking more haggard. Gone was the happy-go-lucky hunter who used to return in the evening to camp with his truck crammed full of game. Forgotten was the jokester of the brush. Leopard on his mind.

He began getting up each day at 2 A.M. You'd see him briefly at lunchtime and then he'd be back out chasing down one of the twelve baits he now had posted for leopard.

One day he shot a reed buck just for laughs.

But his laugh failed to have the old George Black sense of hilarity to it.

Then the final day of the hunt rolled around.

Garcia had confidence. He told George, "Today you'll get a shot at your leopard."

George told him back, "I've had two shots at him already and both times, it was too late in the day for you." It came out like a snarl.

They went out about two o'clock that afternoon. They got behind their blind and waited. At 2:30, just as Garcia had promised, the leopard showed up. Garcia was excited. "Shoot him," he told George.

George took up a position, using a tree as a rest, carefully lined up the shot and then missed. The leopard was gone instantly.

At home that night he simply said, "I hammered it, that's all there was to it. I had a beautiful shot and I hammered it."

There was a touch of whimper in his tone.

George and I had a couple of snorts, he out of his sadness and me out of commiseration. Then about dinnertime Charley showed up and guess what happened?

Charley announced that his elephant had suddenly turned into trophy size and he had arranged to take the tusks home. They weighed eight kilos, after all, and they were his so why shouldn't he take them home. "Anyway, my mother wanted an elephant ashtray made out of one of the legs," he blurted.

Slowly the story unfolded. Charley had gone to Mariano and asked if he could purchase the tusks rather than have the government claim them as was normally the case in an undersized elephant.

"I just checked," he said. "The tusks weigh precisely eight kilos. So we don't have to weigh any flies on them." He was smiling very winningly as he spoke.

My wife, who had been belting Martell's brandy rather decently for a couple of hours, erupted with, "By golly, Charley, you're rotten."

"Wait a minute," said Charley. "All I felt was that why should the government keep those tusks and I went to Mariano and asked if I could purchase them from the government. It was then that Mariano weighed the tusks and discovered they were legitimate."

"Nonsense," said the girl. "You've been hunting for five days illegitimately. Your license was used up for elephant when you shot your mini. You hunted for five more days and when you didn't get another, you and Mariano cooked up this deal over your mini."

She had another cognac.

Charley drew himself up to intone, "Look, it occurred to me that I'd killed this elephant and I might as well take the trophies home."

It bothered me that my super sportsman turned out to be no sportsman at all.

The matter was solemnly concurred by George Black, who noted, "That was usual for him to bring his mother in, did you notice that?"

As Francisco remarked to me, "I wish I hadn't heard what he said the day he brought the elephant back. I'd like it better then. But I'm not surprised. Most hunters are like Charley."

With the hunt over, we stayed up all night drinking scotch and Martell's brandy and Charley got "rottener and rottener."

Remember what Henry M. Stanley said, "The next, is the almost perfect indifference to all earthly things outside his camp."

We chartered a plane and flew out of Nhamacala the next morning and arrived in Beira around lunchtime.

The Safrique people met us, took us to a gourmet type luncheon and then someone mentioned, "That was sure too bad about Kennedy."

"Sure was," I said, wondering how Kennedy crept into the conversation. It was then that we discovered that Robert Kennedy had been assassinated by a Jordanian national in Los Angeles five days before.

It was a reminder that the jungle we live in was far worse than the jungle we'd been in.

8. entertainment

My friend Richard is a guy who delights in throwing parties among the various sexes which usually end in various stages of discontent, and he staged another one over the weekend. There was the normal result although it took a twist to do it.

The pattern was the same. He gets everybody wallowing in cocktails as a psychiatrist loosens up the patient on the couch and this time, he threw in an item mentioned here sometime back.

"This scribbler here quoted something from a book about chameleons," he said. "And I would like to have him requote it since it bears upon our little parlor game this evening."

I didn't remember and cared less so he said:

"It was something about the chameleon and the unpropertied male," he said. Then I remembered.

So he stood me for a recitation and although I didn't remember the precise wording I did manage to recall that it was from Robert Ardrey's book, *The Territorial Imperative*.

The book is a study, and excellent, of the advantages inherent in the defender of one's own land against an invader and how invaders get confused in this, as witness our gyrations in South Vietnam.

How Hitler became confused with it, especially in the matter of Russia . . . these are the main points in his treatise, but of the chameleon, he said:

The chameleon is the only species of animal in which the female is not sexually unresponsive to the unpropertied male.

In other words, if you're poor, your choice of broads is apt to be somewhat scant.

Then he snickered and recalled that a comment here was "All hail the female chameleon" and pointed out that such snide observations aside, it was a three million year old pattern that males collected hunting preserves and territories and even females as property and the females collected males.

And in this game, as he called it, where among the thinking animals, i.e. the ones who speak and presumably also reason, does it end?

Maybe it was an extra martini or two, but oh how eloquent seemed Richard this evening.

"I have carried Mr. Ardrey a step further, just as has the female of the human species," he declaimed. "The male collects property including the female, although the female has considerable voice in by whom she is accumulated. Then there is more property in the form of children and the female has come to consider them as hers. Yet among humans there is such a civilization that there is the property of money."

At Dick's parties there is always the question and then the private voting booth sort of answer where no names are signed and complete honesty is requested and often, under the alcoholic circumstances, obtained.

The question was directed to the girls.

"If you could have your husband's income for the life of your husband, would you leave him, if you had to leave the children also."

I don't know why he put that in . . . about the children I mean . . . women are so daft on the subject of their children.

But the second one was a dandy.

"If you could have the income and the children also, what chance would he have?"

During the answering period as a minion wandered around with a tray and the husbands laughed and told stories, I managed to get in a new definition of "love," garnered from Dr. Arthur Gulick out at Grace Hospital.

"My definition comes from the Greek word Agape," volunteered the good doctor. "How do you like that?"

I liked it pretty good. After all the huff and puff, maybe that's it. The definition didn't go over very well with the other men. They kept bringing up sex which I suppose is a way men go.

The embarrassing answer is Richard's quest at all of his parties and as he read them off there didn't seem to be one. There were several "yeses" to the first question but who knows who answered that way. And there were even more "yeses" to the second one but again who knows who although some of the husbands began beatling at their wives a little.

And then there was an interesting answer: "Since we don't have any children, I'd have to take the dough and run."

Again it was an anonymous answer but the lady, as they are wont to do, talked too much.

Richard laughingly pointed out there was only one childless couple present.

The wife turned livid.

"But, dear, that just means we could court again," she said lamely.

"Yeah, me, and who else," responded the husband.

They were white-faced when they departed.

"How did I know we were the only ones with no kids," she was grating as they walked out the door.

"Did you know?" I asked the host, "anyway, you can scratch them from your next guest list."

"I'm always very careful with my guest list," he replied.

This was the first of a series of parties that my wily friend, Richard, tossed and maybe it was the funniest . . . no games or anything, just the food. Which was enough.

Richard and his wife, Helene, planned it. It didn't work out as planned and things got pretty sticky around the neighborhood for a while, but it did seem a magnificent idea at the time.

There were problems of execution but Helene worked them all out, shuddering and grimacing the while.

It was the worms that got her.

I don't know whether it was the looks of them or the odor from the can but because of my knowledge of Spanish I'd been imported to read the directions.

These were fried agave worms from Mexico so as translator I translated that you should "heat the worms in the can in boiling

water for twenty minutes" but the line of directions that got me
was *Tambien frios son exquisitos.*

They are also exquisite served cold.

Helene bought them at Lambert's in the Broadway Market
along with cans of fried grasshoppers, seasoned baby bees, some
boiled quail eggs. She'd also made a trek to Hudson's Gourmet
Shop and picked up some little delicacies like smoked and sliced
octopus, barbecued snake, and some smoked eel in soy bean oil.

She also picked up a pretty little pacquet called the chocolate-
covered menagerie.

These are candies wrapped in vari-colored tinfoil. The silver
covers chocolate-covered ants, the gold is for chocolate-covered
caterpillars, the pink for baby bees and the green for grasshoppers.

Now, understand that sweets present no problem, in case you
ever have a hankering to give a party like this one, because all
the impending nibbler sees is a square of chocolate with, obviously, some kind of filling which could as well be a date or a
raisin as well as a caterpillar or an ant.

An agave worm looks like what it is . . . a fried, crisp, crunchy
worm with those little body sections by which it locomotes read-
ily recognizable.

And the grasshoppers look like grasshoppers if you're expect-
ing them and not particularly appetizing if you're not, unless of
course you're a nut about grasshoppers. I haven't seen enough
baby bees to judge but they come out sort of soft and squishy
(they not being fried, just seasoned) and as all of us realized they
had to be disguised.

Helene was brilliant. She mixed them in dips and pimento paste
on crackers and sprinkled the trays with watercress and sprigs of
parsley.

Rembrandt couldn't have disguised them better.

A festive occasion of this nature gives you some interesting lati-
tude in your guest list, too.

There are some folks that are keepers, not many probably but
a few and you've got to let them in on it. You've no idea with
what enthusiasm they approach the others with "Hey, have you
tried these, they're great!" On the other side, we had a guest whom
we have come to call, with no considerable degree of affection,

Freddy the Freeloader and it was a thing of crystal beauty to watch him dive into the worms.

To provide a proper denouement for this friendly gathering, you have to save the tins in which these goodies came and the real touch, and don't forget it, is to leave a few of the dried worms and grasshoppers and bees in the can in the kitchen so you can show them around after everybody's eaten.

Encourage them, if possible, to sniff at the can.

This would do it even if they hadn't already eaten 'em.

Well, the whole party was a joy to behold . . . in progress . . . the innocent and the aware and "Do have another hors d'oeuvre while I get you another highball" . . . "Isn't that a fascinating dip. No . . . no . . . it's an old family recipe given by her great-grand-mother the night before she died . . . very hush."

It was simply a cocktail party after the football game.

A quiet, genteel affair with the victims and the apprehensive awares blended in delightful harmony wailing over the outcome of the football game and how the officials are taking over the game and why was Alex Karras so angry with everyone?

Several platters of worms, bees, ants were consumed. I ate some quail eggs and enjoyed them very much and though the eel and octopus and snake didn't get a lot of play, it got some.

Finally the awares kept persuading Helene to tell them what the dips . . . the dips . . . what magic formula had produced the dips?

It took a lot of persuasion for dramatic effect.

Finally a couple of awares, no longer able to contain themselves, went into the kitchen and produced the tins, with their grubby leftover remains, the clearly marked labels and began distributing them about the room among the guests.

Freddy the Freeloader turned a color I haven't seen since the last burial detail during the war.

His wife went first.

As mentioned in the beginning, nothing worked out precisely as planned. The first mistake was that this affair wasn't staged in summer so it could have been held out-of-doors. The second was the mistake of having light colored carpeting.

It's a small house anyway and though there are two commodes, even at three noggins apiece, the plumbing proved inadequate.

I wore a slight mouse under one eye due to the inadequacy of the sense of humor of one guest I never cared much about any-way.

And I personally never even got to the chocolates.

The next day the girl I live with said: You know, honey, you talk about people and their senses of humor and everything. Well, I've been wondering . . . You know that dip you ate last night. I wonder if it would make a fellow sick if he didn't know what was in it.

I felt my stomach do a flip and gulped.

"But it didn't make you sick."

Not last night it didn't.

9. music

The party sauntered wetly along and by now you could see that everyone was going to end up pleasantly hammered, but no one seemed ready to fall into a potted plant, nor decide he was a fighter, either. Someone once remarked that under proper dosage of booze eventually all women decide they are sirens and all men decide they are comedians, but the party had not turned in this direction.

There was an interesting corner populated by Sixten Ehrling, the new conductor of the Detroit Symphony, Leon Fleisher, who was appearing at the piano with the orchestra at the moment, and the pianist Eugene Istomin, who was hosting the blast. It was a corner for learning.

I learned for example that in the old days a conductor led his minions while reading from the musical score but now all of them memorize and conduct. The reason is that Toscanini's eyes eventually got so bad that he threw out the dotted pages and now everyone has to do without.

Stravinsky refers to Winthrop Sargent, *The New Yorker* music critic, as W. S. Deaf and throughout the world of sharps and flats Claudia Cassidy, the Chicago *Tribune* critic, is generally called the Claw.

There was more than an implication here that musicians generally feel that the critics don't come culturally educated enough to be as critical as they choose to be, so a resolution was taken to say nothing about the symphony except that the noises made are pleasant noises.

So pleasant that once, during Beethoven's Concerto in C Minor No. 3, for piano and orchestra, the noise soothed so much I dozed off.

Istomin was a trifle incensed over this; however, he finally concluded—to stay on the critic's theme—

"Look, you slob, if you're going to sleep at concerts, OK; it's been done before and will be again. But the next time you should take a musical score with you and a notebook. Put a pencil in your hand and the other stuff in your lap. Then when you fall asleep, people will think you're a critic and it'll be all right."

The preoccupation here is with Sixten, whom one of the guests kept referring to as Sixtoon, which we explained to him was a complimentary mistake, alluding to America's heritage of the old West and was a combination of six-shooter and spittoon, both honored objects.

Ehrling is a fifty-two-year-old Swede who served a long sentence with the Royal Opera in Stockholm, and throughout his career he has achieved some reputation for an imaginative kind of programming. Instead of feeding you Beethoven, Mozart and such until you whimper, he throws in some younger and less widely known composers.

On opening night in Detroit, he conducted a piece that involved some theatrics. The music faded to a halt, the lights—even the exit lights—were dimmed to a blackout and for two minutes a tape played a raft of jungle sounds which an associate of mine described as sounding like "a convention of werewolves."

The audience didn't know what to make of it, but Ehrling liked the confusion about it. People laughed and giggled among their nervousness. It was different.

To the point that Ehrling took the symphony to New York as part of the International Festival of Visiting Orchestras.

The New York *Times* began with "Only last season the Detroit Symphony Orchestra was, in a way, one of the poorer relatives in the United States symphonic family."

It went on to conclude: "The Detroit Symphony by now is one of the country's superior organizations, ready to compete in any company . . . In short, it is as good an orchestra as one is likely to hear."

Much as I fight any sort of provincialism, it was with considerable pride that I noted his reception in the East. With the Lions and Tigers faring so badly on other cultural fronts it's nice to have some others carrying the cudgel. He was referred to in another review as a conductor of the "no-nonsense school," which brings me back to the corner at the party a few highballs later.

Sir Thomas Beecham, the English maestro, was of the nonsense school, in a manner of speaking. Great, perhaps, but lazy.

One time he arrived in Atlanta to perform as a guest conductor that Thursday evening. He met with the orchestra on Monday, first time either had seen the other. Sir Thomas rose to the podium to address his impending charges.

"Gentlemen," he conned them with dignity, "it is with great pride that I address this great orchestra . . . you polished professionals . . . and I look forward to Thursday evening when we shall play Brahms' First together, at which time we will deliver a splendid professional performance which will be a cause of great satisfaction to all of us and also the audience.

"Since we are of the community of great professionals, and since all of you have played Brahms' First countless times and since I have conducted that tremendous score more times than I can recall, I will not insult either of us by a demand for rehearsal. We shall meet again in the hall on Thursday evening and render a fine performance."

He bowed with some pomp and began to step down. The bony hand of a slender clarinetist was raised in the rear. He nodded his permission to speak.

"I've never played Brahms' First," said the clarinetist.

"Never played it," muttered Sir Thomas. "Unimportant. You have read the score many times."

"I've never read the score," said the clarinetist. "No matter," countered Sir Thomas. "You've heard it so many . . ."

"I confess I've never even heard it," said the young man.

Sir Thomas regarded him solemnly for a moment and then shouted jubilantly: "My boy, you'll love it."

At Masonic Temple a semi-statured graying man whose face remains innocently unlined walked on stage bearing an $80,000 Del Jesu Guarnerius violin. He played this instrument better than any other human being alive can.

This is Isaac Stern.

There was once a Jascha Heifetz, a man who was regarded as the finest technician who ever applied bows and strings together, and a man whom other musicians tend to regard as perfect.

Except to heart dimension.

Stern came equipped with a larger heart, and it is the heart that you will hear speaking, along with technique, and there is a reason for the heart.

Isaac is among those people to whom the world said "no" and who would not accept that monosyllable. He didn't nod back.

After a birth at Kreminecz in Russia he arrived in San Francisco at ten months with parents who were amateur musicians. Fortunately they located across the street from a family that had a son who was attempting to become a violinist.

By the time Isaac was three, he was in tears because he didn't have a violin like the kid across the street. And by the time he was four he had one.

The kid across the street is now selling insurance. The world is grateful that he was originally there.

"He's doing very well at it too," Isaac said as he departed a meeting at the Waldorf after arranging a show for the America-Israeli Cultural Foundation.

"We're going to have a fund-raising event here at the Waldorf," he said. "We're going to put on a Broadway show, and we hope to raise a quarter of a million dollars. The price is $500 a couple and the show is the *Tale of a Soldier* by Igor Stravinsky.

"What's the story?" seemed the question.

"It's about a soldier," he said, "who is coming from a war and meets the Devil. The soldier is carrying a fiddle and the Devil asks him if he could teach him to play it.

"Yes," says the soldier.

"Teach me," demands the Devil.

The soldier tries to explain that ordinarily he wouldn't mind but that he has been away at war and there is a girl waiting at home that he will marry when he gets there and that she has been waiting long.

The Devil contrives to convince him that a violin is an instrument he can learn to play in three days, and such little time should not be an obstacle between them.

"OK," says the soldier.

"Thank you," says the Devil.

So the soldier teaches him and goes home, where he discovers that the three days were actually a bewitched three years and his girl has meantime married someone else. All of Isaac's listeners sighed.

"Leonard Bernstein will direct the seven musicians," said Isaac. "That's how many there will be. Plus three dancers and a narrator."

He and his wife, Vera, were off to see some television announcer about a show to publicize *Tale of a Soldier.*

They—Isaac and Vera—are a story, too.

There was this time at the Prades Music festival in 1950 when Isaac had to depart for Israel to play some concerts. He was after a first marriage at the time and running company with another girl.

A wire arrived in Prades to his friends announcing: CONGRATU-LATE ME. AM ARRIVING WITH FRESH NEW WIFE.

The great woman was with him now: Vera was the girl.

She had been in Berlin, Paris, Stockholm, New York, and some duty in the UN before she ended up in Israel. Isaac married her like a shot.

A friend says of her: "Remarkable. She's not vengeance but steel."

Another friend says, "It makes them a fine pair."

Isaac is a churning energy. If you hear him you will be privileged a distinction. This is the only time that Stern is ever on time for an appointment. Concert time. In all other instances he demonstrates his aptitude for tardiness.

You will hear a man who earns—to use the definition so conclusive in America—probably three times as much as the President. On the other hand he has also spent a lifetime acquiring his skill. No Goldwater would dare play against him. They'd laugh it out of the hall, like they did with Mr. Johnson.

"The most important thing in my life is being a musician," he was saying, "and the second thing I guess is the place that music has given me and what I consider the civilizing force that it is. There aren't very many of those."

"Does your music mean more to you, then, than Vera and your family?" is the kind of square question that you might ask a man on this runaway con.

"Of course not," said Isaac. "Mainly, what I do first is try to live as a decent human being. Besides that I try to use my music as a lever to make for other decent human beings. This is always what I try to do. Isn't that right?"

Isaac is the guy who saved Carnegie Hall from condemnation simply because it was the great musical landmark in the country and people were going to dispose of it . . . politicians and such . . . who didn't understand.

"It was more than the acoustics, it was the tradition," he said at the time.

When you talk to Isaac what you receive back is intensity.

This is the gift that he takes to the Guarnerius. And if you are privileged to hear him, this is what you will receive.

It will be a violin played more beautifully than it can be played by anyone else in the world.

The forty-five-year-old son of a pair of Russian immigrant opera singers named Eugene Istomin played Beethoven's Fourth Piano Concerto at Ford Auditorium with Paul Paray and the orchestra.

I would like to say this was the best it was ever played. I have reason for suspecting this might be true and I shall return and listen to it again.

The reason I do not just go on and say it anyway is that a promise was made here once that there was difference between a fact and an opinion and the reader was entitled to be privy to that difference.

This would not even be an opinion since I am so violently prejudiced in favor of Eugene that it wouldn't be in the least fair and you should get at least fair.

The reason I suspect it's a pretty decent performance is because Eugene thinks it's the best thing he does and also because Pablo Casals wanted to record it with him.

Casals does not record with anybody anymore.

The celebrated Bruno Walter hadn't made a record with a pianist since Rudolf Serkin well over twenty-five years before when they asked him if he would consider recording a Schumann concerto with Eugene.

Bruno showed no interest.

He was handed a record of Eugene's Brahms-Handel variations.

"I will gladly record anything with that young man," he cabled from Germany.

It has been my experience that professionals tend to hang together, professional athletes, newspapermen, pipefitters. It fits.

Eugene's associates in music are the Eugene Ormandys, the Pablo Casals, the Isaac Sterns, the Emil Gilelses.

There was an article in the New York *Times* that began: "If there were a Pulitzer Prize in music it should go to the trio of Eugene Istomin, Isaac Stern, and Leonard Rose."

This is an attempt to justify my prejudice.

It has nothing to do with the prejudice itself.

Istomin is my friend and he lives at the house when he's in Detroit which has been between concerts periodically. Once he suffered tendonitis, just like Mickey Mantle, while touring Europe. He underwent an operation and moved in to convalesce.

It's an experience. The first thing that happens when a pianist moves in with you is that he brings a piano.

An endorsement agreement exists between all pianists of concert status and the Steinway Co. Steinway provides the pianist with an instrument wherever he goes.

This is not a spinet. It's a big Greyhound bus-sized concert grand. Unless you live in a medieval castle all the living room furniture goes to the basement. It makes for an unusual decor.

The next thing is you meet Mr. Allen who is the piano tuner. Eugene's piano has to be tuned so often that pretty soon you realize you have not one house guest but two.

I thought it was a pretty big deal about Steinway always providing a piano until one day Eugene got a bill from them for $2750.

"I thought they gave you the piano?"

"They do. But I have to pay the freight to have it moved. When I was in California playing in the Hollywood Bowl they didn't have a good one and I had to have one shipped from Sacramento."

He's mad at the piano in our house now and is threatening to have one he likes shipped from Chicago.

During one visit he made an East Indian curry and had the house all upset with shredded coconut and scalding sauces and funny Indian bread that smells like you can't eat it. I discovered it's true. I couldn't.

Perhaps he'll forget it—the new piano, I mean. We're stuck with the curry.

It took four days to restore order in the kitchen.

I said it was an experience.

When baseball season is on, he practices with the ball game on television and sound turned off. If it gets hairy, he quits practicing and turns it up.

He brings interesting bits of information home from his tours. He was playing a concert in Orlando when Winston Churchill had his stroke and visiting his friend Arnold Toynbee, the British historian whose ten-volume history costs $75.

Toynbee thought Gandhi and not Churchill was the leading figure of the twentieth century. Eugene wanted to discuss it and then Toynbee told him that the way he, Eugene, was looking at it Roosevelt was more important than Churchill because he was a product of the most important country in the world.

We were at a baseball game one time and a foul ball headed in our direction. While I ducked he tried to catch it.

"If I'd made it," he said when I chided him about the danger to his hands, "you might have seen the quickest change from pianist to conductor ever made."

One time he cut his hand in Tehran opening a can of beans and had to quit for a while. Once I discovered him trying to open some oysters with a hammer and a screwdriver. Oh, well.

A thorough reason—and this not prejudice—why I enjoyed Beethoven's Fourth Piano Concerto so much is it was the first time I had heard it played in its entirety.

For a week around the house I tried to sleep while he played one passage over and over again. I was beginning to hate Beethoven.

This was before the days of Johnson and his grand eloquent barbecues but it was a tiny one in the afternoon at Baton Rouge and the Detroit Symphony orchestra under Paul Paray was a guest at it.

Not only could a player eat. Also could he drink.

Lare Wardrop played his last concert at Ford Auditorium and after thirty-one years a flock of his fellows gathered afterwards to fete him and exchange falsehoods and generally deport themselves as if at a retirement banquet.

Lare was one of the ones who drank that afternoon in Baton Rouge with his duties at the oboe impending for the evening.

He had been playing the oboe and English horn for thirty-one years in the symphony here, working his way through the old days at Orchestra Hall, then through the Wilson Theatre, the Masonic Temple, and finally Ford Auditorium.

If you care more about people than masonry it means through the days from Ossip Gabrilowitsch up to and including Sixten Ehrling.

Almost everyone except the Chamber of Commerce knows that this isn't really the Motor City like it says on the placards and from the lips of automotive hirelings; this is the Labor City.

This is the city of Walter Reuther and the overpass and Jimmy Hoffa and the trucks at night. Although Reuther was a symphony buff it never occurred to him to fight for an English horn player, perhaps because Lare was skilled labor and might take care of himself.

Lare finally quit because after thirty-one years all he could make was $200 a week and that was for thirty weeks of Symphony work.

But then he's not pushing a yankee drill either if there is such an instrument left since my days in a factory.

Ronnie Odmark and Harold Hall, of the oboe, and Charlie Sirard, of the bassoon, and Jack Boesen, fiddler, and Lare were reminiscing about the time an old friend and teacher, the late Dirk Von Emerick, got stiff but still made it to the concert.

The way the story went, Dirk was full of gin but still played the first half. During intermission he was drinking to stay even and he asked, "What did we play?"

"Beethoven's Fifth," he was told.

"Wow," exclaimed Dirk. "Beethoven's Fifth! How'd it go?"

These are the delightful people and if you learned about jazz people first, they're the same but wear their hair longer and the thing they do is more exacting because the composers wrote beyond June-moon-spoon.

"Lare, I thought you quit a couple of months ago?"

"I did. But I called up Mr. Paray and asked if I could play tonight. There's a great English horn part. You should have heard the *Bolero*. I'll bet the audience brought us up five times."

"You think you've really quit?"

"This was the last time. I just wanted to play again."

Sirard, the bassoon man, was saying, "We don't make a lot of money like athletes . . . baseball players maybe. But I'll bet if they didn't make a lot of money they'd play anyway. It's tough to beat it when you like what you're doing."

So maybe a fellow could be wrong to hold a complaint in his mind because money caused Wardrop to take up as a cameraman where he makes three times as much. The cost to have happiness is, I guess, his problem.

Anyway the time in Baton Rouge it was Lare and Ronnie, both playing the oboe that day and at the barbecue they outdid themselves on their own confection which was a drink called "boilermakers" which, as you know, is a shot of whiskey and a beer accompaniment.

Lare and his pal were nodding into their oboes as Paul Paray took the rostrum just above them.

Paray looked at the bowed heads and raised a querying eyebrow.

"Sick," said Lare's cohort and let his head sag again.

"Et vous," said Paray, who hides in his French language.

"Boilermakers," said Lare, and also bowed his head.

"Qu'est-ce c'est boilermakers?" asked Paray.

"Whiskey and beer," mumbled Wardrop.

Paray shook his magnificent head.

"Humph. Make me sick, too."

They got through the symphony, of course, and the more I learn of it the more I suspect that behind the white ties and serious miens, these people have more fun and laughs than us laymen are supposed to know.

Gregor Piatigorsky is a guy, as in the case of the few genuine artists, who is a giver to rather than a taker from life.

He has given a little extra, I think. He wrote a book called, by a strange quirk of circumstance, *Cellist.*

When he first came to this country some years ago, the people who write music fell in love with the habit of saying that "Gregor had crossed the Dnieper River on his cello."

After that reporters used to heckle him with questions about whether he paddled or rowed and didn't a cello have holes in it and why didn't they both capsize or at least in decency, sink.

Immediately before a concert one time, a photographer showed up and over Gregor's protests, demanded a picture of him and his cello.

He finally tucked it under his chin like a violin and posed.

For years he got letters from mothers of tiny urchins complaining that the children were developing curvature of the spine, ruptured chins and other logical maladies from a tendency to be unable to hold the cello in this fashion.

The interesting thing about his book, and I write about it not in review or as a critic but as if it were a thing, a subject like St. Patrick's Day or Selma, Alabama, is that Gregor wrote it himself.

This is the day of the ghost writer but no ghost laid pencil to Piatigorsky.

Grisha is what his friends call him and it was ten years ago or so that Ken McCormick, the editor-in-chief at Doubleday and a true music lover, spent an evening listening to Gregor.

He'll talk you silly.

"Why don't you write a book?" was his final gasp.

"I've been thinking about doing something else," answered the Russian. "I'm awfully sick of playing the cello."

Ken became as upset as he ever gets.

"I had a thought of Picasso suddenly announcing, 'I've decided to quit painting, become a golf pro.' "

The cellist didn't quit the cello and the charm of his book is that you never suspect it's by a professional ghost. A great musician has simply told about himself and the world that surrounds him.

He says interesting things.

At one point he described a tour he made through the rural areas of the United States where, as he admits, many of his audience had never seen or heard a cello. He was interested in the programming of music by his managers, the same old things usually.

"Yet it was true," he wrote, "that many liked to hear the music they knew. In all other things the majority has the urge for the new.

"They would not read the same book or see the same movie twice, or even eat the same dish twice in a row, but in music they seem to want to hear the same pieces all over again, all their lives. Managers and musicians oblige . . ."

It's true.

Given an opportunity to select, the audience clamors for the "old songs."

My companion was Gene Roberts, then *Free Press* city editor now with the New York *Times*. "People feel the same way about poetry," he commented. "They like to read the same poems over and over. But he's right about the rest of it."

He mentioned a concert here in Detroit that some will remember.

"Accidents, the dread of performers, are often the crowd's delight. A broken string or a bow slipped from the hand and its flight into the hall will provoke enthusiasm.

"During a concert in Detroit my starched collar snapped open. Not having time to secure it back in place, with both sides of the collar flapping like wings, I sailed through the concerto. So enormous was the effect that I contemplated repeating the trick later by fastening my collar insecurely, but it never worked again."

This is probably, not the incident but the rest of it, a complete falsehood which is part of the charm of Gregor's book.

A professional writer would have wanted to know when and how many times and such, that he tried it again.

"Facts just confuse him," admits McCormick now. "He's sort of like that legendary jazz pianist and composer Willie (The Lion) Smith.

"He wrote a tune once called *Echoes of Spring* that's very big with Cab Calloway, Louis Armstrong and the rest. He has two stories on how he got the inspiration and wrote the song. It depends on his mood which one he tells. But the magnificent part is that he believes both of them. Grisha is like that."

Everybody's in the book—Heifetz, Stravinsky, Casals, Rachman-inoff, Bartok, Stokowski—everybody.

It's a long anecdote and you come away knowing more about these somewhat strange and bewildering people of concert music.

Stravinsky was explaining to him once following a recording of one of Stravinsky's compositions that they divide the money, 50-50.

"Of course, as the composer, I get 90 percent.

"But we divide the rest evenly. Five percent for you and five percent for me." A good deal of it dealt with his work in Europe and now he is threatening to do a book exclusively on his experiences in America.

It's one of the few times I've enjoyed being threatened.

The privilege was to talk to Willie (The Lion) Smith.

It readorned memory.

Ho . . . fool . . . you've forgotten or are too young to remember The Lion.

The simplest way to explain Willie is to quote Duke Ellington.

"When you came into the Capitol Palace (in 1923) you were either in step with The Lion, literally, or you had to stop and get into it."

Or if you like it better another way, there was Artie Shaw, in his autobiography.

"Pod's and Jerry's, I felt this tiny joint, with its dim lighting, its small bar at one end of the room, its sprinkling of red-and-white checkered tables, was what I had been lookin' for.

"Mainly it was the music for it was The Lion who dominated the joint with his piano playing."

Willie was the guy who carried Fats Waller around with him. Thought he might make it. There were four giants at the piano during the well, up to now, period. What they called the Harlem Stride Piano.

There was Thomas (Fats) Waller, James P. (Brute) Johnson, Ferdinand Joseph (Jelly Roll) Morton and, of course, The Lion. The Lion is the only one still living.

The Lion started blues . . . that's wrong . . . he didn't start it. It was already there in the funerals in New Orleans where Louis Armstrong played the dirges behind the casket . . . the "Didn't he

Ramble" and then the marchers walked home afterward blasting the "Saints Come Marchin' In."

But The Lion made it popular by reproducing the first blues record—"Crazy Blues"—with Mamie Smith right after World War I. It sold everywhere. He got $25 for his piano, as did the other artists. After that, blues was publicly accepted.

Willie lives at 634 St. Nicholas now in apartment 1K, but time has worn on him, as it will on a man, and over at 300 West 151st in Harlem there is the lady he calls "My Madam." She's in apt. 11 and there is a piano there.

The thing that engendered the excitement here about Willie again was that a guy named George Hoefer, who married the daughter of the Detroit sport writer, Frank MacDonnell, did a book with him.

Ellington did the introduction.

The whole thing will make you breathe music.

As Ellington says in the introduction to *Music on My Mind:*

"Like if the cat was weak with the left hand, The Lion would say, 'What's the matter, are you a cripple?' Or, 'When did you break your left arm?' Or, 'Get up, I will show you how it is supposed to go.'"

Willie grew from the piano. He thinks today that any piano player worthy of the name ought to be able to play one tune with one hand and one with the other.

A thing that startled me. This was in his book. He was dubbed The Lion over something that had nothing to do with music.

Willie enlisted in the Army during World War I and ultimately wound up as an artilleryman, shooting 75s at the Germans. He became inordinately proficient at it. One day his commanding officer observed him for a while.

"Willie," he said. "You are a regular Lion at that gun."

It was surprising because back in the '20s and '30s Willie would simply walk into a cabaret and shout "The Lion is here."

At that time, all other piano players better leave.

Willie is patronizing about life now.

But then he was patronizing before.

Ellington also said: "This is the great thing about The Lion: a gladiator at heart. Anybody who had a reputation as a piano player had to prove it right there by sitting down at the piano and displaying his artistic wares."

Duke is a piano player speaking. Among the others who didn't sit down immediately were Waller (The Lion always called him Filthy instead of Fats) and Earl (Father) Hines, who sneaked out of the challenge and the place when he was young and encountered The Lion.

I said it adorned memory and the memory it adorns for me is from around here what we once called Paradise Valley. You don't know where it is anymore.

But on St. Antoine there was a place called the Melody Club where late at night everybody was playing. And across the street was a big red door that led upstairs to Earl Walton's joint.

And around the corner was Slim Jones' Congo Club and up the street from that was Jap Snead's 666.

That was here.

Willie The Lion remembers it all.

Although Harlem was and is his town.

The Lion is aware of race problems now and he was aware of them in those early days. He refused always to play in the South and didn't like road shows out of Harlem.

He wrote a thing in his book that you would stumble over.

"Instead of fights on the street corners after the cabarets closed, there would be people dancing the Charleston."

As Ellington remarked, "I love him—he is wonderful. I can't think of anything good enough to say about The Lion, Willie The Lion, Willie The Lion Smith.

The remark doesn't render the Duke unique.

Vincent Manone worked on the banana docks in New Orleans and in due deference to the Church and his own inclinations bred and raised thirteen children, one of whom was a boy named Joseph Matthews Manone.

Joseph Matthews' childhood inclinations varied against those of his father.

When Vincent looked for this boy child he always found him across the levee playing with colored children and lingering at night, listening to the thump blues music and patting a small foot, and nodding his head and singing along.

"You'll come to no 'a' good," said his father over their red beans and rice. "You stay away from there now. You bad luck."

Joseph's bad luck was compounded shortly thereafter when he scampered across the street in front of a streetcar, slipped and the wheels sheared his right arm off at the shoulder.

Wingy Manone, the legendary trumpeter of New Orleans music, had just been named.

Friends like Bing Crosby, Joe Frisco, and a flock of later thinkers have been sending him the other cuff link every time they lost one.

Sometimes now, he plays the trumpet holding it with one arm . . . if it's a short riff . . . and more often he props it with the artificial limb and a gloved piece of machinery where there was once a wrist.

The music is the same . . . the music he learned on the levee where his father warned him not to be "playing with them colored."

"Louis Armstrong and I left New Orleans on the same train to Chicago," Wingy once recalled at the Showboat on Washington Boulevard. "They had a partition between us for white and colored so we couldn't ride together. When we crossed the Mason-Dixon, Louis slipped up front with me."

He was fifteen when he started playing for Al Capone at the Friars Society Club on Van Buren Street. He began sending a hundred dollars a week home to his father. He was making two-fifty.

"They were great people, the gang guys," he said. "They never hurt anybody but other mob guys who were trying to muscle in. Sometimes there'd be a shooting in the joint and we'd just keep playing."

One night Al Capone came up to the bandstand, according to Wingy, and wanted to sing a song.

"You're crazy," said Wingy. "With the talent we got, you want to sing."

Capone went back to his entourage.

"Don't he know who I am?" he asked the manager.

"Sure," came the nervous answer. "He just don't think you can sing."

Capone thought about that for a moment. His aides watched

him carefully. Then Capone began to laugh. After that, everybody laughed.

Wingy set up shop with his horn after a slightly younger contemporary named Jimmy McPartland had left the Dixieland gauntlet on the floor at the Showboat in Detroit more recently.

He was drinking a screwdriver.

"Booze," he said. "I never went for booze. And booze killed them all. Bix Beiderbecke, Bunny Berigan, Tommy and Jimmy . . . all of them. Booze. What a sweet horn that Bunny played."

You've seen him in movies like *Rhythm on the River, Birth of the Blues* . . . bit parts in a dozen films. Now they're getting ready to do one on him called *Trumpet on the Wing,* based on an autobiographical book he once did for Doubleday which is out of print now just as it is being revived in Great Britain.

"I came here from Vegas, where I've been playing at the Top of the Mint . . . downtown . . . and right now Tony Bennett looks like he'll play me in the movies.

"He spent some time following me around, trying to catch my gestures and things. He's getting them."

10. notions

Defeated again. Diabolically defeated.

It was only an 86-cent breakfast but there I stood before the cashier, crimson-faced speechless, the customers in line behind restless to be on their way.

The cashier's glance was quizzical and accusing and the bill I'd extracted from the money clip was merely a fragment of stationery cut bill-size with a message on it.

"*Remember Watterson,*" it read. It sure wasn't money.

Fortunately a man isn't hanged over these matters and the matter was subsequently arranged but it shows you have to walk pretty carefully around a wife.

This all started when that fellow in California-remember-was told by his wife that he could move back in the house but listed fifteen conditional behavior rules for him if he did.

They were pretty pointed. No drinking. No stopping anywhere after work. You are to let me cash your check or if you cash it, I want to see it first. You are not to see your sister under any circumstances. You are not to do any bragging of any kind to anybody.

There is no point in listing them all but you can see this wife was going to set it down pretty good for this guy and there was to be no nonsense about it.

Well, these are the sort of newspaper stories that are very dangerous because they might tend to give a wife an idea that she hadn't previously owned and there is only one way to combat such peril. This is to take the initiative. Strike first.

So before mine could compose any list of do's and don'ts around the hovel—it beats you why cigarettes in the coffee cups and ashes on the carpet should be such a big deal—I whipped up a taboo or two of my own.

You will agree that they are reasonable.

1. Practice your banjo only when I'm away at the office.

2. Limit telephone conversations to five minutes as it keeps a man on edge to keep getting a busy signal when he is doing the proper thing and trying to call home. Sometimes during these periods he may fall in with evil companions since no man phones from a drug store or a gas station.

3. Speaking of gas stations, when one has used the car it would seem to be simple courtesy to replace some of the gasoline as it is growing into the cold season and it is uncomfortable to walk roads with a gas can in this weather.

4. Stay away from beauty parlors. You're pretty enough without letting those finks put all that junk on you and your hair.

(You will notice how that one was softened. This was very clever because the next one was the one I really wanted to slip by.)

5. It is a matter of simple budgetary logic that it should not be necessary to remove funds from my trousers when I'm sleeping but since this point has been made conversationally over and over, it seems a simple request to at least keep a record of the money you take so that we can try and keep our financial picture somewhere coherent.

Things ran pretty smoothly for the rest of the day. The dinner was as palatable as can be expected. There may have been a slight frostiness around the house but then a man comes warned that there will be days like that.

But then the thing happened with the cashier and no money. Then I called and the line was busy. There was a creeping fear in me that when I got home she would just have come from the beauty parlor and her hair would be piled up on her noggin like a cone of cotton candy.

The car would be running on the fumes. She would still be on the phone and honing that damned banjo with the other hand.

You see, the slip of stationery, among similar slips, cut in currency size that said "*Remember Watterson*" is my own fault.

It happened so long ago but now there is the recollection of the delight with which I told her the story, and it seems foul to use a man's own weapons against him.

Henry Watterson was a very famous editor from Louisville, Kentucky, and one time the paper hired a new auditor. Like all editors, Henry had his idiosyncrasies and one of them was that he had a habit of dipping into the petty cash fund.

He dipped and dipped but he never kept any record of when he did nor how much he took. This upset the new auditor no end. It was also explained to him that if he wanted to do anything to correct the situation he would have to take it up with Mr. Watterson himself.

No one else was going to second him at incurring the wrath of that great man.

The auditor pondered his problem and finally fell upon a decorous manner with which to approach it.

He left a note for the editor—humble and polite—explaining that certainly no one questioned his right to use the petty cash funds but in the future it would be appreciated if, when he dipped, he would leave a note stating how much money he had taken.

The next morning the auditor looked into the petty cash drawer to see how his plan was working and it had worked all right.

The note was there. It read:

"*I took it all.*"

During the riots in Los Angeles which began in the Watts area I kept waiting for a reference to the Watts Towers.

The towers . . . there are seven of them . . . were built by an Italian immigrant named Simon Rodia, a man who died a few years ago in Martinez, California, at the age of ninety.

The heights vary on the towers.

Simon was a tile setter and from 1921 through 1954 he put together these seven of what a building and safety official once called a "pile of junk."

On the other side poet Carl Sandburg called them "remarkable modern primitive architecture."

In 1959 the city decided the towers were unsafe.

Simon built them by his own hand, on his own property, where he lived.

The tallest was 104 feet high, or the equivalent of a seven-story building.

He put them together of scrap iron, broken bottles, dishes, bits of tile and thousands and thousands of sea shells.

You can climb up in them over the rusty rods and irregular bits of cement, footholds and hand grabbings the way Simon did when he was building them.

"No building permit was issued," declared official people and therefore the towers, called Watts because of the area, should be torn down.

There were some who thought they were art.

This is the area of the rioting . . . where the towers stand . . . where the death toll stood at 33, injuries at 862 and arrests at 3124.

This is where a looter stole a pair of shoes, a man hurled a milk bottle of gasoline through a window, where 15,000 National Guardsmen finally prevailed.

Diagnosticians of social harmony, influenced by Tennessee Williams, called it another of the "long hot summers," as if weather is a substitute for law.

About the towers . . .

When the city of LA wanted to tear the towers down, there were those who wanted to maintain them as a public monument.

Simon remarked during the long years he was crabbing up and down them that he was building a "tribute to America."

When the fight started over whether they would remain or not, Simon petulantly declared he didn't care what they did with them.

There were public hearings and Sandburg used the phrase that they "be spared the hand of the wrecker."

Officials must always have a recourse of course, so that they may remain officials.

So on October 10, 1959, they challenged the safety.

A cable was placed around one of the towers.

A truck was attached and exerted what technicians called a 70-mile-per-hour windstorm.

Rodia built these towers without engineering education, machinery, scaffolding or blueprints.

The truck couldn't make the tower quiver.

When Rodia died, there was a memorial service at the towers that coincided with his funeral services in Martinez.

There is a reason why you might wait for word of the towers and it lies in a document by the Italian tile setter who, in his only explanation of his works, said this:

"I had nobody to help me. I was a poor man, I had to do a little at a time.

"I think if I hire a man he won't know what to do. A million times I don't know what to do myself. I never had a single helper. Some of the people say what was he doing . . . some people think I was crazy and some people said I was going to do something.

"I wanted to do something in the United States because I was raised here you understand . . . because there are nice people in this country."

During all of the violence I waited to see if there was some mention of the Watts Towers and finally there was only the mention that they, of course, still stood.

It reminded me a little of another generation and the statements of Sacco and Vanzetti before they were innocently executed.

Of the eloquence that is so simply offered.

". . . because there are nice people in this country."

The towers stand.

I saw an accident on the expressway.

This was no soul-searching deal, you understand.

The two cars careened into one another and the crash apparently startled both drivers enough so that they pulled over. Being a dutiful citizen I pulled in behind to see if I could referee in case either one could stand up enough to fight.

Each guy . . . these were men drivers . . . descended his machine carefully, so as not to stumble, examined his own car, then examined the other car, straightened and one said:

"I ain't hurt so bad, ha'ryu?"

"Mokay," said the other.

They clasped hands amicably and gratefully and, after a few seconds, climbed back into their autos and, after a false start or two, toddled off.

It reminded me of some of the inventions I have been trying to conceive in the auto safety program that the government used to embarrass the automobile companies with recently.

I am working on an atmospheric drunkometer that could work

off the heater or air conditioning system so that when a driver got into his car and perforce, began to breathe his radio aerial would run up a flag.

If the flag was flying just over the fender, it would be a warning to be a little careful. The joker behind the wheel is slightly stoned.

If it's at half mast, give the guy full right of way.

If the banner waves atop the car?

Pull over, here comes a runaway.

I think that this notion became an embryo some years back when Zora Duntov, the Corvette's mad designer, was describing his vehicle.

"What we are doing here is building a forgiving car," he was saying.

"Forgiving?"

"Certainly. Forgive the driver. We have a car so that when a driver makes a mistake, the car will not hold him to it. He can pass quicker, stop faster. Whatever he does, the car will try to forgive him."

What I have in mind is "warning" cars, cars that warn other drivers what kind of a goof is inside.

Like the signs they put on driver school vehicles, that sort of thing.

Running an automatic flag up on the aerial off an atmospheric drunkometer merely handles the matter of the drinking driver.

A driver should be rated as he gets his license.

You could have another aerial on another fender and say he's a Class A driver, he gets a white flag.

If he's color-blind he gets another flag so you should be careful of him at intersections. See how simply it works?

If he's had two accidents and is trying for number three he should perhaps have another aerial on another fender so that two accident stars can be worn. It shows you're meeting a veteran and not some scary kid.

These are the ingredients of intelligence that should be available to a rival on the road.

Perhaps a woman should have a doll's flag to fly although, as someone pointed out recently, whenever you come abreast of a lousy woman driver, it invariably turns out to be a man.

Anyway you can see how beneficial this sort of system could

be on the highways. It's like nature. Why do you think there are rattles on rattlesnakes?

I've come about to the conclusion, as nearly as one can without approval from all of the bureaucrats that could get into a thing like this, that the black flag would be the real ding-dong.

My wife thinks it should be plainer than flags, even flags flying from all four fenders.

She thinks colors should mean something.

In the case of a real road menace, she thinks the whole car should be painted orange. This eliminates a color-blind driver but then, you know how a girl thinks.

There are refinements that can be worked out on this matter and I am taking it up with the Big Three in the hopes that something can be achieved.

Meanwhile, if you see an orange car coming down the street with four aerials up and black flags on all of them . . . a suggestion.

Turn around and head for Indianapolis.

If you're a tree . . . fall.

There must be truth in legends, which is why they become legends. Like Pagliacci . . . the tearful clown. And over the years as a student of laugh manufacturers, I've found that there is a tear in all the fine ones.

Chaplin created a sob in your laughter and Cantinflas is still the poor Mexican pelado when he is doing his best work.

And a man remarked one evening about Joe E. Lewis that, "I'd like to take him home and put him on the mantel."

Which is a way of saying that Sonny Mars was back in town and there won't be too many more times because he has agreed to work out the year for the Playboy Clubs and then he'll settle in Chicago and the Sherman House and the Continental, and spend some time with his Schnauser dogs, and his wife, the former Mary Earl.

Sonny was working at a joint outside Gary, Indiana, when he met Mary nearly twenty years ago. She was a dancer and he tried to get her into his club because she had two weeks off, but the boss couldn't afford her.

"Why don't you take sixty or seventy bucks off my salary and make up the difference, but don't tell her," insisted Sonny.

A week later the boss had to tell Sonny, "I'm keeping her, but you've got to go. Business."

Mary's Irish and Sonny's Jewish. When they agreed to prolong one another, it was the biggest religious war since the Crusades but in this instance the principals won.

"My dad is all right about it, but my mother never has been," he was saying recently. "But my mother-in-law was great. Over the years, I'd write her and I'd send her a yard when I had an extra hundred. When she died, she left me all the letters, all wrapped in ribbon and all the dough, too."

Sonny lost a sister in an accident, and a favorite sister died in childbirth.

"Can you imagine?" he said. "Childbirth. It's one out of six million."

"I know," I told him. "I lost a sister in a tonsillectomy."

His reflexes are Pagliacci's.

"What are you trying to do? Top me?"

But a story about a professional laugh producer should have the elements of humor rather than just the sadness that is such a basic ingredient.

We were discussing squelches, that moment when the guy on stage dismisses a heckler, and discussing the technique thereof.

Jackie Vernon, for instance, never uses the squelch.

"I can't get out of my routine and into a heckler," says Vernon, "and then get back into my act. I just lower my voice and hope the heckler will sound so loud to himself he'll shut up."

The two I remember that Joe E. Lewis used to use . . . the one for women went: "Madam, I wouldn't go down to your house and turn off your red light." And for men, he'd quickly murmur, "My friend, you are not being paid to entertain me, nor are you equipped."

Sonny likes to make arrangements with the management and then engage a heckler in conversation and interpret him by saying "This man wants to buy drinks for everyone. Give everyone a drink on this gentleman, isn't that right, sir? Isn't it? Isn't it?"

Sonny's manner varies according to the room he's working. If it's a big, dignified room he'll do it stand-up and detached, or at least as detached as Sonny can get.

In the small Playboy rooms he sort of wraps the audience

around him like a blanket and everyone becomes his foil. Sit up front and you should need a union card.

He operates as if the audience is interrupting something else he is trying to do. He brings it off funny.

Late at night over the lamb chops and biscuits and coffee, he was remembering the unexpected pitfalls.

The management asked him to introduce a couple celebrating their engagement. He asked the girl to stand up and somehow the wrong girl stood up, a woman seven months pregnant.

Sonny smiled and said, "Well, at least you've already got your engagement present."

Not long ago in Chicago he was playing a room in which a man had fallen asleep on the table. Sonny promptly put him in the act. "All right, enough of that . . . You there, you don't do that on my time. Up . . . Up!"

The man had just died of a heart attack.

He hasn't gotten over it. But maybe that's it.

He never gets over anything. Except love maybe.

With the lamb chops over he produced a letter to his wife. He sends her a note each night after he finishes work.

11. food

"This will involve my sleeping with your wife for a couple of weeks," he said, "but I'm sure that under the circumstances, you'll understand."

It was Jim Beard talking, the man who, as you know, is perhaps America's foremost authority on food and certainly one of its leading chowhounds.

The two of them had begun by discussing diets and ended with Beard describing a pair of hospitals, one in Switzerland and one in Germany, where the plump go to pare it off.

Drugs are administered so that the reducer lapses into a deep sleep for as long as necessary.

The patient is roused and given enough liquid for survival during this period and presumably painlessly, loses the amount of weight he or she is supposed to shed.

"There's a hospital in England where you can lose weight on a water diet, but it always sounded a trifle arduous to me," continued Beard. "You get nothing but water for fifteen days and during that time they make you take constant exercises. It sounds dreadful but I guess it works."

This is the reverse approach to Beard. His dodge has to do with food intake and in the heroic manner in which he goes about it, it becomes part of the package that he will put on pounds. He has written a dozen books on the subject of cookery and completed a series of television shows for national distribution in Canada, New York, and eventually perhaps the rest of this country.

This is not to suggest that Mr. Beard is overpoweringly huge and that you have to moor him, like a ship or dirigible, any more than you have to moor my wife. But he's a big man.

Just guessing, he would go well over 200 pounds and makes a good advertisement for food. After you listen to some of his conversation about it, you're tempted to discard the knife and fork as weapons and order a conveyor belt.

Until now, I have always worked on the theory that food was something you took on to balance out your drinking and most of my memories about this apparent necessity—eating—have to do with the humorous didoes of my companions.

I remember Buster Ramsey, the erstwhile Lion defensive coach, tackling his third plate of crepes suzette one time, remarking, "Best damned flapjacks I ever tasted."

And Bear Bryant saying to the French headwaiter at the posh Pavillon in New York, "What do you mean, you don't have any chili?"

And the notorious autocrat of his own restaurant, Monsieur Point, at the famous place outside Lyon in France where the trout swim in little tanks until you pick the one you want to eat and so celebrated that reservation is nearly impossible.

Monsieur Point refused a second reservation to an American lady because she smoked between courses. One time a man called from Paris demanding a table for four and claiming he was a friend of Pétain, then the head of the French government.

"And who," asked Point, "is this Monsieur Pétain?"

Beard does not smoke himself and for a time I suspected that he was one of those people who had combined with the surgeon general and your doctor to make you give up tobacco but such proved not the case.

"I don't think it has much to do with taste any more than I think drinking a scotch will destroy your taste for a forthcoming glass of wine.

"A dozen scotches yes but not one. I think that some people are born with perfect taste as a musician is born with perfect pitch.

"The best palate in the world for wine, I think, belongs to Frank Schoonmaker and one of the best certainly, to Alexis Lichine.

"Both of them are wine merchants. They both smoke constantly. They don't smoke between wine tastings but they smoke immediately afterwards and while they're going from vineyard to vineyard."

A question seemed, "In your racket, do you ever have . . . let me try and figure how to say it . . . well, a startling culinary adventure?"

"I'm not sure I know what you mean? Can you explain further?" he asked.

"Well, I remember the first time I ever tasted a papaya. It had a familiar look, rather like a cantaloupe, but tasted like nothing I ever tasted before."

"Twice," he said. "I see what you mean. You taste something and then do a double take. The first time was when I ate ortolans. An ortolan is a tiny bird about two inches long and they catch them in nets twice a year as they fly up some occult corridor of their own between Italy and France.

"They are roasted—head and all—and then you remove the legs and pick them up by the head and start at the bottom and eat them up through the neck. The second time was with a fruit I found in Thailand called a rambutan which looks like a dirty potato and has a white translucent meat."

Describing taste when there is no comparison is as impossible as describing color to the blind so we'll let it go at that.

He talked considerably about sauces and how most of them were developed to cover the taste of inferior or spoiling meats, just as the beautiful flavors obtained from smoking, sugar and pepper curing were designed originally to combat a lack of refrigeration.

He disparaged what he called the "cremation school" of outdoor cooking where the guy builds a fire as if he were shipwrecked and calling to ships at sea.

It had been both educational and entertaining and from the beginning I'd wanted to ask him what—if he were in the death house at Sing Sing—he'd order for his last meal.

I assumed that when a guy of this gastronomic training ordered it might mean the end of capital punishment since the taxpayers would rebel at the cost of the meal. At least, it might amount to a stay of execution since it would take so long to prepare.

Wrong again. He didn't ponder more than a moment or two before he answered.

"Bacon and eggs," he said.

When Viet Cong terrorists blew the front off the Victoria Hotel, those worthies who were thrown from their beds onto the shattered window glass and cut thereby received the citation of the Purple Heart.

Just as a soldier or Marine who puts his little tootsie onto a punji stick, those varishaped, whittled-to-a-point booby traps with human excreta daubed on the points for infectionary purposes, also is decorated.

I have a new medal for gallantry which I am proposing, and a very considered proposal it is.

A man should be, after proper performance, eligible for the Nuoc Nam Cross, and I already have two grizzled veterans of the Nuoc Nam campaigns who are entitled.

First, of course, it is necessary that you understand what Nuoc Nam is.

Nuoc Nam is a sauce. It is a sauce that the Vietnamese eat on everything. They eat it on fish. They eat it on rice. They eat it on bats, rats, and they eat it on pineapple.

The best of it is made in a factory on Phu Quoc Island, and no barbed wire entanglements are necessary for a couple of miles in all directions.

The odor protects.

I imagine the worst of it is made somewhere else, but that place is a name not even whispered into the night.

So important is Nuoc Nam to Vietnamese morale . . . it is to the Vietnamese what chili is to a Mexican. A Viet couldn't prepare dinner without Nuoc Nam any more than Pancho Gonzales could prepare huevos rancheros without chili.

So important . . . a stranded Vietnam regiment had to have a planeload of five-gallon vats flown to them in order to maintain discipline and calm. And the story goes that one vat burst in the landing.

The Viets unloaded the rest, but no pilot has been able to re-enter the plane since to fly it back to the base, although all the

windows and doors have been removed and coolies have been
retained to fan it during the scorching noon hours lest it fester.

It takes three years to make a proper Nuoc Nam, and the ingredients are salt and fish. At a distance from the factory on Phu
Quoc, one of the sauciers explained the process.

"You take a layer of fish . . . layer of salt . . . layer of fish . . .
layer of salt . . . layer of fish . . . three layers each," explained my
alchemist.

"What kind of fish?"

"Rotten fish," he said.

"I know, I know it's made from rotting fish. But what kind of
fish do you use to rot with."

He smiled an inscrutable smile.

"With rotting fish it makes no difference which fish rots," he
said solemnly.

Anyway, the layers rot and drain and rot and drain for three
years, and what grandpappy used to call the "squeezins" drain off.

There is as yet no instant Nuoc Nam.

Which brings me to the heroes of this tale, a jg named Jimmy
Hutchings and a Radioman 2nd named Bill Austin, both of whom
are advisors to the Vietnamese junk navy. They live in junks and
sampans with Viets and share their lot. I mean, lives. I mean, table.

"It's not all that bad," reassured Austin. "These are pretty nice
people when you get to know them."

"Who's talking about the people. What about the food?"

"It's OK if you like fish and rice all the time. And this Nuoc
Nam helps. Otherwise there'd be no taste at all. You know they
add peppers to the Nuoc Nam."

"Gee, no, I didn't. I'm glad you told me. Now it sounds deli-
cious." Austin was regarding us both as if we'd taken leave of our
senses.

"Do you eat the bats and rats and everything?" It looked like
ding-dong-bell; Hutchings nodded as Austin waggled his head.

"Do you eat Nuoc Nam on everything?"

Same response.

Suddenly Austin remembered something and looked a trifle
sheepish.

"I don't eat it on pineapple," he admitted. "It's especially good
on monkey."

I have given some thought to the design of the decoration.

I sort of liked crossed cod on a field of bilious green.

You may be familiar with the story about the young lady who entered the public library and asked if she could obtain some information about penguins.

"Of course," said the librarian.

The girl waited for a time and the librarian returned with twenty-seven volumes on the penguin, his life and times, his genealogical history, even down to one novelette entitled *Perry, the Hip Penguin.*

The young lady gulped in embarrassment, blurted, "I really didn't want to know this much about penguins," and fled.

The same thing has just happened to me about the egg.

What do we know about eggs?

That Christopher Columbus stated that he could stand one on its end and then cracked the bottom of an egg and thereby stood it.

This has something to do with the fact that the world is not flat but that part of it escapes me, although I do remember about the egg.

The egg plays a part in an argument that is as pointless as the debate concerning what happens when an irresistible force encounters an immovable object, i.e., which came first, the chicken or.

Some vegetarians eat eggs.

I resent this. I maintain that the collecting of eggs from under chickens is a form of abortion and as any elderly member of the American Medical Association will tell you, this is not only illegal in most places but somehow immoral also, population explosions notwithstanding.

A vegetarian who eats eggs is simply eating a chicken that isn't done yet.

An egg-eater vegetarian is a phony vegetarian.

Anyway, the girl I usually live with had to drive her mother home to Florida which was certainly justifiable recompense for the patience required to put up with four dogs while we went to Europe, but it has posed certain problems in logistics around the house.

After the canned goods were all gone, it occurred, of necessity, that I cook something.

Why not start with an egg?

After all, there were eggs there. And anyone can cook an egg. I've even seen a few anyones do it.

The simplest way, according to my intelligence reports, is to hard-boil eggs. Anybody can hard-boil an egg. Boil the water. Put the egg in for a while. Shuck the egg. Salt the egg. Eat the egg.

The first thing that happened was the eggs got rolling around in the bottom of the pan and then the white began leaking out. Sort of handsome. Spumelike. So I had a pan full of white stuff.

How did this befall me?

Well, like the young lady and the library. I journeyed to the London Chop House to see Lester Gruber, who is stuck with me as a friend as if he didn't have enough troubles.

"Don't feel badly," adjured Lester. "Practically no one knows how to boil an egg properly. I'm serious. What you did was you put a cold egg out of your icebox into a seething boil and it was too much for the egg.

"What you should do is (1) take the egg out of the icebox and let it stand until it is room temperature. (2) Get some water into a rolling boil and then turn the heat down to a simmer. (3) Put the egg in. Let it stay for nine or ten minutes—that long but no more.

"If you leave it too short, it'll be gooey. If you leave it too long it's too tough, hard to peel and rubbery to eat.

"You can put salt in the water and it will flavor the egg slightly and you can boil it in coffee and flavor it slightly and color it pretty. These are refinements."

I began to realize that bringing this problem to Lester was rather like going to the surgeon-general for a manicure.

He took a deep breath, like a man preparing to take a plunge and said:

"Now about the egg . . ."

I tried to interrupt.

"Hard boiled eggs are excellent for dieting. José, bring us a couple of eggs."

He keeps them behind the bar, just like in a corner saloon.

"An egg contains 80 calories, but . . . and this is the important thing . . . you expend 92 calories worth of energy peeling and salting and eating the egg."

"You're kidding."

"I'm not kidding. The exertion balances the intake."

"If you eat a hard boiled egg, then, you should lose about an ounce."

"That's right. If you ate sixteen eggs, you'd lose a pound."

"It doesn't make sense."

"What does? José, another pair of eggs."

He is considering doing a slim volume patterned after the Hip Penguin entitled, *Elmer, the Eager Egg.*

Did you want to know this much about eggs?

12. whimsy

The clock above the Hotel Astor at Broadway and Times Square read one minute to 12 and most of the eyes belonging to what the portable radio claimed as 200,000 people were lifted to the electric ball suspended above the Allied Chemical Tower.

The ball would drop precisely at the moment it became 1965.

The radio said the Knickerbocker Ice Company predicted that 3,000,000 ice cubes would be afloat in New York at midnight, a handsome figure no one would be able to prove or disprove by census.

It also was the day selected by the Distilled Spirits Institute to announce that Americans had set a new course record in the past year—they had outdrunk themselves—by consuming 271,000,-000 gallons of liquor.

"Well," said a man, "gives you something to shoot for anyway."

Most, but not all, of the eyes were tilted up.

Three Puerto Rican teen-agers, stuffed into tight, worn pea jackets shuffled in back of a policeman's horse.

"Stick 'im with a pin and watch that copper go."

"Yeah, stick 'im quick and watch that copper fall."

It wasn't conversation, it was a chant as they shuffled behind the horse in a kind of a dance, their hands feeling one another's arms and shoulders, not holding, but touching and grabbing in a rhythmic, shuffling dance.

"Stick 'im . . . stick 'im . . . watch . . . watch . . . stick 'im."

Like a vaudeville trio, the three done up the same, with the pea jackets and tight pants and hair matted an inch against the backs of the neck, and cut square across the bottom.

Then they stuck the horse, and the police officer didn't know what had happened and began hitting the horse in the head with his gloved hand to wrestle him back under control as they stuck him again.

Then as the officer realized, he wheeled the horse in the crowd but the teen-agers were off, scurrying offstage, laughing into the crowd.

"Tree dollars," said the vendor in a Hungarian accent, proffering the pink orchid to the young colored boy in the white raincoat with the pretty girl on his arm.

"I'll take it," said the boy, handing the vendor a five.

"Oh, you shouldn't," said his girl, then to no one in particular, "That's the way he is."

"That's right . . . five dollars," said the vendor and turned to the crowd. "Orchids . . . Orchids."

"But . . . but," said the boy to the vendor's back and then, shrugging, he took the shining-eyed girl by the arm and they melted into the crowd.

"Where'd ja say ya' cum from," demanded a big guy with an orange hat and horn. "I don't understand ya."

"Nebraska," said the shy little guy leaning against the glass of the Metropole Cafe where, when the doors occasionally open, you could hear the jazz music of Red Allen's Quartet.

"Whyn't ja say so? I heard of Nebraska. Have a drink."

The shy guy from Nebraska took the bottle and up-ended it. When he finally returned it the New Yorker eyed him half angrily and half admiringly. "They grow 'em thirsty in Nebraska, even little squirts like you," he said.

On the inside of the sidewalk a fight started between two paunchy middle-aged men which died of inertia before one of the two hundred extra policemen could get there to halt it.

"They couldn't even swear at one another good," said the cop —Patrolman Scaretti—afterward. "Naw, it hasn't been much to-night. It's too cold for anyone to stay drunk. Bigger crowd than usual. Nothing much has happened where I've been. A few pickpockets."

When the ball dropped, the flushed, shivering mob turned on the simulated gaiety with all of that peculiar false enthusiasm that simulated emotion engenders. It was the New Year and if you had a drink you drank it, and you shouted "Happy New Year!" and if you had a girl you kissed her.

But Times Square on New Year's Eve is not a place of happy people.

For every group there are three couples and for every couple there are fifty guys on the single-o hoping that somehow in the numbers they'll find momentary laughter.

The folks in dinner jackets and evening gowns you glimpse on television must be planted there because there is not a one visible in the street crowd trying to convince itself this is an exhilarating and glorious time.

At five minutes after the illusion had been abandoned and the mob was fleeing the scene and the cold.

I stopped in a dismal little joint called the Roxy Bar just off Broadway where some of the other loners had gone to huddle together for warmth.

It was as quiet as Good Friday between twelve and three.

A big soldier in paratroop boots tossed off a shot.

"Happy New Year," he remarked drily.

"Where you from?" I asked him.

"Andrews, South Carolina," he said. "And I wish I were back there."

The people with homes available were in them.

A half an hour later there was practically no one left from the big celebration.

Getting a cab had become simpler and on the way back to the hotel in mine, the cabby was cursing the pedestrians he was missing with harmless good nature.

"Know somethin'," he said. "A guy comes down here on New Year's Eve, he's nuts." Then he quickly said, "No offense intended."

"None taken," I said. "Happy New Year," he said. "Happy New Year," I said.

The marquee on the Victoria Theatre going by read:
It's a Mad, Mad, Mad, Mad World.

There is little doll in Chicago named Ruth Reinhardt whom Billy Rose once called "The World's Most Beautiful Eurasian."

She presides over a joint called Jazz Ltd. and many years ago she made this point:

"A fella who is passing through Chicago and doesn't stop and visit Jazz Ltd. has got no class."

Ruth has these sorts of opinions and then, after laughing she added, "I'm not suggesting that he will acquire any by stopping—only that he doesn't have any if he doesn't."

A man must protect himself in these matters.

Jazz Ltd. is a huge auditorium—sort of a saloon. It's been moved east on Grand Avenue to where it's now a block off Michigan toward the lake and across from the Sheraton-Chicago Hotel.

It never became a tourist trap, partly because of Ruth, but more importantly because of her husband Bill who presides over a Dixieland jazz band that is so comfortable now that the music laps over you. To hear Mike McKendrick sing "A Closer Walk with Thee" may not make you weep but it will make you drink more thoughtfully.

Bill Reinhardt plays a beautifully fine clarinet with his bulging right cheek and he is the one that has kept the music even and full of integrity.

It's a unique arrangement he's maintained.

When the joint was farther west it was a tiny basement cubbyhole and the walls were made out of spring steel and the music would bounce a customer about unless he was holding on to his companion which made it nice if she were a girl.

That was eighteen years ago and every month or so the band changed. Muggsy Spanier opened it, if memory serves, or maybe it was Doc Evans or Sidney Bechet.

I remember the nights when Art Hodes used to come in for the first set, eyes askew, punch a finger tentatively at the piano and murmur something about "Eye Opener Blues" and start it all rolling upward.

Bill is a solid jazz guy and when they played with him they had to lean into it some because he knew the difference and it was important to them to keep his respect.

Those were the days when it was touch and go whether the joint was going to survive or not and on cold nights when the place was empty but Bechet wanted his money anyway, we all used to have to go around to other places and round up customers and drag them over.

But it worked and the place clips coupons for itself now.

Bill never made a mistake.

Normally a guy plays in the band for a while and then as soon as the ink on the books begins to look dark enough, he lays his bugle down and goes out and greets and sits with the customers.

Ruth doesn't drink but she talks and as stated, she has opinions.

"Did you see where the English are putting a ban on cigarette ads on TV? They're copying the Russians only not so much. For years in Russia they've been putting ads showing what you look like if you have smoked a lot. You know, gray-faced and coughing and skinny lookin'."

"Don't you smoke?"

"Sure," talked Ruth. "Ever since I was fifteen years old. And my Japanese grandmother smoked and my Irish grandmother smoked and both of them lived to be very old ladies. Look at Churchill."

"Doesn't Bill smoke?"

"Sure," she said. "Salems and Newports and all those crazy menthol medicated cigarettes. Not even real tobacco. He doesn't smoke his first cigarette until after sundown. Doesn't touch a drink until after midnight except sometimes with you. Maybe you shouldn't stop by here. You corrupt everybody."

"I haven't done a thi . . ."

"He's a weirdo. Me. I've always smoked English Ovals. I was a flapper. All the flappers smoked English Ovals. Pure tobacco and comes in a hard box so you don't get crumbs in your pocket. I smoke less than a box a day. Enjoy them all. I never had a bad cigarette."

Freddy Kohlman launched a drum ride now. Ruth didn't stop talking but at least you couldn't hear her. The music sort of punctuates Ruth.

"Freddy's been with us nine years. Quinn Wilson, on bass, has been here six years. What I was saying is smoking is up to you. How long do you want to live anyway? Don't you ever get tired?"

Dave Rasbury spoke up now with his trombone—umm, closer walk with thee and Mike McKendrick wasn't there to sing.

"Where is he?"

"He had to have his leg amputated," talked Ruth. "Some circulatory problem. Just below the knee. He'll be back in three or four weeks. After all, he admits he's sixty-four years old."

"What was the circulatory problem from?"

She laughed wickedly.

"Smoking, I guess. You've smoked a whole pack while we were sitting here. I was thinking if they did in the United States like they do in Russia maybe you could get a job posing for one of those commercials on how rotten you look after you smoke."

Like I said, you don't necessarily acquire any class in the joint but you should attend.

It sort of balances you out.

This will eventually end up as a critique of a certain portion of a woman's anatomy and as a casual warning to a man on prospective matrimony but actually it is a defense of a Frenchman named Claude who related here not long ago a French legend.

A man does not invent a tale like this on the spur of the moment and at the time I suggested to him that his was a story he had pilfered somewhere. It had that ring.

His defense was simple and instantaneous.

"A legend belongs to no one except the ages that have marinated it. You suspect that the story of Yvette and the cadet of Saint-Cyr came from a book. I shall now tell you another legend of my country. Please to produce for me the book from which it came. A legend is not a book; it is a piece of the heart of the country from which it came."

Claude's second legend comes from the days of the Reign of Terror during the French Revolution and the wind country of Burgundy where there resided a young and handsome count, a bachelor if you please, much regarded by the minions who worked the land he owned.

Although a century earlier a count had been forced to desist from minting money of his own and from waging little private wars of his own, a count still held considerable privilege.

Henri, however, was a pretty special sort of a count.

He treated his serfs with great affection and solicitude.

There were spectacular fetes on any slight holiday. He clothed and tended medically after his people and was much thought of because he did not exercise his privilege of sleeping with the wives of his vassals on the wedding evening, although some husbands did consider it a rebuke.

He could make a saber sing and those of his peasants who helped him at his hobby of falconry, adored him, and his horsemanship indicated he had perhaps descended from a centaur.

No people had been so blessed as to have a count like Henri presiding over them and, when they poured off the excess from the wine barrels, you could hear the singing and dancing for many kilometers.

But the revolution was in full swing and there were those among the peasants who belonged to the cells, who heard their commands directly from Danton, Marat, and Robespierre in Paris.

One day the order came from the new leaders.

"Bring Count Henri to Paris to the guillotine."

Consternation reigned around the vineyards, the hen coops, and in the roosts where the falcons held sway, open tears were shed.

A revolution is a fine thing as our leaders say, but killing the count? What would we do? How do we tell him what the leaders have decided? What will he say? Perhaps he will be angry? Remember when he rode the little sick *bebe*, Alphonse, to town on his horse and saved his life? And Honoré when he lost the herd that time. How generous he was.

But there was the order.

They all understood that the reason there is an order is so it may be obeyed.

All day they met and fretted and considered until finally a herdsman spoke.

"We are stupid. We will go and ask Comte Henri what to do."

So the cell members banded together for courage and approached the door of the chateau.

"Ah, *mes amis*," welcomed the count. "Come in. Come in. Eh, maintenant. You look so serious. Come now. Nothing can be so as to put such worry on these brows of thine."

They trooped inside, hats in hand, scuffed their feet a moment until the nod went to the spokesman, who, unable to speak, handed over the order from Paris.

They waited anxiously while the count read.

"Well," he said at last. "This is serious, isn't it?

"The guillotine. But what can one do. An order is an order! Wait until I summon the carriage. We must have wine and viands for the journey. I am not enthusiastic but then you have the order, *n'est-ce pas?*"

And they departed, the count with three of the cell leaders in attendance.

They watched him guiltily as he leaned back comfortably in the carriage and napped as they jounced along, a wine glass dangling from his hand, his sword idled against the carriage wall, a lock of hair drifting over his handsome countenance.

"Maybe," said one, "we could produce an alternative so that he wouldn't have to die . . . an alternative punishment? Then we could explain."

"The leaders would not like that. Leaders never like it when you change the orders. Except him. He never minded."

"But suppose he had tried to escape and we'd killed him. He wouldn't have been guillotined then. What do they care? No one cares about him but us."

While Count Henri slept they schemed for an alternative and finally they reached it. Then they awakened him and tendered their offer.

"If you will marry the first woman we meet along the road, we will not take you to the guillotine. We will write and explain and your life will be spared."

The count considered only a moment.

"We shall see who this is, then," he replied.

The cell leaders shouted to the coachman to stop at the first woman.

Eventually the wooden brake screamed against the axle.

A girl of perhaps eighteen was herding her swine across the road.

Count Henri and his wardens descended and one held her for his inspection. "Humm," he murmured, examining her from her muddy toes upward, nodding his head pensively until his eyes reached her face. He looked long, and calmly at her mouth which was a little more than a riven slash of no upper lip at all, pinched, severe, near-metallic. At last he sighed.

"Drive on, coachman," he said. "Drive on."

13. autos

The most amusing account of a transaction between an auto salesman and a victim I ever heard was recorded by Caskie Stinett when he told of parking the car he'd bought a year previously in front of a dealer's and inquiring "How much?"

"I don't seem to recognize that model," replied the dealer. "However, I'm only forty years old."

Eventually they got together. Caskie was allowed one local phone call and no charge for parking on his car.

Which is a fiction of course.

A fact is that one day a guy wearing the name of Roger Hopwood brought a bundle of correspondence into the office. He—purely in the interests of science, he explained—had written to every Ford, Plymouth, and Chevrolet dealer in the Yellow Pages and asked him to quote a price on the then new 1965 vehicle.

Here was the letter he sent to Ford.

Dear Sirs:

My wife and I have decided to purchase a 1965 Ford Fairlane. It is a car for her and an extra family car and there will be no trade-in involved.

She would like an eight cylinder with an automatic transmission, window washers, two speed wiper, white sidewall tires and a radio, a four-door sedan. We understand the color does not affect the price this car will cost us complete with tax.

In other words what do I write the check for complete?

Thanking you in advance for this information.

Sincerely,

Roger Hopwood
675 Sutton Rd.,
Metamora, Michigan

His twenty-eight responses were delightful and perhaps there are many ways to misunderstand this inquiry because that's what happened.

Russ Mile Ford Inc. quoted him a price of $2,371.30, which was the low bid.

Most of the replies made him offerings involving $2400 and some change, an interesting proximity being one of $2474.79 from Bob Ford Inc. and $2473.17 from Leo Calhoun Ford Inc.

There were six fellows who would favor him with $2500 and up—O'Green's Ford at $2504 to Walt Hickey Ford's $2550. The salesman replying from John McAulliffe Ford Inc. wanted $2621.55. Same letter.

"Interesting bit of research, isn't it," remarked Hopwood.

"Very pithy. How'd you make out with Chevy?"

"About the same. I ordered an Impala. I didn't specify whether it should be a six or eight cylinder to see what would happen."

Paul McGlone Chevrolet Inc. was low bidder at $2595 and Kelly Chevrolet went highest at $2955, which is an eight, of course, and has a power-glide transmission added, which costs $163 extra.

Unless you bought the power-glide from Joe May Chevrolet, in which case it would cost $145 or Patterson Chevrolet in which case it would cost $155 or Ver Hoven and Floyd Foren where they concur that a power-glide transmission costs $160.

Roger produced letters showing a low of $2210 from Raynal Plymouth for the "Valiant" he ordered and Johnny Motor Sales wanted $2210.18.

"What do you suppose the eighteen cents is for?"

"I dunno," said Hopwood, "but isn't it interesting?"

"Yeah. But what are you trying to prove?"

"Purely in the interest of science, like I said," answered Hopwood. "But if a man wanted to apply this, maybe this is the way to order a car. Call up a dealer, ask him what the options are and then write all the dealers in the area—kind of like the City Council does—get a sealed low bid. Then you'd have some idea where to start shopping and what things are worth."

"Maybe this confusion has to do with advertising. If you advertise maybe you have to charge more?"

"You think fuzzy," stated Hopwood. "If you advertised you'd sell more cars and then you'd charge less. What's the matter with you?

"I bring you in a scientific premise to pass along to your readers so they can save money for whiskey and horses and things and what do you do? Who do you buy your car from?"

"A guy named Carl Staebler. Runs a joint on Jefferson."

"How do you do with him?"

"I'm not sure. But we've been friends for years and it continues, this friendship. I have my troubles with him though. The last time I bought a car from him, we played gin rummy while they were cleaning up the car and taking the papers off the windows and he beat me for $32.

"Also during this period he touted me on a horse that was running in Chicago and the horse lost."

"I don't think you should be entitled to handle money," declared Hopwood.

"That's what my wife says. But you're trying to take some of the romance out of everything. Anyway, suppose the horse had won?"

Paul was trying to teach me about morals in business.

Paul sells automobiles. In his lifetime he's sold most of them . . . Ford, Chevies, Plymouths . . . and the higher priced derivatives of those companies.

"What's the difference?" he said. "Selling cars is selling cars. You get a good gimmick car on a good year . . . like a Mustang. You sell 'em. I was lucky. I never had the Edsel problem."

He lit a cigarette from another and coughed as if he might vomit.

"It does it to you . . . this business. It's a tough business. You guys all think of the big money in profit when you buy a car. Believe me or not.

"We're selling cars. We make $60. I get $30 and the house gets

$30. You don't believe me, do you? That's because you're the customer."

A point seemed, "Well, you got to have a customer, don't you?"

"Sure. Taking the easy way out, aren't you? What I want to tell you about is the morals in this automobile business.

"In the first place there are three parties involved. One is the customer . . . that's you. One is the salesman . . . that's me. One is the house."

"OK. Moralize me."

"The whole thing is built on lies. You know who the biggest liar is? The customer. You. You come in to see me, I tell you I'll sell this car for $2700.

"You tell me you've been to a guy who's got me beat by $200. Bafta. That's what that is. Bafta. You should get up and walk out."

He coughed affectionately.

"You want to know how I'm so sure. Well, we've got the office wired. All the offices are wired. I get up and I say to you and your wife, boy, can I deliver this phrase: I say, I know that this is an important decision for you and your wife to make. So I'll leave you alone for a few minutes and let you discuss it."

Paul gets up and adjourns to another room. A box on the desk is a microphone. He hears a man and wife talking to one another.

They say:

"If he comes down another $25, let's take it."

"It's a hundred better than anything we've had so far."

"Suppose he doesn't come down. It's still the best deal we've had."

"Let's try somewhere else."

Paul returns. He's going to get the $25.

"I come back and I know what their situation is. We start to talk and the phone rings. It's my sales manager. He says, 'If they fool around much longer bounce 'em.' "

To bounce a customer doesn't mean to throw him out. It means jack 'em a little further.

They are "fooling around."

"That was my sales manager. He says he has a fellow who wants to buy that car. I'm sorry, he's agreed to a price $50 higher than the one we were talking about. If you want it, really want it, I'll go tell them we had already made a deal."

So, a transaction is accomplished.

"I'll tell you something I used to do, one place I worked, tell me if you think it's wrong. We're talking about moral, remember.

"I'd gradually maneuver a guy out toward the parts department. Finally I'd say to him, looking over my shoulder and around, "Tell you what I'll steal you a radio out of here and throw it in for you. You'll have to install it yourself. But it's a $98 radio."

The guy says OK.

When he comes back to pick up his car, Paul looks as furtive as possible, which is not difficult. He has the car pulled up ready to drive away. He sneaks into the parts department and grabs a radio.

He brings it out and hands it to the customer. The customer starts toward the car with it and Paul disappears.

At that point enter the sales manager. If he's at lunch, another salesman will do. He apprehends the customer.

"Hey, where do you think you're going with that radio?"

The customer is allowed enough confusion to get in his car and beat it.

"Who," asks Paul, "has the larceny? The customer has to have some or you couldn't do it."

He thought a moment, coughing the while.

"One place I worked, we used to close deals by offering to throw in the 'overdrive.' And we would, too. We'd hook up the little handle that said 'overdrive' with a wire running to the fireboard. That's all.

"But he'd be getting it for nothing. We'd tell him that it was already adjusted. How could he come back and complain? Most customers think the wheel base attaches off the magneto and needs vulcanizing."

Finally came the question, "Why tell me all this?" and "Does everybody have the microphone?"

"Everywhere I ever worked. We do one thing that's wrong. And that's the blank contract. We'll get a customer to sign a blank contract for, say, $2700.

"Then we'll check the bank, find out we can get $2900, and fill it out that way. If the customer notices, we'll tell him about the taxes, extra equipment, all sorts of things. A lawyer can't help him.

"This is the same guy, though, and always remember and ask yourself this question. Did you ever lie to an automobile salesman? If you haven't, you ought to be put under glass. The customers are the real liars."

He lit another cigarette.

"Why do you smoke so much?"

"I'm nervous from dealing with liars like you."

Paul the intrepid auto salesman called early.

"You know what I said about 'bouncing' the customers. Well I was just using an old term 'bounce.' Nowadays we 'adjust.' It's the same thing but it sounds better, don't you think?

"And, man, you shouldn't have said all car dealers have microphones to listen to the customers. Because maybe some of 'em didn't but now they'll get 'em."

"That's what you said."

"I know. But I have not worked everywhere. Now you've gone and made it true. It's a convenience to know what the customers are thinking and now everybody'll have it. But the word 'bounce' is out. We 'adjust'!"

"OK. You adjust."

He paused to light a cigarette.

"We have other phrases. Like 'If you can't get five, get ten.' 'If you don't write, you're wrong,' is another one."

"What does that mean? The one about 'if you don't write'?"

"Well what you've got to do is hook the customer. So you take his offer and write it down on paper.

"You don't have any prospect of taking the deal as he puts it to you. Like I said the customer is a liar. He quotes you prices you know are wrong.

"Like he says 'I had an offer of $2400.' I know he's going to have to pay $2700 to anybody. I don't know why a customer tries to lie.

"I sell maybe two hundred cars a year. He won't buy that many in a lifetime. So doesn't it figure I know more about prices than he does?

"Anyway I tell him that the price he wants for his old car seems a little high to me but there's a big dealer coming in from Oklahoma on Saturday.

"Maybe this big dealer will pay the price he wants. There is no big dealer, of course. But anyway the guy is instructed to come back Saturday and we'll see."

Now that a useless piece of paper exists between them, Paul asks for a deposit. It's only five or ten dollars and he puts that in his kick.

The customer now has five or ten good reasons for coming back on Saturday—plus hope. Paul takes him all over the bright, burnished car. It helps if the whole family is along. They all fall in love with the car.

The customer goes home. The wife tells the neighbors they are going to get a royal blue convertible. The kids, particularly if there is a teen-ager, talk about the cubic inch displacement and how fast it will go.

On Saturday he returns. Well, as you may have suspected, the Oklahoma buyer wouldn't give that much for his old car.

Paul mentions the price he had in mind to begin with. Then he brings in the "closer," a tall, handsomely dressed, American-boy type who looks sincere.

The two of them have the customer in the office.

"I'm sure Paul didn't include the taxes," says the closer. "I pay taxes. Everybody pays taxes. You know there's a 4 percent Michigan sales tax. You know there's a 10 percent federal tax on an automobile. You wouldn't cheat the government, would you?"

Paul is now standing over the customer, blocking the door. The "closer" is seated across from him.

Small beads of sweat begin to break out on the customer's forehead.

The kids have told the other kids. His wife has told all the neighbors. He is expected to come home with a royal blue convertible with the big engine that will go fast.

So he does. On Paul's terms.

"Always remember," reiterated Paul, "that the customer is a larceny guy. It was the customer who first put banana peels in a transmission to make it sound smooth for a while before it quits working altogether. It's the customer who has you appraise his car and then goes home and sells the tires and brings it back with no rubber and expects the same value. It's a two-way street."

The real victim, according to Paul, is the salesman.

"You remember how I said, there are three parties involved . . . the house, the customer and the salesman," he said.

"Well you got the customer telling you lies on one hand and then the house will boun . . . adjust you, too, if you're not careful.

"You start out and you make a 'minny deal' with the customer. Minny means minimum. You've got a deal with him with his car appraised at $1200.

"Then the house finds it can unload the car for $1400. Do you think you see any of that extra $200? Bafta."

"Your story touches my heart."

"You've got the house bilking you on one hand and the customer trying to bilk you on the other. What chance has a man got?"

"Why do you keep selling cars?"

"Where else could I make $12,000 a year and have such an interesting time?"

"You think it's worse than real estate, or insurance?"

"I don't understand those businesses but I can see lots of room to 'tune' people in 'em."

"Tune people?"

"Man, if you don't know what being 'tuned' is—well, when do you plan to buy your next car?"

There was no intention here to remark any further about the automobile peddlers.

Paul, the intrepid auto salesman, has gone back to work, happy that he is still working.

I had begun to puzzle over the deeper philosophical problem of the horses running at Hazel Park.

As a matter of fact the whimpering Public Letter Box touched me about as deeply as when my bookkeeper weeps, or as my old friend, Antelope Al, the defiant horseplayer who has been working his way north, used to remark, "Is there anything, anything at all as soothing as the wail of a wounded bookie?"

However, the Detroit Automobile Dealers Association requested and was granted an appointment with Boss Martin Hayden. I wonder what they could want with him? I was invited to attend a sales meeting at Joe May Chevrolet. There were other niceties so perhaps a conclusion is expected.

I offer none, for a reason I shall explain in a moment.

The guy who called from May was one Dick Clark who immediately told me, "I'm supporting a wife and children," the inference being, I suppose, that customers do not have this same problem.

He explained some of the facets of car selling.

"I just sold a convertible to a guy for only $150 profit and we have to make $300 on a car . . . On the other hand, 20 minutes ago I sold his brother the same car with a $350 markup. So you see how it works."

"It's kind of tough on the brother," I said.

"He can afford it. He makes fifty grand a year. I sold one the other day to a guy at $150 but two years ago I got $400 from him. But times have not been so good for him. See how it works? A couple of years ago there was a guy in here. He had three children, all of them sick. I talked it over with the sales manager: We gave him a car."

I told him how impressed I was with his beneficence.

"You have to understand that the economy fluctuates with every man's pocketbook. . . ."

"How's that?"

"The economy fluctuates with every man's pocketbook."

There must be a lesson there somewhere.

A letter arrived from Gage Oldsmobile saying simply: Enjoyed your articles one and two on the Perils of Paul, the auto man. Signed Alex Tzouras and Charles Zack.

Another came from a Mrs. R. W. Moss which read:

"Thank you so much for your article of Wednesday, April 21. My husband is an automobile dealer and, although his offices are not 'bugged,' what he has said about the customers is just what you have said in your article."

It seems strange that, despite the fact that Paul remarked that any customer who has not lied to his friendly dealer ought to be put under glass, no customer has rushed forward indignantly to proclaim himself "not a liar."

The hero of this bit of whimsy for me is Mathews Cadillac, perhaps in the person of a Mr. Carl Werner over the hilarious ad placed in the want ad sections. The ad was for A DOC

GREENE SPECIAL. Ford '60 Falcon Sta. Wagon—NO RADIO. NO OVERDRIVE. Standard trans. only. Needs mechanical repairs, also rear deck hinge busted. But price is right. Special only $295. See Carl Werner. Buy from a REPUTABLE DEALER.

Beautiful.

Mr. Werner will hear from me. I've sold one car for him and have a helluva prospect for another en route.

As remarked, I offer no conclusion. A conclusion has been promised by the Supreme Court of the United States on whether GM had violated anti-trust law by preventing the sale of automobiles at discount. There is the notion that a lot of discount selling would correct whatever needs correcting in auto dealing. Who'll correct the customers switching tires, I cannot say.

14. churchill

What an avalanche of memories the headline stirred:

CHURCHILL FIGHTS ON

I took down the fifth volume of Encyclopaedia Britannica to hear the rhetoric again for every listening human has heard that remarkable voice, even me.

". . . we shall not flag or fail. We shall go on to the end . . . whatever the cost may be, we shall fight on the beaches, we shall fight on the landing-grounds, we shall fight in the fields and in the streets; we shall never surrender . . .

". . . Let us therefore brace ourselves to our duties, and so bear ourselves that, if the British Empire and its Commonwealth last for a thousand years, men will say, 'this was their finest hour.' "

Just looking at it returned for a moment the drama that was Dunkirk.

"When the end comes," interjected the companion, "I'll still half expect him to rise up and demand a brandy and cigar."

There was this facet of him that always stunned.

He was things so simply and clearly, large important ones and trivial ones the same.

When he was Lord of the Admiralty immediately before World War I, he ordered a test naval mobilization and then ordered the fleet not to disperse so they'd be ready. He did it on his own.

In 1918 when the war ended it was Churchill running about Paris crying that now that the Allied armies were there, why didn't they go on into Russia and whip the Bolsheviks?

Just successful in their revolution, sooner or later the Communists would pose the serious threat to Western civilization.

He achieved some fame in later life as a painter.

What happened was simply that a painter was commissioned to do a portrait of Sir Winston.

He found him an impossible model. Instead of sitting he spent his time at the artist's elbow, watching him mix the oils on his palette, observing the brush strokes, the knife work, rearranging the colors.

It excited him. And as so many things, he saw it clearly and simply.

The first picture he painted was in oil.

Another time he had some masons in to build a swimming pool on the grounds. Pretty soon he had a hod and mortar and was not only helping but, of course, directing everything.

They finally objected on the grounds that he was not a union member.

It took a few days but he practiced and passed the union test of so many bricks a minute and got his own card and proceeded.

I almost talked to him once . . . or perhaps almost.

Six or seven years ago he had a horse entered in the Washington D.C. International and I decided that a sensible thing to do with the *News*' money was to call him on the transatlantic telephone and ask him:

"How do you like your horse's chances?"

His trainer warned me: "Once he would have dropped everything to talk to you about such a matter. He would have thought it had just the right amount of effrontery."

There was a time some years ago when an interviewer inquired of Sir Winston Leonard Spencer Churchill:

"If you had your life to live over again would you do anything differently?"

With the twinkling whimsy that had become his trademark, he replied:

"Well, yes. I'd have bet the red instead of the black that time in the casino at Monte Carlo."

An odd, tiny thing to think of with this tremendous, roller coaster, Niagara Falls, Taj Mahal, Babylonian Gardens of a man.

Yet when he suffered the last cerebral hemorrhage, I found

myself able to consider little else than the fact of his struggle at the advanced age of ninety.

Considering, that like most of us, he was a man I have never spoken to, heard personally nor even seen from a distance.

. . . never spoken to . . .

A scholar once upbraided him for ending a sentence with the preposition 'to,' just like that and what did he do? He penned an answer.

"This is the sort of pedantry up with which I shall not put."

The thought occurs of his extreme and tenacious battle to preserve life and of the early days when he served as a soldier at the Malakand Field, in the expeditionary force of Sir Herbert Kitchener at the Nile, of the hero he was returning to England after his flamboyant escape from a Boer prison camp in that war at the turn of the century.

How regard so jealously later a life treated so cavalierly then?

"That's because," remarked a companion, "when you are young you are trying to find yourself and you will take the chance but having found yourself you will try to hang on to yourself.

"But now his hearing is going and he's older and he mainly likes to see and talk to very old friends. He's embarrassed about his shortcomings."

I wound up with a butler.

You'd have to say Sir Winston had fewer shortcomings than some.

Lady Clementine Hozier Churchill once told the then Prime Minister of England, David Lloyd George, "If I die, the most important thing I would say in my will would be how to look after Winston."

Then, since she was a woman of humor and taste who would naturally retreat from a statement that might cast her in serious mien, she added:

"The most important thing would be to feed him well."

If I die . . .

But she didn't.

Her husband, Sir Winston, did.

He once wrote, in an autobiography entitled, A *Roving Commission* of his youthful years, this touch for conclusion:

". . . until September, 1908, when I married and lived happily ever after."

Gossips in London on that September 12 rattled their fans and gave the marriage "six months at best."

During this "six months" Lady Churchill bore five children, the son Randolph and four daughters: Sarah, an actress; and Mary, who married politician Christopher Soames; Marigold, who died at three; and Diana, who committed suicide. During the six months, Sir Winston campaigned against the women of Britain ever having the vote. During the same period Lady Churchill toured the London courts helping the suffragettes gain the thing that they did.

Lady Churchill obviously prided herself on eschewing the limelight toward which another might have grasped. She remained, unless her own convictions were at stake, a wife.

There was a conviction one time in 1960 over funds for needy refugees and she delivered a broadcast on British Broadcasting System over which the company later issued a news release.

The BBC, after carefully reviewing the effort for three months, stated that: "Lady Churchill raised 48,000 pounds with the broadcast."

Shortly thereafter, BBC saw fit to issue another release.

"We rate Lady Churchill the second best woman broadcaster in England, behind only Queen Mother Elizabeth."

Unless England has changed since the last visit, this meant that she was the first but it wouldn't be proper to declare it at the risk of offending the queen.

She bore the children and she conducted the dinners, and she nurtured this remarkable man of the twentieth century and you've rarely heard a word about her. But she bucked him over woman suffrage and won.

Another time he mounted the platform to denounce the entrance of women into public life and within a week Lady Churchill had to step forward and receive two of Britain's highest medals for her labors at relief work during the war.

From what you can sense of them, these contradictions must have amused them both.

There was another time when the prime minister's relations

with Premier Stalin had become rock and he received a curt missive.

It must have been remarked that the missive closed with the words, "and my sincerest thanks to your wife for her efforts."

Her efforts had been on behalf of Russian victims of Nazi atrocities of the time.

It was in 1953 that Sir Winston was awarded the Nobel Prize for Literature and when December came—the time for the ceremonies in Stockholm—Sir Winston could not get away.

He wrote a careful speech but it was Lady Churchill who journeyed to Stockholm to deliver it.

She prefaced her rise to the rostrum with an aside:

"I think it interesting that I should be giving a speech for a man who has gained so much attention by giving speeches."

It is one of her few recorded remarks.

Another occurred when Sir Winston was young in his political career and switched from the Liberal to the Conservative Party. You could say it would be like a Republican becoming a Democrat or vice-versa but then who in either party at this moment would you use for Churchill?

He was severely criticized.

She acted as a wife.

Her comment was:

"Some change their principles for their party, others change their party for their principles."

Lady Clementine was the daughter of a Scottish nobleman who had struck it poor, a matter which did not matter to the impetuous man who courted her. The reports give her as "beautiful" and since she's elderly, there are few of us who can speak with any authority except for the lady we see now.

It is pleasant to believe this was true.

I read on the wire stories about the impending loneliness facing Lady Churchill and think about what a day it must have been in Stockholm when she made the acceptance speech for the Nobel Prize.

When she finished, the audience rose in a body and sang "My Darling Clementine."

Somehow she reminds me of the way Victoria was portrayed in *Victoria Regina* when Helen Hayes came back after the parade

through London on her 75th birthday, laughing and chortling
and bubbling:

"Did you see that man, so red faced, and perhaps taken in drink,
when he broke through the lines and came running alongside the
carriage shouting, 'Go it, old girl . . . go it, old girl.'"

15. nuts

There is this long-ago story about the thirteen-year-old boy who picked the wings off canaries.

This was his delight and his recreation, although as it became known to the neighbors, the fact of it became embarrassing to his parents, who were then, in the face of public scrutiny, unable to term it a boyish prank.

They took the child to a psychiatrist.

"What seems to be the trouble?" asked that worthy.

"Tommy picks the wings off canaries," they said.

They left their offspring in the good doctor's hands.

In due time, the boy was returned intact—and unaided. It was the doctor who appeared sullen and harried, and the patient was delivered up with relief and without comment.

The doctor was the first in a series of mental repairmen who undertook the refurbishing of Tommy unsuccessfully, and for a considerable time I could not recall the way the story ended, although I was aware of what brought it to mind.

Not long ago the automobile of a teen-ager up in Darien, Connecticut, was wired with explosives, and although no one was damaged, it was another item in what is rapidly becoming community folklore in that upholstered town.

Already a girl had been killed following a drinking party and it required a court of law to decide that a young man was driving the car. A star witness turned out to be also a drug user.

Then there was a headline in the *Times* that read: "Parents Scored on Jersey Party." It was about a matter in Lake Mohawk,

New Jersey, in which seventy-seven youths were arrested and a police chief named George Geiffken announced that he wasn't letting up on it.

Later, there was a traffic fatality in Lake Mohawk similar to the one in Darien and now Geiffken was saying, "We need co-operation from the parents to stop this sort of thing. The parents are to blame."

A day later in a place called Short Hills, New Jersey, ten teen-agers were arrested following a party. All of this is what reminded me of the kid who picked wings off canaries.

The end of it came later after some of us had wandered up to the Coliseum to see what Cleveland Amory, a humane society director, described as "what promises to be the most extraordinary pet show in American history."

Extraordinary it certainly was.

There were two signs outside that prepared you.

One said: "There is hardly a creature on earth, no matter how ugly or dangerous that some humans do not covet as a pet" referring naturally to the pets on sale.

There were great horned owls, ocelots, iguanas, tarantulas, scorpions, lion cubs, monkeys, hummingbirds, countless varieties of snakes, seahorses, turtles, and many others, most of them for sale.

There were youngsters stirring under your feet wherever you walked, and near the entrance there was a bottle of eggnog with a nipple on it purchasable for 25 cents. This called for an-other quarter deposit on the bottle so that the small fry could feed goats and sheep and calves and miniature horses and other animals that were being supervised and in turn supervised by themselves against overfeeding.

The humane society had a booth set up and was putting the knock on rodeos and distributing a pamphlet entitled, *Is Sport Hunting a Sin?* and generally touching you about things you might favor.

They also had a missive entitled, *Should Elephants Be Kept in Kitchenettes?* This is a ten-part questionnaire designed to tell whether a party is eligible to own a pet or not.

Question No. 1, for instance, goes: Are you planning to regard the new pet as a full member of your family and to be responsible for it 24 hours a day, 365 days a year? And what is to happen when you go on vacation?

They're all like this except the last one, which was: And last, but not least, are you sure that you haven't kidded yourself in answering any preceding question?

This was the last day of the pet festival and the pets had been completely disposed of in the process. Crickets had been marked down to two for a quarter and toads were going for a buck, and a horned iguana had been marked down from $15 to $7.50.

We were wondering how much love you were going to get for your money from one of these when around the corner was spotted a clue to the end of the story about Tommy and the canaries. They had been selling canaries at one site but that, of course, hadn't helped this addled noggin put together the missing pieces.

Suddenly here was a tiger.

And that's the way the story went.

Tommy's parents took him the rounds of doctors and they—all to a man resentful and morose—turned him back eventually, while the parents sympathized with the dear boy and provided him with a fresh supply of canaries.

Finally he had been taken to a psychiatrist of considerable reputation who, as is usual in these cases, was also extremely busy.

When he returned the child, the good doctor did not wear the harried, sullen countenance of his predecessors.

And on the boy's face there could be detected a tiny note of puzzled suspicion, a trace perhaps of fearful uncertainty.

The doctor was exceedingly curt in his instructions:

"Throw him a tiger and let him pick the wings off that."

I knew I was in the wrong joint when everybody looked down its nose some when I wanted to begin brunch with a bottle of beer.

This was slightly before high noon in a watering hole called the Royal Box at the Americana in New York.

At least it was a watering hole the last evening I was here about a year past when the dolls were not only running around without hats, but little else.

Now they were wearing hats because you see that's what it was—a hat show.

Next to the fruit cup where the beer could have gone, there was a folder and on the cover it said:

"You'll love yourself in a hat . . . he will, too."

All I can say is it was a long way from Jasper Abbott's billiard academy on the East Side, or the Ten-Hi Cafe either, for that matter.

I felt like a guy lost in the lingerie department without a paddle. Boy, if the boys at the Lindell A.C. could get a load of this!

The table twittered as if someone had thrown out a handful of birdseed.

There was a tall, reedy guy playing a violin, a squat guy twanging at a bass and a little joker that looked like Peter Lorre was sawing a fiddle . . . background music.

They attracted because the number at the moment was *Anything Goes* which was fitting.

A plump little fellow with dimples and a lisp indicated a model who paraded forth, indicated her hat that is, and declaimed: "This is the crash helmet."

We were seated six to a table and a dowager I'd come to know as Aggie leaned across me to murmur to another portly type she called Judy:

"That's what I call inventive simplicity."

The hat did look like an automobile crash helmet but not as sturdy and although it seemed a crass notion to bring up, I asked:

"Would anyone have a notion what a gadget like that might cost some unsuspecting husband?"

The table twittered as if someone had thrown out another handful of birdseed.

"Between $150 and $200, I'd guess," said Aggie, eying the group for corroboration.

"That would be about right," said Katherine.

A beer wouldn't have helped any on that.

If you've managed to wade this far through the swamp, you are entitled to know actually how a fellow gets to one of these affairs.

Well, it's a short story.

There is a girl around our store who writes about fashion and, besides the fact that Yvonne Petrie is somebody that I both love and respect, she's always hightailing it off to Paris or some such with her racket so maybe there's something to it.

I asked her if I could come because I'd never seen any kind of fashion show and I'll try anything once out of curiosity.

The first time I ever went to a cockfight I won $43, so there you are.

I do think, though, she might have warned me about the beer, considering the unsightliness of the hour and all.

Yvonne brought a real live hat designer over for me to ask things of . . . a lady named Ethel Price who designs for a trade name called Emme and has a lot of awards.

What a rousing silence.

It reminded me of a time over at the late Archie Sillman's gymnasium on Monroe when the collector came around to ask Archie about the rent.

Kid Firpo had just finished going five fast rounds and had gotten dressed and was waiting for his manager Mike McNulty to get out of the stush game and take him back to the hotel.

Archie steered the collector to young Firpo whose English was at best haphazard in addition to which he was as shy as nightfall.

The collector finally left and when we asked Firpo what happened he answered:

"He didn't say nothin' and I din' say nothin'."

Which is the way it went between Mrs. Price and me.

Well, this thing went on and on and on and there was unfurled a parade of baby bonnets and turbans and a doll came out with a chenille dotted veiling so she looked as if she was wearing a bedspread around her head.

This Mrs. Price introduced something in black lacquered leather and there were names I'd somehow heard of like Lily Daché and Hattie Carnegie, not as famous as Henry Yee or Sugar Ray Robinson or Jimmy Butsicaris but you'd heard of them.

Finally a couple of bimbos from *Seventeen* magazine rose to speak and they succeeded in making this wayward child pretty sore.

They think it's indecent that, as they put it, there are 11 ½ million teen-aged girls who don't wear hats.

"Everywhere I go to talk to groups of teen-aged girls—I look out upon a sea of bareheads," said one of them.

"There should be a new word for hat," said the other one.

"One for the rain could be a 'pitter-patter' . . . for blowy days, a 'wind scoop,' 'solar shield,' 'wave-saver,' for dances a 'moon-lighter.' "

A man could become ill. Why louse up the kids any sooner?

Aggie explained politely that the real enemy of the hat designer is the hairdresser.

"You don't want to put a hat over a new coiffure," she explained. "They're deadly enemies . . . hairdressers and milliners."

Man, if there was ever a fight between sharks and alligators it's this one.

Yvonne humanely performed a small rescue and I guess as we got outside I must have been panting a little desperately. She delivered herself of a bemused smile along with the squelch.

"Maybe you could fix it sometime so I could go to a Piston basketball practice. I sure bet that's interesting."

Right from the beginning the Great Jewel Robbery perpetrated at the American Museum of Natural History was one of romance and the standing room crowd that jammed Judge Simon Silver's court in the Criminal Courts Building was sympathetic to the swashbuckling hero, Chief Suspect Jack (Murf the Surf) Murphy.

"They're tryin' to charge 'em with every crime they can't find nobody for," grumbled a standee at the rear of the court.

Murf had also been charged with holding up the Algonquin Hotel for $250 and with pistolwhipping the night clerk and breaking his leg.

Now, out of the latticework, Eva Gabor was creeping, having decided finally that it must have been Murf and his company who held her up for an uninsured and mysterious $25,000 ring at the Racquet Club in Miami Beach.

"It didn't take the Gabors long to get into the publicity act," growled Gilbert Rosenthal, Murf's defense attorney.

Later, Murf and his cohort Roger Clark had been arrested and charged with breaking into a Miami home and lifting $10,000 in jewels.

"It's the insurance companies," amended another member of the audience.

"They're behind it all. They want to get 'em in so much trouble they can make a deal to get the jewels back."

Which brings us back to romance.

It was on an October 28 that the museum was quietly rifled of the Star of India sapphire, the Delong Star Ruby of Burma and assorted other baubles placed in value at $400,000 stolen right out of the exhibition case.

To a slightly lesser degree, it was as if some daring marauder had absconded with the Hope Diamond. It was a crime that smacked of Raffles or Jimmy Valentine.

And who turns up? Jack Roland Murphy, a skin diver with a built-in glamorous nickname, along with Allen Kuhn and Clark, a couple of beach boy buddies.

"Crazy," laughed Murf the Surf to the charges and he laughed even louder when the federal government had to drop charges that he and Kuhn had transported the Star across the state lines.

Eventually the jewels were returned.

The watchers in the courtroom were identifying with Murf and friends.

This was no holdup of a cab driver by a passenger, no have-not stealing from one of his own kind. This was the Blood Red Ruby of Burma with no guard hurt and no person bilked.

A museum and an insurance company make pleasant victims.

The first thought that occurred here at the time of the Star's burglary and the immediate disappearance of all trace of the gems took me back eleven years to a winter in Florida when I worked as assistant to a professional skin diver named Ed Townsend.

We used to discuss how simple it would be to hide something in the ocean. We weren't thinking of jewels but of the smuggling then extant between Florida and Cuba.

A diver will get to know a section of ocean bottom, with its reef landmarks of brain and elkhorn coral, its lobster beds and caves, where sometimes moray eels are wont to lurk, as you know your backyard.

See how easily it lends itself to romance? An immediate conclusion was that if Murf had elected to cache his toys underneath the sea, no one would find them until he decided it was time.

Now that Eva Gabor reared her worn blond head in the affair, there is also a memory of the Racquet Club immediately after the alleged ring robbery.

This is a joint where golfers, football players, swingers, and me live during the winter and I recall that everybody around the club who cared enough about the incident to mention it thought it was a publicity stunt at the time.

One diverting thing happened though on the night of the alleged theft.

Eva came shrieking out onto the balcony outside her room, playing a howling Juliet all the way down the stairs where the first person she encountered was Frank Gifford, the then New York Giant football player, who was talking on the wall telephone just outside the bar.

"Don't just stand there, you halfwit," shouted Eva. "Do something. Call the police."

Frank put his palm over the mouthpiece and replied:

"Mistaken identity, lady. I'm a halfback, not a halfwit."

When the Gotham police charged Murf with the Algonquin robbery, he grinned and said:

"What won't they think of next?"

At last, he spent his first night in jail.

16. mementoes

A friend of mine who was a horse died recently.

I met him only once, it was at his birthday party back in the late '40s at a place outside Chicago called St. Charles which the people who invited me called Baker's Acres.

The late L. J. Baker was privileged to own and associate with him and the colonel understood it for what it was. When he died a few years back he provided the continuity of luxury his horse understood and deserved.

Greyhound was his name and the thing he was put on earth to do was trot, drawing a buggy with a man in it behind him and this thing that he did he did better than anyone else ever, horse or other.

Perhaps I shouldn't really say so glibly that this was what he was put on earth to do since it certainly implies an usurpation of authority but he did it better. Chances are he'd have drawn a plow better or if he'd have had to pull a trace that turned a mill, he'd probably have made more flour by himself than another.

But Colonel Baker had him trot and Sep Palin, full of bourbon and all, was the lucky man to drive him, or guide him, or just maybe go along when he trotted.

By the time he won the Hambletonian in 1935, leaving an aspirant named Warwell Worthy so far behind they had to look for him with searchlights later, everyone knew, everyone in the country, that here was something special.

He made a liar out of people which, though not difficult, is certainly in his favor for it is people with their great wisdom who ordain "Records are made to be broken."

On the windless morning over the Lexington trotting track in 1938 when Sep set him down against the clock, he went a mile— reaching out with those giant 27-foot and some change strides— in 1:55¼.

No one has touched it.

They called him the Grey Ghost and he has sixteen records like that one that no one has been able to measure. The evening I celebrated his birthday with him I had the impression it didn't matter to him although there was a thing, which I'll come to in a moment, that did.

Bill Connors, the racing secretary if you choose to categorize him thinly, called when he learned the big horse died because we felt that way about him and Bill used to talk a lot about him in another time when both of us cared seriously about harness racing.

"I saw him a lot," he was saying, "and even though my boss owns Speedy Scott, that grey one was something else. I saw him a lot. I saw him three times at Springfield back when racing there was everything. Old Sep and his bourbon and the grey baby strid- ing out."

Greyhound was thirty-three years old and some computer put in the wire story that this converted to 132 years in a human being.

This particular animal would have thought it the other way. "If there was a 132-year-old human being, he'd be as old as me."

"Baker only paid $900 for him," said Bill. "He wasn't thought much of at the sale. He was kind of a dirty black colt then. It wasn't 'til later that he turned grey and then when you saw him, of course, he was snow white."

Buggy racing is peculiar in the records they keep.

They will record the happenings of a horse on a half-mile track, in a team, under saddle and they joke about records "when the driver had a crick in his neck" or Sep "with only a pint in him" or "Greyhound in a slow rain."

Sep set one with him hitched alongside a thoroughbred runner. I can't recall the time now but Bill saw it and told me the last half-mile Greyhound was dragging the runner.

"When he was a two-year-old," said Bill, "he and Sep fell in a ditch at Indianapolis or someplace and they were afraid he was hurt. He showed class right from the start, probably thought his price was a joke. They were worried but it never affected him any."

One time Ted Williams was telling about seeing Jim Thorpe on the street up in Boston. This was during Jim's bad times when he was fighting whiskey and poverty in tandem but as Ted put it, "You knew he was something different. You knew he was somebody. And you knew he knew it."

That was the way Greyhound was at his birthday party, the important thing.

His coat was perfectly white then and the hair had grown long but he was barbered neatly around the fetlock and where it hung over the hoofs. He still wore shoes and he ate blackstrap molasses and ground hay with the guests.

Colonel Baker made a speech and the rest of us applied ourselves to the intoxicants and fell into the potted plants. The women's mascara and lipstick ran and I shudder to think of what the horse thought.

But he knew he was somebody all right and then Colonel Baker took him out on the track, ribbons in his mane and tail and an exercise boy trotted him a mile. He creaked but he pranced, too, and held his head like the champion who raced himself out of competition in six years.

He was a gelding, as you may know, and I said to Palin once, "Man if he hadn't been a gelding, what a sire he'd have made."

"If he hadn't been a gelding, he'd have never gotten to the races," replied Sep.

Bill assures me this is a fabrication. A horse is gelded because a human can't handle him and they couldn't handle Greyhound when he was a yearling. He was too much horse then. So he was gelded which is why he merely brought the $900.

He won slightly over $50,000 which mattered neither to Baker nor him and it would have been a million today with purses what they are. There's no telling what he might have commanded as a stud but as I peer around harness racing as it is now with all the Adios horses I think it's nice that he wasn't a stud. There was really only one of this trotter and it's sort of nice not to have the landscape cluttered up with Greyhound Boy and the like.

The ceiling of the reception hall at No. 16 Gramercy Park in New York City ranges upward 40 feet or so above the fireplace and there stands a full length portrait of an ascetic featured man,

aquiline-nosed and of Byronic brow, who surveys the guests below
with warmth and a vaguely patronizing air.

On a slab of burnished brass is inscribed the following, printed
in what passes for Olde Englishe:

> Goode frend for friendships sake forebeare
> To utter what is gossipt here
> In Social chat lest unawares
> Thy tongue offend thy fellowe plaiers

To begin with, let's ignore this warning since it was no more
than a cane's length from the plaque that a dialogue ensued between a pair of aging theatrical folk which contained this nomina-
tion for the most savagely cynical—but memorable—remark you'll
come across in this and perhaps any other year.

The two were discussing the cast of a bygone play, ruminating
over what had become of their fellows from that day.

"And whatever happened to so and so," asked one.

"Didn't you hear? He committed suicide. Discovered that he
had contracted cancer. Took a pistol and blew his brains out."

"Hmn," said the first, "that was his talent, then, marksmanship."

This then was the Players Club on an afternoon and the patri-
cian in the painting is Edwin Booth who presided there during
the latter part of the last century and donated the elegant mansion
for use as a club for his "fellowe plaiers" shortly before his death
in 1893.

The club has been usurped now by a smattering of television
and advertising urchins, but the membership remains largely of
the theater and this impertinence of times doesn't matter really.
Mr. Booth's house is so laden with stage artifacts that anywhere
you go you rather expect a stage manager to run by calling, "Stand
by for second act curtain."

There are cases and cases of Booth's old costumes—the raiment
of Richard III, Macbeth, Richelieu, Shylock. In the dining room—
converted on this day into a movie house—a pair of stained-glass
windows face each other, one of them a leaded picture of Richard
Mansfield as Richard III and another, a parody, of David Garrick
in the same role.

A handsome, 10-foot image of Cyrano de Bergerac looks dis-
dainfully down on the guests as if he's about to whip out his

epee and start challenging: "Ah, my old enemies. You . . . coward-ice—you prejudice . . ." stabbing at the air.

On the first floor, shelves of theatrical jewelry line the walls and as a companion commented: "You know this stuff looks pretty good after all these years for what is literally costume jewelry."

The swords and daggers used in ancient *Hamlets* and *Mac-beths* are untarnished as were the scales and knife used by Shy-lock. There is an entire display devoted to Edward Hugh Sothern (1859–1933), very impressive, and it depressed a couple of us who did not recall the name except as a fellow who used to go up to Saratoga with an actress named Julia Marlowe and bet the horses and drink champagne. There's a plaque up there about him.

The purpose of the gathering was the showing of a silent mo-tion picture starring John Barrymore, Mary Astor and Irene Rich entitled: *Beau Brummell.*

"Is there some pertinent reason for this affair . . . an anniver-sary of something perhaps?" was a question.

"Around here you don't need reasons. I'll bet half of the people here knew Jack intimately and that blond lady with the teased hairdo is Ethel Barrymore Colt, Jack's niece."

Down the aisle, but within earshot, a fellow was telling of how Jack Barrymore was suspended from the club for a year. He had been standing at the bar, some taken in drink, and had abruptly taken his walking staff, leaned over and swept the bottles on the backbar crashing to the floor.

A year later, when he was readmitted, he was standing again at the same site and it was commented to a stranger-guest that this was Jack's first day back after his year's suspension.

"Oh rally," remarked the stranger politely, "and what were you suspended for, Mr. Barrymore?"

"This," said Barrymore, seizing his staff, leaning forward and sweeping the backbar clear of bottles again.

There was a lot of giggling and chattering in the audience as the film got under way. Here was the old organ music background you'd forgotten and the subtitles, well, one went like this, Barry-more to Astor.

"I did not think to find you wearing wedding dress for another."

Another time, one of the actors uttered the exclamation: Egad! It broke up the house.

There were two intermissions but no butcher wandered the aisles selling candy and pictures of the stars as they once did. And the film broke twice. It took you back, all right.

It wasn't until the final scene when Beau, old, sick, mentally deranged and confined to a debtor's prison in Calais, is reunited with his loyal valet and begins to see the ghosts of the Prince of Wales and lost love Astor, that I recalled seeing the movie. I dread to remember how long ago.

A silent movie—they perforce leaned on acting—and there was neither chattering nor giggling during the final scene.

By the time Beau fell across the table in death and a superimposed young guardsman rose from the old carcass and walked away with a superimposed young Mary Astor, there wasn't a dry eye in the house. Corny but it still worked.

I realized I hadn't grown up much. It got misty the first time I saw it.

One weekend a greyhound named Caesar's Delight assuaged the frustrations of generations of dogs, when on the back stretch at the Miami Beach Kennel Club, he caught the electric rabbit.

That this was due to mechanical failure is not important.

A racing dog caught the lure.

The discomfiture of the thousands of patrons who had wagered on that eighth race when the event was declared no contest mattered not a hamburger to him.

If there is a special niche for heroic canines in dog heaven, there is a special place assured for Caesar's Delight alongside Fala, Rin-Tin-Tin, and Lassie.

Which serves to mention the matter that four distinguished members of the Michigan State Senate have seen fit to ally themselves with Bill No. 104, which would enable us all to participate in dog gambling.

If you don't already, it is necessary to understand why the term is not dog racing.

There is no law now to prevent dogs from racing against one another. It is merely illegal to wager on them.

Horse racing is really horse gambling.

Some years ago when betting on horses was abolished in Texas, an optimistic promoter concluded to his subsequent dismay, that, since Texas is a horse country and has cowboys and such, that people would come out simply to observe horses running in contest against one another.

The meeting folded the second day. It offered further proof, to paraphrase James Thurber, that a true horse lover is a horse that is in love with another horse.

Not long ago a member of the promotional group that seeks to add dog racing to our culture solicited my editorial aid in trying to bring the dogs to Michigan, and added:

"Although I know you're partial to horses."

He is correct as far as he went. I have enjoyed many horse races, although my interest is mainly on the people you encounter around the track. I have also enjoyed a few dog races.

Actually, although I try to enjoy the things in the world around me that I cannot change, I'm not sure, after some years in attendance, that I favor gambling on animals—horses or dogs or fighting cocks, although no senators are currently sponsoring a bill for fowl warfare.

There is a reason for this.

Until a horse or dog whispers it to me, I'm convinced that the animals do not enjoy what they are forced to do.

A horse, by and large, runs out of fear and panic.

Some assistant starters cram him into the stall of the starting gate and close shutters in front and behind him.

Then the starter pushes a button. A bell rings in his ears and a little gnome the horse did not request as a burden slashes him across the rump a couple of times.

He did not request the saddle, bridle or the pack of extra lead weight either, but come one, come all.

If his knee is sore, a trainer may stand him in a bucket of ice for a few hours, not so that he will feel better or that his knee will improve but so that he will not feel pain and favor his knee while he's running.

A jockey will take a handful of coins and, when his steed shows signs of flagging, he will rattle the coins in his ear which panics him again.

In the gallant stretch run, he is getting his fanny slashed every step of the way.

If he likes any part of it, he really is a dumb animal.

Mesh Tenney, the man who trained Swaps, Candy Spots, and some other illustrious horses told me once:

"A horse won't do anything unless you make him. He'll stand under a tree in the shade if you allow it."

A dog runs because he's hungry.

He's been trained to chase an electric rabbit and the reason he's chasing it is because he thinks he will catch it and because he's been locked in a cage overnight without anything to eat.

The reason he thinks he can catch it is because he's caught some.

A racing dog is trained on live rabbits, sometimes cats when no hares are available. He gets to catch them to make him optimistic in the future.

The roar of the crowd in what Eddie Arcaro once called, referring to the stretch at Churchill Downs, the "tunnel of noise," or the same on the Rickard Course at the Kennel Club, must frighten an animal witless.

The dog promoter seemed a trifle bewildered.

"Then you're against racing," he said.

"I didn't say that. I said I wasn't sure I approved of gambling on animals."

"You like horse racing; you're always talking about horse racing," he insisted.

"Don't tell me what I like or dislike. But, as a matter of fact, you are correct, in part. There have been many horse races that I've enjoyed and, with luck, I will again.

"I enjoyed the whole setting, the people in their gay attire, the trumpets, the jockeys in their silks and there's nothing quite as handsome as a thoroughbred horse.

"I have seen a couple of greyhounds I thought were handsome, I say a couple because I haven't seen as many dog races as I have horse races."

"Will you write something to help us get dog racing?"

"Dog gambling. You want to be a bookie like the horse people are."

"What the devil are you driving at anyway?"

He was annoyed now.

"All I am doing is stating some things about what dog and horse racing are, and what you are or anyway hope to be.

"I mean the same thing when I sometimes refer to a saloon-keeper as a caterer to human frailty.

"I'm not against it, it's just that occasionally I like to see things presented clearly and without hypocrisy, if you'll pardon. This is one of those days."

Incidentally, it didn't hurt Caesar's Delight when he overtook the rabbit and it discomfited a lot of humans.

17. racism

The Sir John Hotel is located just off the corners of 10th Street and Northwest 3rd Avenue in the land of the coconut and the orange and the bikini. There is a near-Olympic-sized swimming pool in the patio with a shuffleboard court to one side and the owner is a white man named Dave Probynski.

The Sir John was, at one time, the luxury vacation spot for a Negro family that attended the annual Florida winter sun rites, and on Saturday nights the place leapt and thumped.

There was still a lot of leaping and thumping around the area recently. Dave has a spot next door called Knight Beat where the carrying on held some of the old fierceness and Clyde Killen, who used to manage the Sir John for him, had opened a nightclub nearby where Jackie Wilson was holding forth and the line to get in never seemed to end.

But Jackie Robinson was in town and attending Hialeah some with his cronies and he was staying at the Hampton House, an integrated hostelry closer to town.

Joe Louis was in town and he was living on Miami Beach where not long ago a black man had to have a permit to appear on the streets after 9 o'clock—a work permit to show he had business there.

These are famous citizens, of course, and fame has long been a key to many doors, but the Sir John is not the only place you have to look now if you want to find a Negro party in Miami.

With so many Southern cities obviously dragging their feet over what is the No. 1 social problem in the country, the winter playground wears a changing face.

The rather glorious part of it is that Miamians tend to deny this happening.

"You'll notice that colored people still ride in the back of the bus down here. There's no law about it any more but they do anyway," said one antagonist the other morning.

"You can go down to the courthouse and you'll still see the signs over the lavatories . . . white and colored . . . and they're obeyed, too."

"I don't think the public accommodations act," offered an attorney, "is constitutional. I'm not discussing the moral issues with you. By the Constitution you have a right to discriminate if you want to. You have a right to select your patrons. The Supreme Court is all wrong—I don't mean wrong, maybe—but illegal."

"If you look around Miami can you see any difference?" asked a real estate dealer.

A couple of us decided to look around.

Some colored folks rode in the back of buses and some did not. There were no signs in the courthouse. There are Negro patrons in the supermarkets, a few, and a Negro girl was pushing a baby buggy up the mall on Lincoln Road. A white fellow picked up a black fellow on the curb in front of the McAllister Hotel downtown on Biscayne Boulevard.

"They might be baseball players and that doesn't count," said the Miamian who was being dragged along as a witness.

"What's the matter, was your mother frightened by a baseball player?"

By a fortuitous circumstance, I encountered a friend named Jimmy Wilson who has been working in Miami wintertimes for twenty-eight years. He works at Hialeah racetrack just as he works at the tracks up North during the summer.

"Things are changing, all right," he said. "A black police officer can arrest a white man now and he didn't used to be able to.

"Before, a black policeman had to call a white policeman and let him do it.

"We can go to the dog races now and we didn't used to be allowed. The running tracks are open without much prejudice. You can go around without getting bothered much. It's better. We can notice it.

"Don't think I'm trying to make it sound better than it is. I'm a mutuel clerk up North and this year eight of us put in for clerk here at Hialeah. We belong to the union and we've been here a long time. They told us 'it isn't time yet.'"

This practicing cynic was prepared to accept the native story that no real changes have been made and it was heartening to discover improvement.

A Negro fellow who works over in the county building told me once: "All I really want is to be able to buy anything I can afford."

Nobody in the world can afford the Gold Coast on Miami Beach, but if he wants to go get it, he sure can.

And the Sir John doesn't mint money anymore on prejudice.

It stirs you a little.

Not jump up and down, perhaps.

But a little.

A Unitarian minister named James Reeb lay close to death in a Birmingham, Alabama, hospital and a few of the group gathered on the steps of Brown's Chapel AME Church were badged with bandages after the troopers' clubbings on the last Lord's Day.

These memories lent truth to what was otherwise an almost comic unreality.

The Reverend Martin Luther King had departed the church at 4:30 and, when we asked him, "What is the plan now?" he answered:

"We'll march at five o'clock."

He went away and never returned. He never planned to. It was to harass the vigilantes—keep them alert and annoyed.

Attempts at an earlier march had been confined to a block of Sylvan Street, the one the church is on, just the block between Jeff Davis at one end and Selma at the other.

A hundred trooper cruisers ringed the area and, when City Police Chief Wilson Baker said no one was going any further, no one went, except some of the youngsters from what they call Snick (SNCC).

This is the Student Nonviolent Coordinating Committee and some of them flitted between houses and up alleys to the center of town and gathered around the Dallas County Courthouse.

They wore a great mien of "We showed 'em" while the troopers wore a great air of patience. They were preventing marches this day and they prevented them.

It verged on seven o'clock when King's aide, the Reverend Ralph Abernathy, formed his collection of visiting sympathizers, who seemed to outnumber the Selmans, and provided a final, as one correspondent put it, "Come on I'll show you a confrontation!"

The aspirant marchers were fortified four or five abreast and perhaps a thousand strong and they combined with the troopers and local police to form a T on Sylvan Street—troopers crossing it with their human barricade across the pavement—and Baker announced again through his microphone:

"You can go back into the church if you like, or you can stand there, that's your choice."

They stood there.

The visiting clergymen took turns in prayer. No one was denied his voice. Then the singing started. All things begin and end with "We Shall Overcome."

But the—I keep wanting to call them a congregation—got into "He's Got the Whole World in His Hands" and made up a lot of insulting verses for Governor Wallace.

"He's got the Ku Klux Klan in his hands, the Citizens' Council in his hands,"—things like that.

The troopers relaxed across the road, angry, bored.

One of Sheriff Jim Clark's deputies finally spoke. Mainly no officials speak to foreigners, reporters especially.

"What does it mean?" he answered. "I've been here since January 16 and I still don't know. But I know this, that if all you outsiders would keep out of it, we'd handle it. You a reportah?"

This had happened earlier. Upon arrival in Selma, here was a sudden fellow with a plastic covered badge that said Press Pass on it and naturally I'd inquired what it was.

"If you want to move in this town, you'd better go the courthouse and get one," he'd answered.

At the courthouse, it went with a burly deputy precisely like this.

"A reportah from DEtroit, eh, boy? What you goin' to write

about us up theh? Sumpin bad ah bet. What'd you-all come down heah foh but to write sumpin bad?"

But he got me Badge No. 193 which I mention so you'll see it's a popular place.

What does this entitle me to, if anything, seemed a question.

"It's foh youah protection, boy. They clubbed a lot of reportahs ovah in Marion. Didn't yoah heah, boy?"

Anyway when Clark's deputy asked a question he got a proper answer and then he said:

"I don't know what's happenin', but I'll tell you what ain't gonna happen.

"If those people"—he gestured with his billy club toward the singers—"want to mix together, white and black, they can do it anywheah they want to. But not heah. They ain't evah gonna do it heah. Evah."

No evangelist ever spoke with more sincerity.

But the unreal touches that hinted at the commies were on the Brown's Chapel steps where a man wore an arm band with Lenin's name on it next to a guy with a pointed red beard and where people you didn't know rose up and took charge.

"We'll keep those troopers here all night . . . they going to earn their money tonight. And if they fail we'll march over them. Are you with me?"

Hallelujah . . . yea, brother . . . amen.

Clapping of hands. A lively segment of the crowd were children. They were having a wonderful time. It was a picnic for them.

"Who is that fellow leading things?" was a question.

Not one of the five people I asked had any idea but they yea-brothered him anyway. A Snick girl from Texas named Casey Hayden, with a camera strung around her neck, explained.

"I'm making a film strip for the rural areas of Alabama. I work out of Jackson, Mississippi, normally but this one is for the rural areas here.

"It's filmed because so many don't read very well and you can get to them easier with pictures."

The rednecks were collecting on the corners now too but no one seemed to think they'd be as violent as the night before when four of them attacked the three clergymen and dismantled the Reverend Reeb.

Three of the attackers had been arrested.

"Are you for this?" pointedly asked a clergyman from Christ Church in Chicago.

"I just got here," was this answer from a guy who had become tired of edgy questions.

"You're an American, aren't you?" he persisted. "You're an American?"

"You're damned bet you and resenting pushing all the way. May I ask where the churches have been for the last hundred years in all this?"

They kept standing. Someone started a rumor there was a bomb in the church. The troopers had to investigate. More harassment.

Eventually a reporter broke out his scotch. Governor Wallace apparently is at war with the distillers too because the only brand down here is a poison called Jamie O'Six which is a distant cry from heather.

"One thing," he said, "you now qualify as a member of SCREW. There's UNCLE and Sigma Delta Phi and the Hockey Haters Association of America, but now you're also a SCREW."

"What does it mean?"

"A guy from the New York *Times* organized it and has even had cards printed up. It means Suffering Correspondent of the Racial Equality Wars."

I wonder if there are lapel buttons?

In the second floor corridor of the Post Office Building in Montgomery, Alabama, a uniformed officer of the state police was presiding outside the doors of Judge Frank M. Johnson's Federal Court.

Judge Johnson conducts his tribunal without interruptions and spectators are barred from entering once his session begins until witnesses are changed on the stand or until there is a recess. There are foot square glass windows through which an observer in the hallway may witness the proceedings.

A would-be spectator who had arrived late approached the window.

"You can't stand there," said the trooper.

"Who's that on the witness stand?" asked the man, stalling for a moment.

"Some nigger preacher from Atlanta," answered the trooper.

"Who's that questioning him?"

"That's his nigger lawyer," said the officer.

The point of repeating such a dialogue is to mention that the trooper spoke courteously and in no way disparagingly of the people to whom he was referring. By his own rights, education, and environment he was merely replying to the questions.

By the same token, when Major John Cloud addressed the marchers just over the bridge across the Alabama River outside Selma, saying, "Your march is not conducive to the public safety; you are hereby ordered to disperse," he was merely carrying out the orders of his chief, Governor Wallace.

After the ensuing mayhem that ended with eighty-four injured Negroes, the same Governor Wallace offered from the gubernatorial mansion that "We saved their lives by stopping the march. If they had gone on they could have been attacked by angry whites along the highway."

His position may have been based on the voter registration figures from Dallas County, which encompasses Selma and Lowndes County which lies on Highway 80, the road to Montgomery.

Dallas County with its 353 Negro voters is a veritable electoral stronghold by comparison. There is not a single one in Lowndes.

Then, as you may have heard on television, this same Governor Wallace seemed to found his remarks not on what is happening in Alabama but what has happened in Harlem and in New York's subways and at Detroit's high school basketball games, as if this had any bearing on his own problems.

This is the situation that exists.

And just as a student might come to the conclusion that he had encountered an impenetrable barrier, history—recent history—comes to his rescue.

It was in 1957 that the big government got into a head-on collision with a state government. It was Little Rock over integration of the schools.

Five years later in Oxford, Mississippi, there was a quarrel over the integration of a university.

Then it was Birmingham and the matter of public accommodations and the integration of hotels and restaurants and rest rooms.

Subsequently, the result was the civil rights act of 1964.

This issue is the most important for every official that is currently in office in Alabama and other Southern states since he is battling, not only over the matter of segregation or integration, but over his own survival.

With everybody voting, Sheriff Jim Clark of Dallas County will become citizen Jim Clark as quickly as the ballots can be counted.

The happenings at Selma seemed especially horrible to us at that moment because they were freshest upon us but remember the church bombing and the children and how ghastly were the occurrences at Oxford.

With history on your side you can only wonder why it has to move along with such terrible steps.

Yet it was a leading citizen of Oxford, Mississippi, of all places—Mr. William Faulkner—who expressed it as he did so many things in his lifetime when he accepted the Nobel Prize for literature.

He concluded his acceptance speech, stating that he was convinced that the human race would "not only survive but shall prevail."

It's just that prevailing has been so difficult, lately.

18. hijinks

Marian Fodel works as a waitress at Bush's Bar on Woodward where the councilmen and judges and clerks assemble to exchange lies and other pleasantries late of an afternoon.

The day bartender, Bill Casey, had been stricken in the heart on Sunday evening and Marian sat up most of the night with him and most of the day on Monday so that it was an effort to make it to the waiters' and waitresses' ball at Cobo Hall in the evening.

"I wouldn't have missed it," she said from around the tired eyes, "and isn't it a good party? Bill's at Park Community Hospital. You should drop him a note."

It was the golden anniversary of Local 705 and the union turned it on with considerable splendor.

Ray McKinley had what he chose to call the old Glenn Miller band sounding from one bandstill while Jimmy Wilkins was holding forth down the hall.

They alternated and successfully bracketed the guests with music.

There was a sign outside the entrance warning that no alcoholic beverages should be brought into the hall.

The amenities were thus observed.

The sign dismayed no one.

Governor Romney and Mayor Cavanaugh elected to make it and the mayor even stayed for the first installment of a Miss Waitress contest which involved twenty contestants.

Their service may have been just as good as ever around town, since every employer knows that Myra Wolfgang, the Little Shepherdess of Selden Street, wouldn't inconvenience an employer except for money, but the service would not have been as scenic as usual.

A girl named Kitty Tabor finally won it but, as someone remarked, "She's from the Playboy Club and starts off with an edge because they pick 'em for looks there in the first place."

Before a flock of assorted newspaper and television stiffs got around to voting a $250,000 Haps-burg tiara onto the noggin of Miss Tabor—very momentarily for there was a Krandall there from the Sidney Krandall jewelry house to whisk it back to the vault after pictures—another queen was called.

She was Miss Union Made, a little gal who works keeping house at a motel and she earned hers in a competition making beds at the London Inn last weekend.

Serena Allen is her name and she made a bed in the quarter finals against 40 contestants in a minute, 48 seconds.

The judging included equal parts for speed and perfection and Serena had to put those tight hospital corners to the sheets.

"In the finals I did it in a minute, 34 seconds," said Serena. "But I guess I got better under pressure. Actually I felt like I was taking my time because I wanted it to be a good bed."

Housekeeping heads from various hotels judged the competition.

And then there was a distinguished man in a dinner jacket whom you've seen so many times around town, if you've survived for any distance at all, that you automatically nod to him and assume him a friend.

"You haven't seen me for the last two years," said Leon Mitchell, "because I retired then. I was eighty-three years old on Saturday. I worked at the Book the last five years."

He's been a waiter since some friends talked him out of joining the Navy when he was fifteen.

That was in New York but he's been in this town forty years and the Sheraton-Cadillac will always be the Book to him. And always may be a while yet.

There's never been a notion here that being a waiter was as health-sustaining as say being a lumberjack or a professional golfer, but Leon suggests the possibility.

"When I wanted to join the Navy you had to get somebody to

write a letter to the Secretary of the Navy," he was saying. "There were no recruiting offices. You had to have pull to enlist. After my friends talked me out of it and into a waiter's job at the old Waldorf, the boss fired me three times the first week."

The other waiters wouldn't let it happen. They explained they'd talked him out of the service so they were responsible. It was the beginning of unionism for Leon, on the simplest basis.

Leon remains a union guy to the last.

At the moment he is corresponding to the Internal Revenue Service with a complaint.

Waiters, as you know, must declare their tips as income.

However, their social security money after age sixty-five is based not on their total income on which they paid taxes, but only on the income issued them by employers. Leon is fighting to have this changed.

I pursued this with an employer and one of his headwaiters afterward.

"That's right," said the waiter, "but you see the employer would be affected if a change was made."

Of course.

Social Security is taken from both for the employee.

"You've got an owner's lobby in Washington to save the money," was this comment.

"Not me personally," said the employer. "But yes, we have associations who have lobbies, but don't cry, baby. The unions have lobbies, too, better ones."

Justin Roderick Strunk is a young banjo player, poet-at-large and skier who up until his thirty-fourth year had demonstrated an almost uncanny talent for failure.

He worked for the Republican Party during the 1964 presidential campaign in the state of Maine, wrote the campaign song "We're Gonna Carry Barry to the White House," which he rendered on his banjo and vocally thereby contributing to that great success still memorable to us all.

He also toured Maine with a candidate Clifford McIntyre who was trying to unseat Ed Muskie as junior senator.

As they went from town to town, Jud, which is what he answers to, would walk onstage and deliver some light songs and patter including his own composition which was "Mac Is the Man" and then he'd introduce the next senator.

"I cost him Rumford," he was admitting not long ago.

At the time Jud and his candidate visited the paper center of the country, the mills were on strike and the unemployment was beginning to chafe.

"Jud," said the aspirant senator. "Go out there and say something funny and soften 'em up."

"Yessir," responded Strunk, thinking madly about the few facts he had on the residents (a) that a paper town reeks of unpleasant odors when the mills are working (b) that the town was on strike.

"I found a fellow prone on the street," he pattered, fingering a chord on the banjo. "We got him a doctor." Another chord. "You know what the diagnosis was? He was overcome with fresh air."

Not only was there no laughter. Subsequently there were no votes.

Senator Muskie still represents the state of Maine.

Flushed with success, and exhilarated with visions, Jud and his wife, Marty, repaired to New York where she got a job at Wanamaker's and he sauntered off with his banjo in search of supplemental income.

He hooked on with Fred Weintraub, who owns that joint in the Village called the Bitter End. Not as an entertainer but writing songs on Spec. This means speculation which also means that you get paid if everything works out grandly.

Jud was retained a few years ago by that fellow Clifford Prout who rather hoaxed the country with his aim at clothing animals. You'll remember that a great many animal lovers took him quite seriously.

Jud lasted with him long enough to compose:

> There'll be habits on rabbits,
> Aprons on hogs,
> Stretch pants on elephants,
> Swim suits on frogs.

His ventures have the common denominator that they expire quickly.

While Marty was striving at Wanamaker's Jud tried out for an off-Broadway play called *Beautiful Dreamer*.

"What do you do?" asked the director.

"Sing and dance," said Jud. He'd forgotten his banjo.

"Sing Swanee River," said the director, and afterward he said "Dance whatever you can." Then, "What do you really do?"

"Play the banjo," allowed Strunk.

"You're hired," said the director.

It was then that Jud discovered it was a play about Stephen Foster and, of course, they were searching for banjo players.

"I was the E. P. Christy Minstrels," he explained. "Casting is economical off-Broadway. It was a funny part, I came on stage as if I was coming up the streets in Pittsburgh and around the corner, I had to sound faint at first. I would start in a closet with my back to the stage, slowly walk on."

The play lasted six weeks. Jud considered it a triumph.

He bought an island in a river in Maine with an old house on it for Marty and the kids. There was no plumbing, electricity, telephone or other such nuisances. He worked hard, installed them all, deposited the family and went off to seek his fortune again. He received the message "Call home immediately."

By the time he called there was no communication. The river had flooded and his family had been evacuated by plane.

Jud composes quickly. He appeared on the Catherine Allen Cooking Show in Seattle at the time the city was having a problem disposing of its garbage. The dump formerly used at sea was filled and disposal had become a political item of some importance.

Miss Allen was interviewing him primly when he suddenly invented:

> Won't you take the garbage to the garage, mother,
> You're filling up the living room and den,
> Though you've tried to be discreet
> And lugged it to the street
> The city boys just bring it back again.

Miss Allen gave a tight-lipped smile and gasped, "I hope we don't hear from the mayor."

"I hope I don't hear from the police," answered Jud as the cameramen fell over one another.

Anyway, what I've been trying to get at is that Jud Strunk is mainly a ski nut and he's taken a job with the U. S. Ski Team and is editing their monthly magazine and touring the country trying to raise money to keep the skiers competing internationally until the next Olympics.

He is permitted to ski and he plays banjo for the ski team. If you want to send money to the U. S. Skiing Association in Denver, Colorado, it's all right with me.

However this should be done quickly if Jud is to receive any credit for it.

You see, in the Christmas issue of the ski magazine he wrote a parody on *Twas the Night Before Christmas* in which he had the resort owner asking hopefully for students, and the publicity man wistfully for press guys, etc.

He built their hopes to a climax as they sang their wishes and then he closed it with:

> I then turned and left them with voices all straining
> For soon they would learn that outside it was raining.

It hasn't snowed in the East all season and his association bosses are not sure that Jud is such a riotously funny man.

With his sure touch for success, had Jud been on the *Mayflower* the history of our country would have been different.

A crisis spreads many wings.

At an early hour recently a DRS bus had managed to render itself a casualty on Fort Street.

Then a trailer-truck jackknifed behind it and there ensued a confusion that had happened also somewhere else a few minutes ago.

The traffic did what traffic would under the circumstances—jammed up behind these impediments for considerable distance.

Then bureaucracy set in.

No tow truck could touch a DSR vehicle except a DSR tow truck, so the fuming and fussing was against the city and its regulations.

The snow had halted by this time, so the inconvenienced could stand outside their autos and complain to one another, acquiring a sort of brotherhood and unity thereby.

A wing of crisis is a holding of hands.

It takes many faces.

The kids next door erupted out of the house and into the snow caroling "School's out . . . school's out" and began to plunge about into the sculptured snow created by the wind.

One of them, a girl named Tina, watched her elder brother stand in front of a drift taller than his head and cry "Look at me" and flop backward, disappearing into it.

Tina, half his size, lined up before the next segment of the drift, cried, "Watch me," at which point a worried mother came out and retrieved her brood.

The drift was twice as tall as Tina.

The kids loved it.

It was the parents who were concerned.

The policemen who were on duty when the snow really began to take hold agreed to work the next shift until, when and if the replacements could arrive.

In the fire department it was the same.

As the policemen waded through the snows to get to hospitals, tired but trying, no one was calling to complain of "police brutality."

They were helping people regardless of race, color or creed.

"Hey, I don't have to go to work," said Al Tabachi, the bartender at Frank Gagen's. "Frank's not going to run."

He was talking to a bar-owner friend.

"I own mine and work behind the bar myself, so I'm going to run," he said and he did.

The big supper clubs closed because the help couldn't make it to work.

A girl that lives with me, who was raised in Miami and suffers from great inexperience at snow, thought it was delightful and, over the protest of the Detroit-breds, elected to walk to the grocery store in early afternoon.

She lives in Lafayette Park which is what former Mayor Cavanaugh sometimes boasted of as a prize of urban development.

None of the streets are priority thoroughfares.

It could be Maple Lane in the country.

She stepped into a depression in the ground that had drifted over and found herself over her head suffocating.

There was no tragedy, as happened with the heart attacks suffered by shovelers. She managed to extricate herself and get back to her home.

"You should have convinced me not to go out," she accused.

"Would you go out in a hurricane in Miami?" someone asked.

"Of course not," she snapped.

"This is our hurricane," she was told.

In the extreme winds, an elderly woman was having trouble crossing the street and a man took her by the arm and, sheltering and guiding, helped her make it.

She thanked him. Later she admitted how offended she'd have been under normal circumstances.

The people who man the public services stayed downtown . . . the radio, TV, newspaper, telephone people.

They used up all the available hotels and then cots were placed in some of the offices to insure working communications.

Factories closed, cinemas closed along with everything else including, for the first time, J. L. Hudson's but there was a touch to it in one that stayed open.

The Flower Show at Cobo Hall survived.

It reminded me of a thing a poet said:

"God gave us memory so that we might have roses in December."

And, man, was it December.

Walasse Ting is a mid-twenty-year-old Chinese boy who paints pictures and lives in Paris and is a member of a small group of artists who have assembled there under the general flag of the name Cobra.

The name derives from their origins—Copenhagen, Brussels and Amsterdam with the first two letters of the first two cities and the initial of the last providing the name.

He has recently published a book entitled *Ic Life*.

"I am a painter and not a writer, I think," Ting said to me once. "But I have many things to say and so I have written poems to go with all the paintings in my book."

He writes a poem called *America* and the first part read:

> brain made by IBM & FBI
> stomach supported by A&P
> and Horn & Hardart
> love supported by
> American Telephone & Telegraph
> soul made by 7 up
> skin start with Max Factor
> heart red as U.S. Steel

Ting and Pierre Alechinsky were visitors in our village at the home of Brooks Barron and his wife Florence, to whom Ting's book is dedicated.

At a party for them, the guests were pleasant but faintly supercilious, gracious but patronizing when the back was turned.

Ting writes another:

> everyday I look self in mirror
> I never believe i was a child
> i don't think i will turn old man,
> don't tell me if you know something else

"I like to think I write with Chinese grammar," said Ting. "Anybody can write poetry. I don't say good poetry but give a pencil and anybody write it. I am painter."

They were pleased at the prospect that Albert Landry might have an exhibition for them.

"This is important," said Alechinsky, "I sell anything to collectors. Very expensive, but lithographs a young man can afford. A collector I know in Chicago buys with a truck. A young person you must make contact. He will buy a single thing because he wants it. It is important."

Ting and Alechinsky have painted fifteen paintings together, the first of which was called *Peinture à Quatre Mains*, painting with four hands.

"We confuse collectors," Alechinsky was saying, through his French. "They buy Ting signature. They buy my signature. They don't know how to buy both."

Ting interrupted with, "Two paintings in one. They don't understand."

"Unusual, yes," said Alechinsky. "But it is important that an artist not always be alone. No man alone ever plays a symphony music. I make movies to be with other workers. Why shouldn't two people paint, one do his, the other his thing that he understand."

A man pointed to a pepper mill and asked Alechinsky: "Could you paint that?"

"I have no sense of urgency," he said.

He looked down at his watercress salad and held up his fingers to form a rectangle.

"I might find something to paint in there," he said, looking through his fingers. "Something to tell. An artist must have something to tell and then hope he can tell it."

Ting pointed at a poem in *Ic Life* that he liked:

> Take good care of self long journey ahead
> keep strength ideas love in heart
> hatred bury in deep earth
> spread self like giant to four winds

Mrs. Barron had the paintings around her house and no one ever uttered word of either praise or distaste about them as if fearing, and in this company it could have no other than, a polite recrimination.

The artists seemed to be being held up for inspection like cabbages at market, albeit with great genteelty.

It is easy to chop up a work someone else has sincerely attempted.

And at one of the pop art extravaganzas in New York recently where a fellow had reproduced a Campbell's Soup label in a frame, one critic commented, "I like mine when you get the soup, too."

Similar comments were forthcoming.

A poem can be quoted but a painting you must see, so if you ever have the desire you can go look when the works of this pair are returned.

Wallasse is self-conscious but Pierre has outgrown that, if he ever had it, but both are trying very, very hard to communicate something.

I found myself siding with them.

Just trying is important.

19. vietnam

A young man named Roy Davis for whom respect and affection is held here traveled to Washington, D.C., for the teach-ins, sit-ins, and "the march on Saturday" protesting the war in Vietnam.

He was nineteen at the time.

He was then a student at Highland Park College.

He was very serious about his thoughts and as a poet once remarked, "The thoughts of youth are long, long thoughts" and this is mentioned without the slightest insinuation at the deprecatory.

Roy checked in at the Detroit committee offices on the Wayne campus, the Committee to End the War in Vietnam.

The workshops and discussions were held in Lincoln Memorial Church and in the Mayflower Hotel.

This is a time in your life when you stay up all night arguing religion and politics and fidelity as applied to girls. It is an important time and as I remember and realize it is important to you to understand why you must go to war.

"What do you think you'll accomplish?"

This was a discussion and not an argument with me trying to understand. I could never have become involved in a mass movement where I could see no way of success, and I do not think now that the State Department would be influenced a nickel's worth by all the students in the country on parade.

"I hope I understand better," said Roy. "What I hope to accomplish personally is to inform myself more. I am against the American position in Vietnam. I think that we are meddling in a

Vietnamese problem where we are not wanted and are unnecessary.

"But I assume I'll understand more because there are people there who know more than me. I think if you're not informed you have no business to like it or not like it. If you are going to protest you should know why."

We chased that over for a moment.

"But what will you accomplish insofar as affecting others?"

"What I hope," said Roy, "is that we can stir up enough with our protest to get other people confused so that they have to think about it too."

He paused.

"You know if you believe everything the government tells you it may make for a harmonious society but might still be wrong."

A question seemed:

"Suppose you get drafted?"

He smiled.

"Well, the CO bit is about gone."

"What do you mean by CO?" Whimsically enough, I remember it as standing for Commanding Officer.

"Conscientious objector," said Roy. "I don't think you could get by with that anymore. If you just refuse to go you could end up with as much as three years in jail. I can't see myself doing that. I imagine I would take my chances in the Army."

I suggested that it might be difficult to accomplish anything at his workshops and discussions since everyone going to Washington on this project agrees with one another anyway, that it might be just a huddling together for warmth, a self-congratulatory bit of rationalization.

"You're right that we agree basically, but I'm sure we'll find out additional things that will strengthen our position."

He said he preferred not to be "government conditioned."

And I agree with that.

My quarrel with the State Department is the refusal to explain precisely what we are trying to do in Vietnam, and I'm not a protester. Maybe this is exactly what we should be doing. The greatest thing.

I try to think that we are doing in Vietnam what all the Allies in the last war should have done when Hitler took over Czechoslovakia, Austria, Poland, and the rest . . . that maybe a scrap over the Czechs might have been a deterrent to what subsequently happened.

But no one explains it to me that way.

It can occur to you that General Eisenhower made a mistake, and then Mr. Kennedy and then Mr. Johnson and now Mr. Nixon can't suddenly pull out and say, "Look this was a crock. All these people who have died . . . this was a mistake and I'm now rectifying it."

"I wouldn't have felt this way about World War II," he said. "We were attacked. We had to win it. But Vietnam is something else. My going to Washington probably won't affect anything."

You could tell he'd like to think so.

I do not suspect him of anything so base as cowardice.

And I respect, as Voltaire remarked, "his right to say it."

Advocates of culture our country over will be pleased to know that the troops in the Vietnamese war speak better.

Perhaps they do not speak culturally. However, they do speak less profanely in some matters, which is certainly a giant stride forward.

For example, in a war I remember there was an expression of sympathy so often used that it had been reduced to an abbreviation.

I refer to the initials TS.

TS was offered in kindly sympathy over all manner of serious matters, from the cancellation of your rotation back to a rest area to a Dear John letter from your wife.

You could be awarded a TS slip from your chaplain, a TS slip from your CO, meaning in this case commanding officer rather than conscientious objector.

TS, as mentioned was an abbreviation of two words unsullied by gentility and any male of mileage can give you a more precise definition. Suffice it here to state merely that it was not an abbreviation for toasted scampi.

The phrase that has replaced TS is "Sorry about that."

On Okinawa recently a corporal wandered in the barracks at Camp Courtney bewailing the fact that "I didn't get my transfer."

Four of his brethren offered "sorry about that," and one was even ". . . really sorry about that."

As was TS previously, it is true expression of sympathy and made the corporal feel better.

Later in the evening, while a little drinking was going on there was a word without which no sentence was complete in another war. Charles McCabe, the San Francisco columnist, refers to it as the word that won World War II. It slipped out only once.

There was a flock of conversation which I had a little difficulty following because of references to "ranchers," "rustlers," and "cattle thieves."

It's like a tobacco or horse auction, it doesn't make much sense at the beginning but if you listen long enough, a light eventually falls.

A "rancher" is a guy who has successfully established a certain rapport with an Okinawan girl. The "rustlers" and "cattle thieves" are intent upon replacing him.

As you can see, none of the situations have changed basically but the terminology has improved.

Since Okinawa was a place where I fought once, a Marine gunnery sergeant named Van Beulwitz wondered, and he had a jeep to accredit the offer, if there was any place on the island I'd like to revisit.

"Yesterdays are no big deal with me," I told him, "since they have very little market value, but since we've got this jug and some time, I'd sort of like to see the 6th Division cemetery, just curious about who stayed and whose folks brought 'em home. Do you know where that is?" The gunny laughed.

"Sure. It ain't. They moved all the bodies back to the Punch Bowl in Honolulu. A long time ago."

"Well, then. That handles that. Maybe we could go and see a place named Sugar Loaf Hill. It's not very big . . . it wasn't . . . but maybe they put up a marker or something on it. I'd like to see what it looks like with grass, when it's not all dug up by artillery and rockets and bombs."

(Greene, a Marine in World War II, was wounded and won the Navy Cross at Sugar Loaf Hill.—*Editor*.)

The gunny exchanged glances around the room.

"Never heard of it," he said.

Neither had any one else.

"What about this Courtney, the guy this camp is named after. Who was he?"

I thought I knew.

"There was an article about him and how the camp was named in a copy of the 1st Division paper they put out on the island, just a minute."

A corporal got a copy out of the files. This was only the second issue so it was handy.

"All the camps here are named after Medal-of-honor winners," said the gunny. "Hansen, McTureous, Hauge, Schwab. Yeah. Here's the story."

The paper was called *The Word*.

This amused me. The "word" in the Marine Corps is something you always have if you're hep and didn't get if you're a foul-up.

There is a legend dating back to the famous naval battle of the Revolutionary War when after hours of fighting, a Marine musket shooter in the rigging overheard John Paul Jones shout, "I have just begun to fight." He threw his weapon down growling, "There's always someone who never gets the word."

The gunny was reading.

"You know you're right. There was a Sugar Loaf Hill. This Courtney got killed at it. That's how he got the big medal. I still don't know where it's at. And I still never heard of it."

After we finished the jug and made an appointment for the next morning, he escorted me to the door.

There was a twinkle in his face and in that of the corporal with him.

"You know, sir, about your hill?"

Then they said it in unison.

"Sorry about that."

20. men

Funny name maybe . . . Redwine!

That's the only name anybody knew until he died and until they took him off to burial at Acacia Park Cemetery.

Kenneth R. Redwine, it turned out but no one ever called him anything but Redwine or Red and when you made out a check to him and asked how he wanted it, he always replied:

"I'd rather have cash, but if you've got to write a check, make it Redwine."

Red was a bookie.

He was also a rather unique bookie because he had the entire Hearst newspaper empire fronting for him during his salad days.

Red was on the payroll at the old Detroit *Times* as a mailer. I almost said he worked on the *Times*. This wasn't true. He was a mailer and was supposed to look after the discharging of newspapers from the mailing room, but he didn't: he booked horses.

He booked football, baseball, hockey, basketball, boxing.

Red would bet you tomorrow wasn't Friday if he could lay the odds.

He wore a bluish type overall shirt and trousers and carried 10 grand in his pants pocket on a slow day.

When you bet with Redwine you called WO 3-8800 and a girl said: "Detroit *Times*."

"May I have the mailing room please?"

"Certainly. One moment."

After that a male voice said:

"Mailing room."

"Is Redwine there?"

The answer, during the betting hours from noon to five, was always either, "Just a minute," or "He's on another phone, will you wait?"

What a front!

In the early '50s a racetrack executive came into town from Roosevelt Raceway and asked if he could make a $5000 bet on the Giants in the World Series.

A photographer at the *Times* told him, "Sure," and called Red.

"Will you take 5 G on the Giants?"

He listened a moment and nodded at the executive. The bet was on.

A moment later the photographer was taking pictures when the man from the East asked, "Is he good for the money?"

The cameraman looked him over.

"Red is. Are you? He's taking my word for you."

A hood decided to roll Red for his walking around money one evening as Red was entering his house out on Vaughn. Red decked him and ran in the house.

A day later he had a gun with a silencer.

You can go to jail just for owning a silencer.

He shot it for us one time so we could hear it.

A silencer allows a noise that doesn't sound like a shot . . . sort of chugs.

He was a beautifully profane man and he drank whiskey as if they might have stopped making it the night before, but he never used it during the magic noon-to-5 hours.

He was funny, too.

I introduced him to a guy one time and okayed him.

The guy bet him sixteen straight times without losing and he was betting $600 and $700 a shot.

Finally one day, Red called up.

"That guy you sent me, John. What about him?"

"What do you mean, what about him? Does he owe you?"

"No. But I'm getting humpbacked carrying money to him and I just wondered if he had any to pay with in case he lost which he maybe isn't ever going to do."

There was a Friday in 1959 when a horse named Rutland Arms, that C. W. Smith owned, was transported to Atlantic City, not

entirely for the amusement of the Atlantic Cityans. He paid
$17.80 and a guy came down to the old Times Square Bar the
next day to collect on a $300 bet.

Red always paid immediately. If you wanted to pay him, he'd
often say, "Wait a while. Maybe you'll win it back."

That Saturday the winner . . . $2670 . . . bought Red a couple
of drinks. This was difficult, Red never accepted anything from
anyone if he could help it. Finally he said:

"Look that Smith friend of yours has got a horse named Hillsdale running today at Atlantic City. If you're any kind of loyal
you should bet."

The winner felt sheepish and bet $200 on Hillsdale.

Hillsdale paid $20, so Red peeled off another $2000.

"It'll teach me to tout," he complained later, but then he
smiled. "I love to see a winner. There are so few."

A player could owe Red and bet him and collect as if he didn't
owe. He was unique that way. He often said that the big problem
of a bookie was that when a better owed him, he lost his business.
He tried to fight it.

Many people were hurt by the folding of the *Times* but the guy
who took the worst financial beating was Redwine. His front was
gone . . . his office . . . and a lot of his customers.

At the funeral home his wife, Sue, who divorced him three
years ago, was back with him again.

"What happened?" I asked.

Red used to call up after she left and cry on the phone.

"After the *Times* folded," she said, "Red was never the same.
He . . . you know how he could be . . . he was unbearable. But
I'm happy now, and I think he is too."

A bunch of us called a horseplayer in Florida who bet Red a
lot, to tell him.

He was silent for a minute.

"Probably a good thing for him," he said finally. "Where he
goes they won't let any liars in and it'll solve a lot of his
problems."

A varied collection of friends spend their Sunday mornings as
the adjective suggests . . . in various ways, and sometimes when
morning health permits I join them.

I sometimes attend church, sometimes walk in the sun, not ever over a golf course unless they are considerable friends, sometimes attend the morning "hangover" club at the nearest saloon, but mainly I go along with God.

I rest.

It's the seventh day.

A Sunday several years ago was one of those rest days with complications, a primary complication being the reading of the papers.

A quotation by President Johnson attracted first, which said:

"The whole nation can take heart from the fact that there are those in the South who believe in justice in racial matters and who are determined not to stand for acts of violence and terror."

The "those" is named Frank Johnson the federal judge in Montgomery, in this instance.

Judge Johnson has been threatened and detested by a lot of his immediate society in Montgomery, and it showed me a little something this time, so far as the people he has been standing up against.

I stood outside his courtroom one day and chatted with a state trooper.

"What kind of a guy is Judge Johnson? How does he go?"

The trooper looked up and down.

"You don't know Judge Johnson, eh? Well he runs his own stick. The judge does . . . he runs his own. You go in that courtroom and you know who's runnin' things. Ain't nobody runs Judge Johnson's court."

This was a time immediately before the Selma march and in Johnson's court the witnesses were Martin Luther King and Sheriff James Clark and the sides involved on the legality of whether the march was proper or not.

A guy with a sunburned face and a blue, open-throated shirt interrupted to say, "Judge Johnson's tough but he'll decide" . . . whatever that meant.

A woman came over to deliver an opinion.

She was wearing a kelly green dress that was cut six inches above her knees and six inches down into her upper cleavage, which was abundant.

I do not suggest that the bedroom was her workshop or that

she was a prostitute or anything like that, but if you had to paint a picture of such, she might have been a way you painted it.

"He's been tough . . . tough on me even, maybe . . . but he's fair."

Well, this isn't even the type case that a federal judge oversees, but it was a way Frank Johnson is regarded.

It was recently that a Dr. Steve Gurdjiian here in town was remarking that "you bet on a man" rather than an electronic system, a project or a national law.

Right after the doctor said that, there was encounter with a guy, a schoolteacher-football coach who runs a program in Cleveland for high school dropouts.

He puts them back in school and gets them jobs.

Dr. Mauch, who controls the money from Washington, went to Cleveland and examined what they were doing with federal funds and asked to inspect the dropout program of John A. Spezzaferro.

He returned to Washington, allocated $225,000 a year for two years to John's program, nobody to touch the money but John.

Seventy percent of John's students are colored. There was a day when several of the black racist organizations declared a strike on the schools. Families were ordered not to send their children to school.

The organizations sent a representative to every school to stop any children who showed up. A man from CORE arrived at John's school, went to John's . . . the principal's . . . office, and explained his presence.

John is as peace-loving as a cobra about his own convictions.

"Look," he said. "My people have already been out of school. Every mind I've got has been devoted to convincing them that they must not . . . MUST NOT miss school. Take your campaign somewhere else."

"I've been ordered here," said the man from CORE, and took up his position outside the front door.

John tried to stay away but couldn't stand it.

He finally went out and joined him.

"Every kid is going to walk by both of us. If he wants to go to school, he's mine. If he doesn't he's yours. If you try to threaten or dissuade him, there's going to be a new hole in the window over there where I threw you through it."

The kids came along and said, "Good morning, Mr. Spezza-ferro," and the man from CORE went back to report, "If everybody in the world is like him, the place is OK. He's for right."

I'm reminded merely because when Judge Johnson sent the jury out and surely everyone in Alabama must have known that if the three Kluxers were pronounced guilty they'd get the ultimate ten years, they sent back in four hours and said, "We're hopelessly deadlocked."

The judge sent back, "You haven't been out long enough to be hopelessly deadlocked. I command that you strive for a verdict."

It's no revelation that the men make ships go.

It is pleasant to know they still exist.

Since it is pleasant as well as necessary to tend a friendship, Freddy and I occasionally spend an evening just wandering around this town that has nurtured us both.

More time than either of us chooses to admit anymore walks with us, enough so there is no compulsion to talk and the memories form pleasant ghosts.

He joshes me sometimes about the kid days when I carried drumsticks in my pocket, back when Paradise Valley existed and Slim Jones ran the Congo Club, and Earl Walton presided behind his red door and the Melody Club was full of freedom of music.

"He was hoping somebody'd ask him to sit in," he relates.

And sometimes they did.

I josh him about the Yankee baseball team and the years and years when he'd go to New York when Don Newcombe and Jackie Robinson were starring for the Dodgers and he'd bet the Yankees and hustle a ticket or two. He'd sympathize with his victims. "Too bad about Jackie," and "Newcombe didn't have it today."

"You're a race exploiter, Freddy."

"Green is my color, man. Green."

Freddy doesn't drink or smoke but his wife Mike and I handle this department. But Freddy helps, helps everybody he can, and as Mike carried it one day when I asked, "Where's Freddy?"

"He's down at the corners helping 'em stand around."

Anyway, once as we were enjoying a brief silence together, he broke it with, "Did you ever hear of Naomi Long? Her married name now is Naomi Long Madgett."

"No."

He quoted a poem, "Woman with Flowers" it was called.

> "I wouldn't coax the plant if i were you.
> Such watchful nurturing may do it harm.
> Let the soil rest from so much digging
> And wait until it's dry before you water it.
> The leaf's inclined to find it's own direction;
> Give it a chance to seek the sunlight for itself.
> Much growth is stunted by too careful prodding.
> Too eager tenderness.
> The things we love we have to learn to leave alone."

Between the next two saloons, he pressed a volume of Mrs. Madgett's poetry on me, a thing entitled *Star by Star*. I then remembered another book by this lady, a title like *Songs to a Phantom Nightingale*.

"Who is she?"

"A friend of Mike's and mine. She's an English teacher out at Northwestern High. She worked some for Reverend Hood during the election."

He had halted without being finished.

"What else?"

"I've got a cousin . . . Louis Wanamaker, who is assistant pastor to her father, Clarence Long, in New Rochelle, New York. She won a $10,000 fellowship in English from the General Motors fellow . . . Mott . . . and she's spending this year out at Oakland University."

It was approaching that hour when both of us would have to attend our jobs.

I examined the book . . . Harlo Press, 16721 Hamilton . . . $3 . . . A note said that copies of this book may be ordered directly from the author at 18080 Santa Barbara Drive, Detroit.

I read one of my own, "Destiny."

> "How near we are to paradise
> Fate does not deign to tell,
> Or what direction peril leads
> The descent into hell.

Or whether spring's capricious breath
Blows promise to the sun
Or flings away a sterile seed
To earth's oblivion.

By what improbable design
The grasses part our way,
The brooding stars of destiny
Have never stooped to say."

There was an immediate thought.
"Sounds a little like Emily Dickinson."
"If you say so, ole buddy."
He stood up.
"Gotta go to work. See ya'."
"Thanks for the book." "Okay."

21. more men

A man died a couple of years ago who was a combination snob, phony, genius, autocrat and entrepreneur, but he may have tasted your hamburger.

He was to food what Beau Brummell was to fashion.

Henri Soulé was his name and he came to this country in 1939 to open Le Restaurant du Pavillon de France at the New York World's Fair.

He was the man that football coach Bear Bryant insulted by saying, "Well if you don't have any chili, let's get out of here," and left.

This was at Le Pavillon, the restaurant he conducted.

After the Fair disintegrated, Henri stayed on to open two of the most famous restaurants in New York, both of them the most expensive, the most exclusive and both with (with certain exceptions) the finest food.

Le Pavillon was one, La Côte Basque the other.

Caviar distinguished both.

Henri was recognized as the complete authority on caviar and each day he would go to the importer and sample the sturgeon eggs that had been flown in that day.

His belief in his own autocracy was total.

He was impervious.

The purveyor would open twelve canisters of caviar and Henri would stroll the lot with his single hygienic spoon and sample. Finally he might decide to take three or four cartons.

An ounce of caviar cost $10 at Pavillon or La Côte Basque.

Once a canister had been sampled, it was no good to the next buyer. The seller always had to cheat and get a mash from another, put it in where Henri had sampled and then smooth it over so it would look untouched.

Only Henri could get away with this.

Henri was a professional snob.

Mrs. Edsel Ford entered Pavillon one time with her granddaughter Jody and Henri made some fuss over them.

"You're in Pavillon now," said Mrs. Ford. "What will you have?"

Jody didn't even look at the menu.

"Can I have a chicken sandwich and a glass of milk?"

Henri permitted. He was a great liberal as far as labor went, too.

After he deserted his own country to prey on New York, he stole all the kitchen and dining room help he'd brought over from France for the Fair. Among them he had the secret of cuisine, the chef.

Pierre Frenay provided the food.

Henri Soulé provided the romance.

Then there was a kitchen workers' strike. To Henri's astonishment and dismay, Pierre sided with the kitchen workers. Pierre had to depart.

Pierre had been making an approximate $25,000 a year. He was promptly hired by the Howard Johnson chain as a consultant for twice the amount.

People that quit Soulé have been responsible for fifteen or twenty of the best restaurants in the country, among them La Caravelle, Grenouille, Mistral, LaFayette and many others of which you also have not heard.

Le Pavillon was and is the most expensive of this country's restaurants, the responsibility, of course, being Soulé's.

After he died, I was discussing with Les Gruber, who was his friend, whether the food was really any better.

"I can tell you two stories," said Les. "One afternoon when I was at lunch at Le Chauveron I had *moules marinières* (that's mussels), and because it's my business, I noticed that it cost $3.50.

"That night I dined at Henri Soulé's and they had *moules marinières* and it cost $5.50. So I had it again."

"How was it?"

"It was $10 better."

The next time Les tried shrimp, similarly overpriced, and they were worse. You are entitled to this concern over the passing of this sort of Barnum of the kitchen for this reason.

"Because of him, a chef supervises the kitchens of Howard Johnson, and from La Caravelle, Mistral and some of the other derivatives of Henri Soulé, others have disseminated over the country."

One time he stuck his little private spoon in the vats of caviar but on that day the owner had had enough and picked up a vat and doused it in his face.

His autocracy had momentarily run out.

But he ruled his kitchens with an iron fist . . . so iron that a lot of people left . . . but they were able to get pricey other jobs because they had worked for Henri.

A decent hamburger you and I get or a bowl of soup on a turnpike, descend from this dictatorial Frenchman.

Back in the genealogy of quality . . . unheralded and unsung . . . there is always a tyrant.

The best barroom fighter I ever saw was a guy from my youth named Irv Sterling who tossed a guy through the plate-glass window of the 10-Hi Cafe on East Jefferson one evening.

Irv was not angry, simply annoyed.

He thought the guy had insulted his girl and under interrogation the fellow failed to understand.

This is important because the second best had a chance at a saloon fight in the Playboy Club recently and walked around it.

He didn't walk away from it. His eyes flashed once and I thought, well, bye-bye-tootsie. But then he simmered down and there was peace.

Gene is his name and, like Irv, he grew up tough around St. Jean and Jefferson and sand mountain where you learned to swim and Jasper Abbott's poolroom where you learned other and perhaps more important things.

What he was doing was standing at the bar in the Playboy with his wife and half a dozen friends and there was a girl in his party standing on the end of the group.

And, of course there were a couple of guys around the bar, perhaps incented by the Bunnies, one of whom had decided he was the young Lochinvar come out of the West.

He leaned over and breathed on the girl.

Gene looked over to see.

A Puritan he is not. If it was all right with the girl, it was all right with him.

It was not all right with the girl.

Gene leaned across the interloper.

"This jerk isn't bothering you, is he?" he asked for the benefit of both.

"As a matter of fact, he is," she said.

The bar at the Playboy is a clean, well-lighted place and it was interesting to surmise the impending event.

Gene is the second best I ever saw and has a great spirit of instinctual efficiency about these things. He is great with his knees and will hook you as hard as he once did in boxing rings where he'd learned that a punch to the chin is not aimed at the chin but about eight inches beyond the chin. A punch is intended to carry through the whole head, which professionals understand.

The interloper, it developed, had a friend, and he brought him in for support.

I watched Gene examine the new one and place both positions on the floor. I waited in quiet anticipation to observe an artist at work.

Both of the amateur antagonists took succor from one another. Heroes.

"Would you move over here?" asked Gene, thus placing the girl in question away from the problem.

I wondered what had happened to my barroom anesthetist.

The action was slow.

The next thing, one of the heroes had grabbed Gene and was explaining how his friend had had too many and wasn't everybody a nice guy and couldn't they all shake hands and be friends.

The original interloping creep got out a hospital certificate from Harper to show that his wife was in maternity and therefore he should be excused.

They all had a quick drink together.

My notion had exploded.

Gene suggested they go home and they did.

No action. No bodies. No blood.

I sought Gene out and asked when the change had taken place.

"You know it didn't matter to me in the old days. We were in joints. You whipped a guy and they threw him out in the street and you didn't see him again.

"Did you notice this. I spent as much time talking to these two jokers who I'd never seen and couldn't care less about to prove I'm a nice guy which I'm not. But what should I do? Knee this guy? Then I'm a bad fellow. These polite places are tough."

We lit a cigarette over that and I had a question.

"Is this the new Gene? Is this what age does? Or is this prosperity? Now you're making dough and you're genteel?"

He laughed right down to his soles.

"I haven't belted anybody in a couple of years. I was down visiting my brother in Pennsylvania a couple of years ago and he took me down to the saloon and we fought with a couple of steelworker friends just for kicks. They liked it and we liked it, although them less.

"In these cushy joints, there isn't anybody'd understand a knee in the groin. Anybody watching, I mean. You got to change. None of these guys want to fight. They want to talk. And that's the worst thing. Look how I spent five minutes having a drink with those clowns listening to 'em tell me how we were all nice guys, I gave it up."

He was quiet a moment and then he said:

"But you know something. If I knew that when a guy got smart and I hit him he'd disappear . . . not be around telling me what pals we were later . . . both them guys would have been belted."

The peace conference is reached in strange ways.

Disappear.

It ain't possible, but what a thought.

I have come recently to realize that I could never have handled a Miss Lonelyhearts column, could never have been a Dear Abby or her sister, Dear Ann.

Did you know that in every readership survey taken in the country it has been discovered that more people read this sort of column than any other?

Me, too.

I read it. Sometimes I wonder if the letters weren't contrived, as everybody must. And I admire the answers. So glib, so quick, so funny, sometimes.

"My boy friend seems to have trouble keeping his hands off my best girl friend! She has trouble keeping her hands off him. Does this indicate something?

Curious.

Dear Curious: Keep your hands off both of them.

It's great entertainment.

Then the other day a great friend called and told how important it was and we sat down. This a deeply religious guy, successful, family and all that. I've been teaching his oldest boy, ten, to scuba dive.

There was a little garbage in the opening conversation, which made you wonder and then there was the pointed question:

"Do you think it's possible to be in love with two women?" he asked.

The way he said it you knew it was a conversation you wanted to avoid.

But he waited.

Finally I had to say something.

"I guess you're asking . . . or saying . . . that you're still in love with Midge, but there's somebody else and you guess you're in love with her, too."

"I'm in love with both of them. That's right."

I thought about saying, "If you'll tell me what love is, then both of us will understand this conversation better," but I didn't.

What is it? How much sex is in it? How much of it is shared crises, shared memory? How much of it is children? If there's new love, how much of it is freedom, a new sensation of touch and a new reaction to your own old personality, new to the new but merely accepted by the familiar love?

I played it quiet.

"I suppose you can be in love with two women," I said. "Most of us guys are in love . . . I mean that with the great respect, affection and all that . . . with more than one other man. We have more than one fine man friend. I cannot regard the impossibility of having two fine women friends. It's the same thing, I think, without the sex except that after sex, if the principals are intelligent, they're better friends."

He jumped on it quickly.

"That's what I mean. A guy has a lot of male friends. Why can't he have a lot . . . or another . . . woman friend?"

He was really leaning on it.

"Well, there's little Roddy for one thing. Maybe you can explain it to me. Maybe you can even explain it to Midge, your wife. But how do you explain it to Roddy who's only ten. You'd be asking him to understand a lot. As a matter of fact, you'd be asking him to explain something you don't understand so much you're asking me, and anybody'll tell you how goofy I am. Anybody at all."

He clung to the fact of the male friends.

"You're right though. A guy has a lot of other guys he's close to, it's just as natural for him to be close to more than one woman."

"Suppose Midge would like to be close to more than one man? That would have to be proper, too, or are you now invoking the old double standard, men are entitled. Women have to be locked up in chains and sold as virgins. Are we going the logic route or are you just asking for somebody's approval?"

He sipped morosely now on his old-fashioned.

"I said one time about this, that my friendship you can't ever lose because I have given of it, but my respect you can lose."

"What do you mean by that?" he asked.

"Nothing much. I was thinking about Roddy that's all."

He didn't answer.

"On the other hand I have never been able to plumb the human heart with any degree of accuracy even my own. I hope you can plumb yours."

"What are you saying, really, you . . . ?"

"I'm wishing you luck. That's the very simple thing that I'm doing."

It got very rough at the end.

I kept remembering about the Miss Lonelyhearts business and also a thing John Ciardi said not long ago about "Fools give short answers to long questions."

And I wondered where that left me.

And him . . .

Being a chalk-eater anyway, which is horse racing jargon for a guy who must bet on the favorite . . . the one that adds up best figuring with a stub of chalk . . . I'd already sent it in on Bold Lad in the 90th renewal of the Kentucky Derby.

There are many ways . . . some of them even interesting . . . to lose a horse race and I thought over the years I'd examined them all.

Everybody has bet in an office pool where you put up your dollar or whatever and slips of paper are placed in somebody's beret and then you pick out your horse by lot and if you get a dog, well, that's the way it goes.

A man had talked me out of attending this affair for the first time in several years which was not really a very difficult proposition.

"You'll see it better. They'll run it back over so you can see what you missed the first time. Eddie Arcaro will interview the winning jockey afterwards and you should see it once on the boob tube anyway. You owe it to your education to share this magnificent experience with the countless other millions around the country who will be watching on TV. Besides you'll get to play in one of my auction pools."

None of these reasons had much bearing on my decision. It was pure sloth. For at whatever risk of boasting, I'm as good a man at sloth as any man alive, sloth being, according to Webster: habitual disinclination to exertion.

Anyway, eight of us ended up in this guy's recreation room which he has done up like an Irish Pub. The first thing he does is lubricate the guests slightly to turn them properly festive.

Then he scribbled the names of eleven horses in the Derby on slips of paper and began to explain the advantages of bidding high at the beginning of the sale since obviously the winner was surely among the slips nestled in a silver trophy that a horse named Miss Mommy, that this guy used to own, had won once.

Atmospherically, as you can see, it was exciting.

Even though the winner was there, bidding started off slow and it took four bids to get it to three dollars. The auctioneer suddenly bid five.

Well, by now, I was convinced that the first draw might be Bold Lad and for six dollars I could get him and then quit this peculiar nonsense.

It wasn't Bold Lad, at all, it was Swift Ruler.

Bilked again.

"Now you don't tell anyone what horse you've got," he instructed, "because even though you've got Bold Lad, or Lucky Debonair or Tom Rolfe or one of the live horses, you mustn't let anybody know or they won't bid as much."

It was a winner take all and even an addled head like this one could figure that he couldn't buy them all, so I waited out a couple of rounds, one of which went for $7 and the other for $9.

Then I'd sit there and look at these buyers as they opened their slips and try to figure what horses they'd drawn.

My wife bought the fourth round and then wouldn't tell me who she had. Divorces have occurred over less. I'd have showed her my Swift Ruler, and as a matter of fact, tried to but she wouldn't look.

"Try and play it fair, will you," was her comment.

Well, the auction wandered along and somehow this guy managed to convince you that everyone was the winner. I succumbed a couple of more times, once getting Tom Rolfe, who was a live horse and finally we were down to the last slip.

There must be something about the last chance.

It was the high bid of the afternoon.

I had to go to $15 for it but determination won the day.

The name was Narushua, the goat who eventually finished last. As I look back on it, I'm not sure the auction wasn't more fun than the race and it turned out they didn't run it back. The sound track went out and all you saw were a lot of strangers whose lips were moving while they peered intently at one another. Arcaro wasn't there. Also, I was surprised to see it wasn't in color like the World Series.

"That's because it's CBS," explained somebody.

"They can afford to buy the New York Yankees, they can afford to put on the Derby in color and get the sound track right with it," I thought.

Anyway, what with one thing and another, the total pool amounted to $137. An eloquent auctioneer. A bimbo named Patricia or something won it all, and she only paid $6 for a single ticket on Lucky Debonair.

If she'd bet it on the horse, she'd have only won $25.80.

"Most of the money she won was yours," accused the wife.

"There must be a lesson here somewhere," I said defensively.

"There is," she said. "You sent the bet on Bold Lad and then you went for three horses here by lot. The lesson is that you're neither smart nor lucky either."

"I have days like this," I said.

"Why so often?" she asked.

The General stuck a bayonet into a native at Dakar during one of his hitches in the French Foreign Legion. Unfortunately the fellow died of it and the legion could not view the incident as a simple boyish prank as was usually the case in those times.

The General was court-martialed and sentenced to a year building roads in a prison in then French Indochina.

The bunks were of wood and suspended from the wall in such fashion that when they were lowered the slab of timber rested on a three inch slant toward the floor, so that in order to sleep the General had to cling to it.

The work shored up what was already a magnificent physique which has served him well during his drinking years in the French capital, but what he considers a trick of the service made him leave the legion.

During the year in Indochina he was comforted by the fact that it was the last . . . give or take a month . . . of his six-year hitch and when he returned he could get some furlough and re-enlistment money and divert himself after a long period of alcoholic celibacy.

The "trick" was that prison time didn't count on enlistment time, so when he returned to Africa he discovered that the year had been on him.

This offended the General's sense of fair play.

When he finished out that term, he abandoned the legion and returned to Paris. This was a dozen years ago and it will not be until two years hence that he becomes eligible for a small pension for the time he did serve.

The General, rather obviously, was not a general at all.

His name, however, is Paul Maréchal which in French means marshal, so he thereby acquired the nickname.

He holds forth daily in the park, just off Champs Élysées, where the theater of the Marigny is located.

The chef at the posh Restaurant Berkeley feeds him from the kitchen with the stuff tourists are paying 50 francs for out in front.

In return the chef is rewarded with the charm of the General's company and very charming company it is, indeed.

The bartenders along the street are not as charitable, or rather not charitable enough for Paul's requirements.

So there must be money.

Paul developed his own business. In France there are no parking meters as we know them here. However, every motorist must carry a small, yellow colored, rectangular-shaped cardboard clock with an hour hand on it.

When a motorist parks his car, he sets the cardboard clock at the time he parked and he is permitted an hour's parking immediately thereafter. When the yellow clock shows he has been away from the car more than an hour, a gendarme tickets him.

For a modest fee, Paul watches the cars and when the hour is up and the man has not returned, he sets the clock ahead another hour and so on.

He is very careful and has never been caught changing the dial and considers it an honorable manner in which to survive, and certainly more gentlemanly than horsing around with a bayonet.

In addition, the General has sponsors.

Eugene Istomin, the pianist, is one. For several years Eugene has been sending the General $20 American every month. When he was in Detroit recently playing his concerts there was a day when we had to go to the bank, change a twenty into 97 francs and mail it to the General. Very urgent.

"Why not mail him the $20 and let him change it?"

"You don't know the General. It would confuse him."

After Eugene conceived the idea of giving Maréchal some economic stability, Paul managed to convince some others that this would be a noble project for them, too.

How many remanded, no one knows.

Charles (Chickie) Sherman was sentenced to a year and a day in prison for income tax evasion.

Chickie has been a practicing bookmaker for many years and is one of the honorable men, as much as you say it when a guy has been convicted of not picking up his part of the tab for that soldier or Marine who died in Vietnam yesterday.

He did a short stretch before when he didn't have the $50 stamp that the federal government instituted for bookies a decade or so ago.

It was one of the more violent legal tricks.

If you didn't buy the stamp you were bait for the feds.

If you bought it, you were an admitted bookie for the locals.

It was sort of like mortar fire used to be in the war. When a mortarman was trying to get on target, he'd often drop a shell over . . . then adjust . . . drop a shell under range . . . then adjust.

You were then bracketed. The next one was for you.

At this moment, wise sergeants suggested loudly, "Let's get the——out of here."

That was what the $50 stamp did. It bracketed bookies.

Chickie didn't have the chance . . . alternative if you prefer . . . that a normal businessman has when he errs in taxes. They don't send businessmen to jail every day for less than Chickie did. A normal businessman is called by a different name and is permitted to pay, along with his back interest.

Personally, I've never understood why they sent bookies to jail. Money is their line and it has always seemed that you should take money from them in a fine instead of fining taxpayers with room and board.

But then a real estate operator once said to me in a dispute, "Well, that's the law."

"There used to be a law by which you burned girls as witches," I said.

"I wouldn't burn a girl," he said.

So there you are.

Chickie wasn't ever going to attack anybody, or make the streets unsafe but none of this is really what this is about.

What it's about is a coincidence.

On this day that Sherman's life was inconvenienced a pair of horseplayers won $9391.60 in the twin double at Wolverine Harness Raceway.

Four horses . . . and if you care about this sort of thing, their names were Ethel Attorney, Debbis Jeno, Fortarios, and Henry's Dream . . . combined for this handsome return on an investment of $2.

A friend of mine won it.

I'd mention his name except for one thing and it has nothing to do with any duplicity with the government. He's a young fellow who lives at home with his folks and he told them he was going to the movies because race horsing is not the sort of thing in which they prefer him to indulge.

Perhaps if they knew the amount, they'd change their minds.

Money is such a terrible persuader.

Anyway, this guy is a perpetual loser.

He is hereby awarded the counsel that he should save his losing tickets, and I hope he's saved them up to now. The tax law is that you must pay tax on your gambling winnings. If you just lose for the year, that's your baby child.

But you can subtract what you lost against what you won.

If any.

Wouldn't it be pleasant to have this problem, and furthermore, the last race didn't even matter. By that time, since the earlier horses had paid long prices, there were only the two tickets alive in the twin.

The ticket was good before the last race was run.

The coincidence of the tax evader attending to prison and the tempted tax evader preparing for it is too much for me.

And too fresh in memory is the scene in the British Isles where bookmaking is not only a legal but a respected profession.

Over there a bookie wears a cutaway, striped trousers and a top hat.

It's a shame about certain laws.

I'd give a bucket of champagne to see Chickie in a cutaway and topper.

In Lansing, Michigan, the day of final passage for legislative bills had ended and now Senator Michael O'Brien was being feted on his 25th legislative year by a gathering of his peers.

He had just launched into affectionate reminiscence of the days of the $3 per diem. Haskell Nichols, who has been up here for thirty years, had already spoken and the mood in the basement of Dine's restaurant was mellowing happily.

Then Stash Novak looked across the table and spotted Senator John Bowman. He cast a reflection in earthy terms upon John's ancestry, lurched around a couple of chairs and pushed Bowman off his chair.

It was about as exciting as Clay and Liston, but at least Stash demonstrated intent, and this was Stash talking now, not Senator Stanley Novak.

Peacemakers intervened immediately of course, but his intent was reestablished the moment they relaxed. This time Stash was guided to the bar, where he elected to "go home before I get in some trouble."

Senator Bowman journeyed to the O'Brien table and apologized for the altercation on such a tender occasion.

"He'll have forgotten about it tomorrow," said O'Brien. "What was the matter?"

"It was the Sunday liquor bill," answered Bowman. "I'm sorry."

"It's forgotten," said O'Brien.

This was the climax to the final day in the Senate and that august body had decided again, agreeing in spirit with Melina Mercouri and Grecian moviemakers, that as far as booze went it was to be never on Sunday again in Detroit.

Stash had had a tough day of it.

He began the morning with a roster of the Senate on which he had checked off 22 certain votes for House Bill 2149 which would allow the question of whether liquor might be sold in Wayne County on Sunday to be placed in public referendum.

He needed only 20 to pass.

It had been months and a flock of politicking but now Stash had it knocked.

Stash was the only one who was certain.

Mayor Jerry Cavanaugh had calls in to Beadle, Bowman, Brown . . . just starting down the list of senators . . . but wasn't getting answers. He placed a call to his friend George Fitzgerald and got none.

Bowman eventually called to tell him he was voting against it. When the bill came up for passage Bowman voted nay, Fitzgerald voted nay and Garry Brown wasn't present.

The vote was 19-18. Stash was a vote short.

About that time Garry Brown wandered in and Stash exploded with joy. Here was the 20th vote. Forget Fitzgerald and Bowman. Then Brown voted nay.

In the meanwhile, Carl O'Brien decided that if it wasn't going to pass he didn't want to be on record in favor so he changed his vote. On the second time around Roger Johnson changed his ballot also.

It was gone now and Stash knew it. He went back to his chambers and fumed. Then he dictated a speech and had Owen Deatrick, the retired *Free Press* correspondent, polish it up. Then he went back to the floor and motioned for reconsideration of the bill.

He realized it was gone but he had some things to say to the Senate. As soon as he was beaten in a roll call to reconsider, he took off on his fellows.

"Welshers," was one of the things he called them. "Those senators," he said, "who gave their words and flunked their character tests."

He reverted back to his labor union days.

"Finks," he shouted.

I was sitting with a lobbyist in the gallery as he spoke.

"He really means that," said my companion. "This guy's word is just like gold. I had his promise on a vote once and he changed his mind. Just like apparently some other senators have done here. Novak came to me and asked to be released from promise.

"No, I told him.

"He didn't want to, but he voted with me."

We adjourned to Novak's office.

He fumed for a while, returned periodically to the Senate floor to vote on subsequent bills, returned to his office to brood.

A thing that defied understanding was that on the previous day both Bowman and Fitzgerald had candidly remarked that they

would vote against it. Not just to me but to anyone else who inquired.

Stash waved it aside.

"I know who promised and who didn't," he said.

"It's a matter of simple economics with me," Bowman had explained, "I represent Macomb County. Why should the saloonkeepers across Eight Mile Road have a break over mine? If I were
four or five county lines away, I might change my mind. But then
I have the church folks to think of, too."

Fitzgerald applied the same logic, mentioning "my Belgian
saloonkeepers."

A strange and unnatural thought occurred to me.

If the bill . . . and this is what it was . . . intended only that
the people of Wayne County be allowed to vote on whether they
wanted to do something or not, wasn't it sort of undemocratic to
deny them this simple democratic process?

This, of course, was hooted down.

The scene at Dine's didn't seem to reflect great dignity on the
Senate, but then . . . happy thought . . . suppose as Stash was
leaving he'd met Fitzgerald coming in the door.

Pow.

Just judging from his name, Inspector Peppino Puleo has very
little chance of being a Greek, yet he told a Grecian fable about
justice.

The inspector was very careful to state that this was a story and
not a policeman's philosophy.

The conversation had been of the store booster, which is a professional shoplifter, and the snitch, which is amateur like your
wife, perhaps.

Assorted shapes and sizes of patrolmen . . . Jim Balaze, Jack
Glisman, Myron Dobryden, Bill Grunis, Bill Kennan . . . were
around and the stories were going about the woman shoplifter
who turned out to be a man when searched, and the girl with the
shopping list who was filling it.

"Doing your Christmas shoplifting early?"

Apropos of nearly nothing, the inspector launched into his story
of Athens in the centuries ago.

It was during the Hellenistic period when beauty was rampant and the fathers of the town decided that a new edifice should be erected . . . a single glorious building to replace the courts, the police department and the jail.

Instead of a varied collection of ramshackle buildings, there would be the one grand monument to justice and the law.

It so happened that Athens' finest architect was also the city's most famous philosopher, a man of great distinction and a man held in deep regard.

The city fathers approached him and after the proper preliminary rituals, they explained the need of the city and begged the great man to entertain the task.

"I shall walk in the garden and contemplate," said the architect-philosopher, stroking his beard, "and I shall return with my answer."

After a proper period of contemplation the great man returned.

The fathers waited, sipping wine.

"I shall build you the building," he said. "However, I shall discuss it no further with you. I shall think heavily over my plans, then I will call upon your builders and erect the temple of justice. Only then will you see it. If that meets with your approval, consider it done."

Apparently second-guessing has been around for a while.

The fathers were overjoyed.

"Agreed," they cried and repaired to the nearest temple to be anointed with oils.

The great man labored long and carefully, drawing his plans.

Then he summoned the builders.

The city fathers watched gleefully as a magnificent marble palace grew before them.

They conjectured among one another on what this pillar meant, what that mighty wing would house, enjoying themselves and waiting.

Finally it was finished.

All of Athens turned out to behold the temple of justice.

A great feast was spread.

There were athletic games and races between chariots.

The great man, aged and exhausted from his labors, took the city fathers through the edifice.

They clapped their hands in excitement and delight until the tour ended at the top of the building, where the jail rested.

The jail consisted of a single solitary cell.

"But you have room for only one prisoner," cried the fathers.

"Trouble me not," answered the weary man. "It is all you will need."

And he repaired to his home to rest and refresh himself from his labors.

Although the fathers were alarmed that a single cell had replaced the large prison previously available to the town, they installed the police and magistrates and waited.

It was at the end of the first week that a thief was arrested in the marketplace, where he had bludgeoned a stallkeeper and made off with his wares before his apprehension by the police.

He was duly tried and convicted and sentenced to prison, whereupon he assumed occupancy of the single cell.

The jailhouse was now full.

Three days later the police arrested a rapist who was likewise haled before the court and convicted.

What to do?

The city fathers went to the now rested philosopher.

"What will we do? We have had two crimes in four days and both men have been convicted. One occupies our only cell, yet you said that one would suffice."

The philosopher regarded them quietly.

"Take the man in the cell and hang him," he said.

Inspector Puleo eyed his audience, his patrolmen who may have heard the story many times and this unwary interloper.

"They didn't have any crime for a long time after that," he said.

It reminded me a little of the commissioner's credo that there are two kinds of citizens . . . the lawful and the unlawful.

Perhaps that's the way it should be with a proper cop.

And after that, a magistrate decides.

You hang around . . . you hear stories.

22. books

At whatever risk of shocking the reader, there has come under my hand a book over which we must now harmonize.

It has a title.

Liquor: The Servant of Man.

Little, Brown issues it at $4.95.

The first time I've seen a price put on justification.

The dust jacket is a drawing of bunches of grapes and sprigs of rye and a corn leaf here and there.

The flyleaf begins:

"Throughout history man has made use of liquor. No other human custom—save sex—has persisted so long and has been subject to so much myth and misapprehension.

"Dr. Morris E. Chafetz, an internationally known and respected authority on alcoholism, now turns his attention to the long-suffering misunderstood and often forgotten great majority of non-problem drinkers."

I also commend Dr. Chafetz for bringing up the subject.

Dr. Chafetz is assistant clinical professor in psychiatry on the faculty of medicine at Harvard University and director of the Acute Psychiatric Service and Alcohol Clinic at Massachusetts General Hospital.

The doctor reminds me a little of the late H. L. Mencken, who wrote many years ago his suggestions to the world diplomats that they all stay happily squiffed and then they'd get along better and so would the world.

The memory revolves around all of the people Mencken infuriated with his dissertation, that, of course, being Mencken's hobby, infuriating people.

I'm pleased that the doctor's credentials are so presentable, for he says that 95 percent of the people who drink have no alcohol problem, and this will annoy everyone who disapproves.

When he quotes Winston Churchill's famous remark, "I have taken more out of alcohol than alcohol has taken out of me," he is bearding those he describes in another sentence:

"The emphasis is all negative; the don'ts drown the do's. It is as though a minority of scared, unhappy people have successfully attempted to kill the pleasure of us all."

I would not discourage a crusader against booze from reading this book, since there are things in it he will be able to carp at.

Dr. Chafetz quotes, for example, an unknown sage of 1690 who presumably said: "You say man learned first to build a fire and then to ferment his liquor. Had he but reversed the process we should have no need of flint and tinder to this day."

A dissident may thereby throw up alcohol as an obstacle to progress.

But the weight of the book provides an interesting and obviously carefully considered discussion of liquor and sex, crime and liquor, motoring with it and the rest. The thing that Chafetz does is refuse to lay the blame simply.

Like all thinking men, the doctor is against drunkenness.

He discusses the uses of wines and liquors and an interesting point he makes is that drinking is more pleasurable when accomplished leisurely.

Chafetz never loses sight of the fact that drinking can be dangerous and at one point goes out of his way to point up that:

"Unfortunately, the narcotizing effect of alcohol is greater than its caloric; brain and muscle are numbed by alcohol simultaneously, but the brain is controlling."

Yet as he hastens to add: "The same . . . occurs without liquor; any potent distraction from fatigue has a similar effect."

And though my approach is mildly frivolous, my conclusion is that it's a book worth reading, even though I'm aware that publishers these days are cascading us with gimmick books.

If you're any sort of pro football addict, and why not, and if you survived the days of Bobby Layne and company, you will be interested in some seriously produced understatement.

"All day long," writes Chafetz, "the athlete in training must drive himself under physically and emotionally tense conditions. Then comes the evening meal, a little relaxation and an early bedtime. Why not some wine with the evening meal, or a highball before retiring? The relaxation and appetite stimulation that liquor can supply would be invaluable."

The copyright on this book is 1965.

Bobby Layne came out of Texas University in 1948.

You would have to say that Bobby anticipated him.

A highball before retiring.

Man!

The punishment for theft in Saudi Arabia is to cut off the hands of the thief.

Justice Cornelius, the chief justice of Pakistan, was pointing out the other day that this system of punishment has greatly curtailed theft in that country.

He was pointing it out to the other judges at the Commonwealth and Empire Law Conference in Sydney, Australia, in his own behalf.

No, Mr. Cornelius hadn't stolen anything.

But the previous day he had suggested that the criminal be punished by loss of limbs.

Well, can you imagine how big this went over with a flock of jurists who don't hang, draw and quarter people any more and recently have decided not to simply hang them any more either.

"Inhuman" was one cry. "Reactionary" was another.

It interested me that the Pakistani didn't back off much.

"I am not inhuman, I am not ruthless," he said. "I suggested a practical solution to a serious problem."

He explained that he was not advocating amputation but surgery on a nerve or muscle to incapacitate a criminal temporarily until he reformed.

Referring to Britain's "Great Train Robbery," he remarked:

"Instead of jailing them, they could all have had their legs taken away. The organized criminal does not fear prison. Nowadays they look upon it as a tax-free holiday."

Then he made his reference to justice in Saudi Arabia and both sides withdrew, complacently secure in themselves.

Whoever espouses a cause different than another's is always deemed wrong, just as a man who does differently.

To render an absurd example, a man in white tie and tails is improperly clad at a miner's labor meeting while if he showed up at the Met with one of those torches on his noggin, they'd want to arrest him.

All of which brings us, by circuitous route, to a volume published by Wayne University Press, with an assist from the Ford Foundation and written by Frank Hartung, who was associate professor in sociology at WSU at the time of the writing.

The name of the book is *Crime Law and Society* and I'm grateful to a guy named Mike Ware out at the Press for sending it along, because at $9.75, I'd have had trouble managing it, although now that I've read it, I would buy one if I lost it.

Hartung is concerned with the concept of responsibility for crime.

For instance at one point he uses the familiar billiard table illustration whereby:

"The individual is likened to a billiard ball that is knocked around the table by forces beyond its control . . . delinquents very soon learn to conceive of themselves in this manner.

"Whether they in fact believe it, or use it as a manipulative technique, or do both, is still moot."

I'm exaggerating, of course, but Hartung reminds me a little of Justice Cornelius in that he is suggesting a lot of things that sociologists do not propound, criminal lawyers will resent and criminals, if they read, would recognize as to be not in the criminal's best interest.

Here are some sentences from Hartung:

"Juveniles learn reasons and justifications for committing their delinquencies from psychiatrists, social workers and sociologists as well as from other delinquents.

"Psychiatry, the courts and the law are subversive to society in the extent that they have greatly increased the kind of ordinary and normal conduct classifiable as irresponsible.

"Whether a woman is classified as a thief or a kleptomaniac

often depends as much on what goes on in the head of the examining psychiatrists as it does on what goes into her purse.

"The criminal and delinquent are normal, no matter how repug-
nant humane people find their conduct to be."

One I particularly enjoyed was:

"The concern with mental health and mental illness is a social
movement rather than a scientific development."

I know of a couple of people personally who have committed
homicide and for temporary insanity are now loose.

I see them occasionally and am convinced they were the recip-
ients of the aforementioned "social movement" plus excellent
legal counsel.

I hope the book gets around to some judges.

But you never know how people will react to things.

The girl I live with walked by a while ago and asked what was
happening at the typewriter and I showed her the clipping about
Justice Cornelius in Sydney.

She read it and said:

"Ugh. I'm glad he wasn't my teacher in school."

A book arrived entitled *Football and the Single Man* which
brings me to a favorite subject.

Girls.

In this instance, a particular type.

The book is an autobiography of the guy they've called Golden
Boy. Al Silverman, the very capable editor of *Sport* magazine,
wrote it.

I used to think that an autobiography was the memoirs written
by one's self but it says on the jacket "as told to" and then it says
"A candid autobiography," so there you are.

Paul Hornung.

In case you don't keep up with children's games, you still know
Paul, not perhaps as the Heisman Trophy winner from Notre
Dame, or a man who did the option play at Green Bay so well,
but at least as the fellow who bet when he shouldn't've and then
admitted it.

He was grounded for a year because of it. Remember?

Anyway, Paul talks a lot about his various "fiancées."

At one point, he says, "I think that still I would rather score a touchdown on a particular day than make love to the prettiest girl in the United States."

You notice this is not a flat statement. He prefaces with, "I think."

An entire chapter is called "The Subject Is Women" and he talks about his little black book and recalls a true story of a couple years back when there was a rumor that the Giants were trading end Del Shofner for Hornung.

Former Giant Coach Allie Sherman squelched the rumor at a team meeting, saying, "I wouldn't trade Del Shofner for Paul Hornung and all his girl friends."

Modzelewski of the Giants jumped up shouting, "Wait . . . Wait a minute, coach. Take a vote, take a vote."

Silverman wrote this book as honestly and as well as he could and it is the first time I've ever seen women mentioned in much detail in a book about an athlete.

There is usually a great deal of piety on everyone's part about presenting an athlete in hallowed inspirational light for the sake of the youth of America and what comes through is a square-jawed, clean-shaven type, some statistics and the personality of a wooden Indian.

Hornung points up a type—the sport broad. They call them "jocks" too. They are to sport what camp followers are to wars.

There seems to be no great common denominator except that they are addicted to sport figures.

You will normally find them at whatever bar in a particular city at which athletes congregate after a game.

In baseball, particularly, they are not interchangeable. A certain group of girls will have it for a certain team.

There are places in this town into which I could walk, if I'd been away and was unfamiliar with the baseball schedule, look around the room and say with complete accuracy, "The Yankees are in town," or "the Indians," etc.

It's the only time all year when you see this particular group and, when the game is over, the athletes come and get them.

They come from every family background: from Birmingham and from the Town House and from Third Avenue. There seems to be no pattern that way.

I am reminded of one girl in particular, who for purposes of identification I shall call Alicia.

She accomplished a unique distinction among the "jocks."

I have heard them compared to the kind of men who attend burlesque shows in the afternoon.

About that I couldn't say. Nor have I seen many signs that any of them ever suffered very much.

By that I mean simply that at least they are not discovered moping tearfully about in public.

It's an arrangement that seems to keep all sides contented, for whatever that's worth, and I've never been presumptuous enough to inquire into any of the matters personally.

There's one young matron-about-town who persists in having athletes over to her home and it doesn't make much difference which kind. She entertains football players, golfers, baseball players, all shapes, sizes, and complexions.

I see her at all sorts of events.

These are the stage-door janes of the male singers, cast in a different vein.

Most of them are relatively attractive.

Hornung was staying at the Racquet Club in Miami, which he mentions, at the same time I was, about the time of his reinstatement in 1964.

He introduced various fiancées during that week. All of them were lovely and pleasant.

I mentioned Alicia because she married a football player here. It was a surprise to all of us.

But they are apparently very happy.

We got a card just the other day. He's been traded now.

They just had a baby boy.

I found it rather touching.

23. nonsense

Just a short while ago I heard another lumpkin say, "If you can't say something good about someone, don't say anything at all."

Show me a man who uses this hoary nonsensical axiom and I'll show you an innocuous jerk, aye, perhaps even a dangerous one.

Perhaps the subject is a man who's a cheat.

So our hero says nothing and you are permitted, in your innocence, to deal with the subject and be cheated.

After that, if you complain "Why didn't you warn me?" he shrugs and replies, "Well, that's business."

Business is not, or at least shouldn't involve, cheating.

But one good cliché deserves another.

"If you can't say something good . . ." deserves "Well, that's bus . . ."

Which are maunderings that have been running through this swampy mind all the way from some business over at First Federal's new bank building on Griswold and Woodward, where, for one reason or another, Bill Veeck had been holding forth.

Veeck always leaves me more than a little refreshed and one of the reasons is that he is a complete opposite of the "jerk" I was mentioning above.

If a fellow is a faker and his name comes up, Veeck is very apt to describe him as a faker. This directness is in such short supply that it invariably causes me to catch my breath.

Somehow the name of Mr. Avery Brundage cropped up in the conversation. Mr. Brundage having been, as you know, the chief bottlewasher, authority, front and pooh-bah for the amateur athletics and the International Olympic Committee for many years.

Brundage has been easily identifiable over the years for the stuffed quality of his shirts and a certain sanctimoniousness of manner in all things.

Since Veeck has been writing a once-a-week column for Marshall Field enterprises, he has fallen into the habit of referring to Mr. Brundage as a prominent saloonkeeper.

This upsets Mr. Brundage and the first time it happened he called Mr. Field to complain. Mr. Field had been alerted.

"Veeck called me a saloonkeeper," he objected.

"I noticed," said Mr. Field. "But isn't it true that you own the La Salle Hotel?"

"Yes, of course," said Brundage. "Everyone knows that."

"Well, isn't it true that there is a saloon in the hotel. As a matter of fact, isn't it true that there are several saloons that you own in the hotel?"

"Yes, but . . ."

"Then isn't Mr. Veeck within his right to identify you as a saloonkeeper?"

"Well, why does he have to bring it up?" said Brundage.

Which somehow got Bill on an incident that happened in 1959, the year Veeck found his way back into baseball as owner and operator of the Chicago White Sox.

After having been run out of baseball when he wanted to move the St. Louis Browns to Baltimore, and having seethed on the outside for a few years, all the satisfactions were his.

His first year back, he won the American League pennant.

Toward the end of the season, after the Sox had clinched the pennant, Bill was doing everything he could to stimulate attendance at what were now strictly noncrucial games at Comiskey Park.

The country's champion tumbling team happened to be in Chicago—amateurs—and Veeck contracted with them to stage an exhibition before one of his baseball games.

He had also rented several floors, the ballroom, practically the whole La Salle Hotel to make it World Series headquarters during the games scheduled between Los Angeles and Chicago.

The word came down to the amateur tumbling team from

Brundage that they could not perform at Comiskey Park in conjunction with those filthy professionals. Such word was communicated to Veeck.

Veeck called Brundage, but was unable to contact him personally.

"Would you give Mr. Brundage a message?" he asked.

"Certainly."

"Would you tell him to cancel all of the arrangements made by the Chicago White Sox at the La Salle Hotel. We are moving headquarters somewhere else."

Veeck sighed happily in the recollection.

Within thirty minutes Mr. Brundage's office was on the phone.

A great change of heart had transpired.

There had evidently been some misunderstanding.

So the amateur tumblers were permitted to tumble.

And the White Sox kept their arrangements at Mr. Brundage's Hotel.

It's rather an uplifting story.

Around the table, as he was telling it, were a couple of people who seemed a trifle shocked to hear Mr. Brundage treated in such frank and rather disrespectful fashion.

"If you can't say something good" . . . but then "That's business."

I found it heartening.

24. dogs

A sinister thing about dogs is the soft-eyed manner in which they look at you.

A dog can really pour on the silent affection.

I used to think that all dogs were rather like Robert Browning's Last Duchess who "had a look, how shall I say, too soon made glad but she liked whate'er she looked on and her looks went everywhere."

This isn't . . . . simply isn't so.

Pete bit the mailman again recently. He bites the paper boy all the time. He only weighs five pounds and he doesn't really rend anybody. I haven't found a single arm or leg under the bed yet.

But his victims do complain.

I explain about the evolution of dogs. Large dogs like St. Bernards are so gentle because over the hundreds of years that they have been dogs, every time a mean one came along he was killed. How could you handle a mean St. Bernard?

But Pete is a Maltese and since at his fighting weight he is still not very dangerous, he has survived with a little ferocity left in him. A five pounder you dropkick across the room when he becomes obstreperous. With a St. B this is impossible.

"You know," said the milkman over a conciliatory beer, "it's a good thing Saints didn't always carry flagons of brandy around their necks or the mountain drunks would have defended even the mean ones . . . in case one was carrying the balm . . . and some of them might still be ferocious."

Anyway, you can see the diplomacy that even little Pete requires.

My wife got back from driving her mother home, arriving simultaneously with a quaint letter from the Nichibei Trading Co. Ltd. in Japan.

The letter read:

"Dear Sir.

"We had a great pleasure to find your name and address in the 'Popular Dogs' July 1965 issue. We think your Am. Can. Ch. Bobbelee Meringue, Maltese an excellent dog.

"Would you be so kind as to give this dog to us?"

That name that sounds like a pastry is Pete's square monicker and although he seems pretty ordinary to the milkman, the paper boy and me, he has somehow become a champion show dog in Canada and here.

He even won four pewter beer mugs in Canada so he's not all bad.

This was not a Nip looking for a handout, it was merely a confusion of tongues. The letter continues.

"We are eager to import a male champion Maltese as soon as we can. Would you please offer him to us with his photo, pedigree copy and minute show record, and also let us know his price, weight, and so on.

"We will be greatly happy if we will be able to get him. Trusting to hear from you a good news immediately by return mail and thanking you in advance for your great kindness."

I was rent asunder with the mixed emotions of an international livestock tycoon and the effrontery of some stranger trying to filch my mutt, even if he does bite people.

"The Japanese are very big on buying established champions," explained my girl, "they pay a hundred dollars a point and Pete's got fifteen for his American championship and ten for his Canadian. That's $2500.00."

"You're kidding."

"I'm not kidding. That Mr. Calvaresi who runs Villa Malta in Massachusetts sells champions to the Japanese all the time. He never gets less than $1500.00."

I got up and walked around Pete once.

"Man! $500 a pound and they aren't even sure what he'd taste like."

As a guy who bought Trans-Cuban Oil Stock just before Castro took over, it looked like I might now make my financial move.

I called up a friend of mine who trains and breeds dogs.

"Sure. Dog people are all nuts. There was a guy lived out here worked for a bank and embezzled money to buy a dog. The bank caught him and before they could redeem the dog he'd strangled himself on a barbed wire fence. It was in all the papers. Chances are she's right."

I asked about the freight rates to Japan.

And then she began to yell and shriek and Pete got excited and started to bark and run around.

To sum it up, the Nichibei Trading Co. blew it.

I got no dinner and am back with the hard-boiled eggs.

And Pete sits and looks at me.

But it would have been helpful at the bank.

25. thoughts

There is no suggestion linking this sick story and the NBC American White Paper, which occupied 3½ hours of our lives one evening several years ago.

"There was this frontiersman," began Neighbor No. 1, "and what he did was buy a bell and rig it up in the yard. There had been a massacre a month before and it tended to make the wives edgy.

"The frontiersman explained to his wife and children that the bell was an alarm and, at the first suspicion of Indians, whoever was nearest should tug the bell rope and he would hear it from wherever he was and come running and defend them.

"Forthwith, the settler repaired to the north 40 and set about his plow.

"He had no more than begun his furrow when the bell pealed from the cabin.

"He threw down the plow, grabbed his musket and hatchet and set off at a run down the grade, forded the stream, slithered through the woods that screened the cabin, gasping now for breath and using rubbery ankles, emerged into his own clearing to find the children playing, his wife scouring the skillet."

" 'What happened?' he choked. 'Where are the Indians?'

"His wife looked over her shoulder and laughed gaily.

" 'I wanted to make sure you could hear the bell,' she explained.

"He remonstrated with them over the seriousness of the bell as not a toy and then trudged back into the fields, grumbling the way."

Neighbor No. 2, who has a son in Vietnam and somehow blames me for it, had brought a notebook and pencil to NBC's class.

I read him a quote from Cleveland Amory in an issue of *Saturday Review* on President Johnson in which Amory wrote:

"I was for Johnson for vice-president in 1960 and I'm for him for vice-president now."

Just trying to shift the heat from myself. I didn't send his kid to Vietnam.

We got the glasses and ice arranged in the first aid stations since this was to be a show like Cleopatra for length but with no intermission.

"He had no more than got back to the field than the bell rang again," continued Neighbor No. 1.

"Up with the musket and tomahawk, down the grade, across the river and into the trees, twice as tired this time and into the clearing to glimpse little Roscoe fingering the bell rope. No Indians. A really angry lecture ensued this time before he set back to his toils . . ."

And now Big Daddy was talking about our commitment in Vietnam, just as 3½ hours later the program would end with his talking about Peace as the most important word in our language at this time.

No cudgel has ever been carried here on behalf of television when it spits on its hands and runs back to do an important spectacular, and this is not the time to begin, but the show was exceptionally well done.

The White Paper had a lot of whitewash in it and at one time when an observer at the Dominican Republic business remarked, "In my opinion President Johnson had no alternative but to do what he did," Neighbor No. 2 nearly threw up.

But as mentioned, like Cleopatra it had a lot of nice stuff in it, with no double entendre intended.

A documentary like this reminds you of the bricks along the way that you have forgotten, when it is well constructed and this one certainly was.

You suddenly recall Truman giving aid to Greece and Turkey, thereby establishing a precedent.

There are the great shots of the warheads rising up out of their launch pads around the country and then being put away after the

Cuban missile crisis and you remember how close we were to oblivion.

There is fine coverage of our early missile failures, recalling the realization felt then but no longer of precisely how far behind we were in the space race with the Russians.

You can feel the somewhat shame again that we did not lend some of the support to the Hungarian revolt that we have provided in other places.

There is the immediate reminder that the Indians and the Pakistanis are fighting a war with equipment provided by us and isn't that a pithy notion?

And that in Korea there were fifteen nations represented by troops on the side against the North Koreans and what has happened since?

There is David Brinkley, who must write or edit his own bits in a montage like this, because they smack of the dour realism that you receive from him on his daily shows.

The sum of it, graphically done, is of course that we are trying to contain communism in the world and are being successful to a degree.

Chet Huntley closed with the assurance that the problems we have will continue for the rest of our lives although I think he injected a "probably."

When the networks take this trouble it usually will not harm you and this one was better than that, granting that it's like a James Bond yarn where you know the going in the U.S. isn't going to ever look really bad.

The scotch plasma was running low after 3½ hours but Neighbor No. 1 remembered to conclude his tale.

"The warning bell rang in late afternoon and the woodsman dropped the plow, gathered his weapons and padded his circuit back to the house.

"His wife wore an arrow buried through her forehead and the kids had been dismembered about the yard.

" 'Well,' said the frontiersman. 'That's more like it.' "

I warned you it was sick.

It's a simple matter of a cough I want to get rid of.

The doctor asked me the other day, "What do you do for exercise?"

"I cough," I said.

"I'm serious," he said.

"So am I," I said.

"What I mean is," he said, "is that coughing isn't exercise."

Here's a man who never coughed.

If a man has a dedicated cough, morning is his time of day.

Arisal in the morn.

My medical friends who superintend me around the saloons, on the subterfuge that they are caring for me, tell me that there are three kinds of coughs:

(a) The nervous cough, (b) the cigarette cough, and (c) the whiskey cough.

Naturally, I hold records in all but the first category.

Nerves are convenient for some but have come late to me.

But the basic and beautiful thing is the "cough."

We, and I'll explain here shortly who else is involved, have decided to get rid of our coughs by recording in competition with the Beatles and the Idiots and some others. Loose the coughs into space and lose them. We got an offer.

The recording company wants to call us the Cacophony Coughers. Catchy, isn't it?

Every family that has ever encountered the common cold will want one.

Playing our numbers could become a breakfast ritual.

Even a child listener will tackle his cereal better for this cacophony.

Hey, you think this isn't going to be a record?

You've heard Sounds of Sebring and listened to the Ferrari scream and the BR burp and rattle and the Corvette pride before quitting time.

You've heard the Sounds of the Sea Lamprey Making Love and the Battle of Beta Spendens, the Siamese Fighting Fish.

Coughing belongs to us here in America.

Air pollution is ours. Water pollution is ours. Nicotine "fits" are ours. We are admirers of booze. And who developed nerves? Just take a small gander at Washington.

We must lead this new musicology.

At the moment I am coughing alto, John Lundblad, an itinerant builder from Dearborn, is coughing tenor, and Dale Shaffer, the top horse at DRC, is coughing basso.

We have a girl soloist who coughs under the pseudonym of Cathy the Canadian.

We are recruiting a fifth member to make a quintet.

Any of you who feel qualified may apply. Just send in a resume of qualifications and if they muck out, the company will call you and allow you to cough over the phone as a test.

There are no tricks or treats about this offer.

The phone call will be made to you at your best.

Gurgling coughers need not apply.

A gurgler must go his own way, doomed.

This is flu-time of the year, explains Roger M. Featherstone, the organizer of the Cacophony Five, and the best time for recruiting.

Listen about the house.

Here is a profitable way to get rid of your cough.

Join the coughing chorus, for fun and profit.

Roger is seeking harpists and kettle drummers as accompanists.

He is organizing this parlor group under the auspices of the Smith Bros.

Participants are permitted, if not encouraged, to wear bears.

You should have been there to see us cough "Onward, Christian Soldiers" yesterday.

It was our finest rendering since Wooley-Bully.

A seat is open.

Cough a little.

Tone is terribly important.

You always remember how it happened to you.

The first time you skipped rope with a girl down the street who grew up to be monstrous but who was so beautiful then, the way a fig tasted, how you got fired, what it was like the first time at the controls of a plane.

It isn't profound but it's a true report because it isn't hearsay or an editor telling you what you should look for.

This is the way it happened in your own mind . . . not much of one maybe . . . but yours.

It was about 5:30, I think, and I was reading the paper about Dorothy Kilgallen dying and thinking about what a great guy her dad is and also how the *Journal-American*, the paper for which she worked, was treating her so grandly and how they had quotes from everybody in the world . . . Robert Wagner, John Lindsay, Angie Dickinson, Governor Nelson Rockefeller . . . everybody . . . and I turned to make a cynical remark:

"It's too bad Ike was under an oxygen tent because I'd've appreciated knowing his sentiments on this grievous mishap to all of us."

The lights flickered.

The girl who traveled with me said:

"I always told you that someday you'd say something awful like that and a thunderbolt would come down and clap us both right between the eyes."

The lights flicked again.

The lights went out.

"OK," I said. "Cut the clowning, turn 'em back on."

Both of us understood that there was a temporary power failure in the hotel and that in a moment the lights would resume.

I held the paper in my hands and waited.

After a while the girl said: "Got a match?"

"Just a lighter but it's about out of fuel."

She went to the window. I grabbed the telephone and called the desk.

"I know," said the clerk, "the lights are out. They're out all over this section of the city. They'll be back on in a minute or two."

Fifteen minutes later, the girl said:

"I think there's a liar downstairs and, if we're going to make dinner with that editor to whom you owe so many apologies, better start trying to move around some."

I can testify that shaving by matchlight is not impossible if you have a helpmate to hold the matches. We scavenged some.

She ran her lipstick nearly up to her eye.

This was the Algonquin Hotel, the haunt of Dorothy Parker, Robert Sherwood, Alexander Woollcott and Bob Benchley who, when he was in Venice, sent a wire back saying:

STREET FULL OF WATER, PLEASE ADVISE.

"The phone works, honey," I said. "Please send a wire saying: 'All full of dark. Please send Indian.'"

Nobody laughed.

"I'm glad this is an old hotel," said the girl.

"We're only on the eighth floor. Suppose we were in the Roosevelt or Pierre or someplace where you might be high up."

A belting came on the door.

"It must be a marauder," said the girl.

"What the . . . ? He's showing light under the crevice." The janitor provided a candle.

I was able to inspect the damage of the matchlight shave.

Inspect but not repair.

"Do you think you can make it down eight stories?" she inquired sarcastically.

"Do you suppose the bar is open?" I asked her.

I did and it was, but unfortunately there were a lot of people . . . intruders off the street . . . and you had to use semaphores over their heads.

We went out into the street.

"Any chance at a cab?" was the question to the doorman.

He laughed a tired laugh. We started walking and finally we were walking up Madison Avenue toward the engagement for dinner.

A guy named Dick Bower, who used to work at Ford's but now toils for Volvo, came out of the dark and said:

"Wow. Imagine meeting somebody in the middle of a black-out."

"Why haven't you got a Volvo with you?"

Press relations guys always explain:

"I've got one but it's on the fourth floor garage and I can't get at it."

The taxis were either loaded or wouldn't stop or wore off-duty signs.

A motorist stopped at a corner and became amenable over a tryst with Dick's $10 bill.

"A thing like this pulls people closer together," said the driver, friendly now over his sawbuck.

The radio assured there were auxiliary electric systems in hospitals, the city wasn't going to be attacked and the lights would be on almost immediately.

Consolidated Edison issued a report that it was ready and functional and whatever trouble there was lay on some other culprit.

The restaurant kitchen was closed but the guy finally fed us.

When the realization finally came that the lights weren't going on again, it became apparent that one of us (guess who?) was going to have to go out and tour Harlem and Brooklyn and the Bronx and look for looting and that sort of thing that normally transpires during this type crisis.

There was a broken window here and there but there were more policemen than anybody and generally, just folks being nice and commiserative with one another.

There was no rioting.

Some teen-agers had made funnies with a bucket of paint.

The girl I travel with had been deposited at Toots Shor's . . . closed but open, after a fashion.

When I got back Eddie Arcaro was pleading for a sandwich.

"Shut up," Toots explained.

"The thing I can't understand," he said after a minute, "is how all the hundreds of people who are trying to fix these lights can't fix them. This may be a real great lesson in this country."

He had just echoed some sentiments.

"If a guy tries," said Toots, "he could get stiff by candlelight too."

To almost any accusation, a normal reply from this quarter is, "Usually I'm guilty but this time I'm innocent."

It's no fine, probing, original line, but it has sufficed over the years and kept me out of Criminal Court more successfully than it did Juvenile, which is, as you must admit, something in its behalf.

The latest charge was that I turned out the lights in New York City, this mishap being coincidental with a visit of mine.

I would like to straighten out this base canard.

The reason for my visit was not to put the lights out at all, albeit the temptation is always great and I must confess that I enjoyed the fact that if they had to go out, it was in New York Ciy.

There is a mildly provincial reason for this.

If the lights had gone out in Chicago, or Detroit, or Los Angeles (if you choose to count that as a city), or San Francisco, or Memphis, or New Orleans, this ridiculousness would have been because of the intrinsic stupidity of these cities.

As any New Yorker will nasally tell you, it couldn't happen here.

Of course not.

As the girl I live with remarked at the time:

"They've got no water, you can't get across town except by heli-copter, now there are no lights and not even the saloons have class enough to stay open."

This bimbo is from Miami, though, and she's spoiled.

The reason for my visit was to attend some of the listenings at the United Nations, where various folks were debating again about whether Red China should be admitted to their august body.

You needn't remind me that these debates have been going on since 1950, but it's like the fighter who got up after the third knock-down and said, "I wanted to see what would happen next."

The secret of learning, I suspect, is to retain naïveté.

Read and listen as if you want to believe. You'll soon find rea-sons, usually, why this is impossible.

I was just giving it another try.

The basic reason for the United Nations is to have a quarrel without guns. Sure, they run an international postal system so you don't have to pay a quarter to send a letter to France against a dime to Denmark, but the other thing is why they're there.

Let's hold this to a basic line of thinking.

Who fouled up the League of Nations by refusing to enter? Us! We, baby!

Now we resist the entry of Red China again.

What does it matter except that if they enter they are there and you can talk to them, as we do with that great ally, Russia.

Strangely, Russia is not the one plumping for Red China this time.

It's a flock of Asian-African powers urging admission.

It baffles how we can deny a country freedom of speech.

I may as well tell you that the listening was the same and the confusion remains the same. As a matter of fact, the only singularly interesting statement heard down there was about Rhodesia, with their white order of independence just declared.

"Rhodesia is the first country to declare itself independent from Britain since the Colonies," observed a diplomat.

"As a matter of fact," said another posing over his cigarette, "doesn't it resemble the U.S. government and its attitude toward Alabama?"

Anyway, Arthur Goldberg, presenting the Washington viewpoint, said the UN couldn't admit China because "it would encourage her present path of violence" and that an acceptance now "would be . . . yielding to undisguised blackmail."

A few Chinese aren't to be allowed to talk?

Diplomacy exists incommunicado?

Have you ever heard such guff?

Anyway, what I was trying to do was explain that it wasn't me that stuck the penny in the wire.

I may act like my lack of understanding of profound things such as who threw the switch and why it wounds to have another fellow talk in an assembly upsets me. And this is true.

So yesterday I went back to an old hunting ground and watched the Lions lose it to San Francisco.

I don't understand exactly why that happened, either.

But I beg absolution on all counts.

I didn't put the penny in, have no vote against Peking and it was not my play-calling that kept Gordy and Schmidt and Williams and Walker and Marsh and the pensive Terry Barr and Milt and Studstill from scoring another.

And as the lady said as she came by:

"If you keep listing the things you don't understand, you'll be there until Christmas."

26. dreams

There was a Grandma McGuire lurking around in my family when I was a little kid and it came as a great disappointment to me when I discovered that this was merely an affectionate appellation and that she was not related to me at all and therefore I wasn't any more Irish than, say, Martin Luther King, to pick a name at random.

She was, it seemed to me, a remarkable woman and she actually came from Ireland and talked strangely but charmingly and spoke to me with great wisdom.

She used to say, "If a man isn't in luck's way in the mornin' and God's favor with him, ye can't hope for much that day."

And she knitted me sweaters and socks and things and told me that "the best knittin' is done in the evenin' because the sheep are asleep," and that "Ye must never step on a cricket because the other crickets will eat up your socks when you're abed."

Well, as someone said once, a man is nothing but an old boy and I've never been able to entirely escape from the Irish and have read them and listened to them and disliked some and forgiven most.

I discovered that St. Patrick didn't banish the snakes from Ireland at all because there were never any snakes to banish.

And in the chill light of reason I came to realize that the Irish were in many ways prodigious liars where the truth was not important, and sometimes when it was.

Johnny Maher, the Lion halfback's father, used to conduct a saloon out on the east side and he used to remonstrate against his race.

"What is all this nonsense about the Irish?" he would wail on St. Patrick's Day, which he liked to celebrate 365 days in the year. "All they could ever do on that lousy little island was grow potatoes and go into the bogs and get peat. They could grow potatoes because all it takes is a spade.

"And they get drunk and fall down—I had an uncle who was drunk all his life—my aunt always said he had the 'failin.' In any other race he's a drunken bum but if you're Irish you've got the 'failin' or the 'curse.'"

A thing to remember is that the "lousy little island" has produced greater literature per capita than any other article of geography. It's a tiny little mote to show Sean O'Casey, Paul Vincent Carroll, John Millington Synge, George Bernard Shaw, James Joyce, Liam O'Flaherty, Elizabeth Bowen, Brendan Behan and the rest.

"That's because there is a great brotherhood in poverty," explains Tommy McIntyre, thereby demonstrating the truth that logic is not necessarily a predominant Irish characteristic.

But then he explained also how St. Patrick's Day became a legal holiday in Boston. The New England Yankees were having no part of making saint's days legal holidays since every day belongs to a saint and they weren't having too much of the Irish anyway because it was in Boston the saying originated that "the wheelbarrow was invented to teach the Irishmen to walk on their hind legs."

"The turkeys scurried around in their history books," said Tommy, "and discovered that March 17 was the day the British evacuated Boston. With a little connive the Irishmen managed to get British Evacuation Day declared a legal holiday, which it remains. They just call it St. Patrick's Day by coincidence."

In the old days no St. Pat's was complete unless a man on the east side paused at Broderick's saloon out on Kercheval, presided over by the late John Broderick, a man of such dignity that the scene lingers of hustling an obstreperous drunk onto the street with the drunk protesting, "but Mr. Broderick . . . but Mr. Broderick."

And downtown no St. Pat's was complete without a pause at Tommy Long's when he had the place on Fort Street. But Mr.

Broderick has passed on and Long's disappeared from Fort many years ago.

The second thing and more important, although some days it's been hard to tell for some, was the step a little further along to Holy Trinity Church which boasts the only rectory outside of Mexico where you might imbibe tequila.

St. Patrick's Day at Holy Trinity has become as Fr. (now Msgr.) Clement Kern puts it, "a prayin' kind of thing" which is the way generations of Irishmen and would be Irishmen have wanted it, with a noonday Mass.

A wispy Dublin lady named Susan Cullen begins teaching the children of the school all the Irish songs, ones you know and ones you've never heard, for a rendering on this day and a thing gotten up by Harry LeDuc and Bill Coughlin and other alumni of what used to be Corktown called Sharin' of the Green brings in money.

"We live from St. Patrick's Day to St. Patrick's Day," the father was saying last evening. "The last report I got we've raised $5800 and what with some other things that aren't in yet it should amount to $8000 when we're finished."

It's the 131st year of the parish.

"It started in 1834," said the father as we were leaving.

My Grandma McGuire, who really wasn't my grandma at all, used to say, " 'Tis a glorious milestone but 'tis even a greater hurdle."

Frenchy LeCompte was a fine Morse Code operator for Western Union around New York some years ago and he was the guy we all referred to when an example was required of someone who upped and unexpectedly seized something he wanted.

He was the one who grabbed at the chalice, caught the brass ring.

I've heard Frenchy called an "escapist" which at one time was a very ugly thing to say about anybody because it implied that he was a fellow who ran away and didn't stand up to his responsibilities.

I always considered this a bad rap against him because he stood up under Western Union until they pensioned him off and how much responsibility must a fellow absorb.

Anyway, Frenchy in addition to his talents with a Morse key, was a great student of Persia, the country and its language. In those days, I already had the habit of carrying books around with me in case there was a traffic jam or somebody else was late for the appointment. One day it was the Rubaiyat of Omar Khayyam with the classic translation by the English writer Edward Fitz-Gerald.

Frenchy snatched it out of my hand and before I could wiggle had written a correction into the margin of FitzGerald's translation. I checked it with a college professor I knew, who checked with some other sources and it turned out the excitable Frenchman was correct.

When it came time to recite LeCompte could have stayed on since Morse operators are vanishing much quicker than Indians because they have to work indoors but Frenchy's decisions had already been made and his bridges cremated.

"I'm moving to Persia. That's where I'm going to live out my life," he told us.

"Have you ever been to Persia? How do you know you'll like it?"

Nobody could conceive of such a thing.

"No, I've never been there," he said. "But a've been waiting to go."

He was our special hero for all the mountains we'd meant to climb and rivers there'd been an intention to swim until Merle Oliver chucked it in.

The former boss, Martin Hayden, had been sheafing through Merle's records, thinking, after something Merle had done, that he ought to get more money. While wrestling with this unnatural thought, he suddenly noted that Merle was about to be sixty-five which according to the personnel department of most corporations, including that one, renders a man instantly useless.

Ho, thought Hayden, reverting to class. I won't have to give him a raise after all. I'll permit him to stay on. After all who else can cover cancer and arthritis and rheumatism and write about farming, too. Aren't I grand?

So he called Oliver in to dispense his largesse.

"I've already sold my farm," said Merle, "and bought the tickets."

"Tickets?"

"My wife and I sailing Friday the 19th to the Seychelles Islands."

Oliver is not the sort who jokes over serious matters.

One time when he was a student reporter at Michigan, augmenting his income while he collected a degree in electrical engineering, he was covering a football game when another reporter showed up late gasping, "What's new?"

"Nothing much," replied Oliver. "Quarterback broke his leg."

The late arrival laughed and went about his chores.

It was a little while until he noticed that the quarterback in question was in fact absentia, he had broken his leg.

Merle became a considerable student of farming and its facets.

A woman exhibitor doubted his knowledge of cattle and at the show ring at the State Fair one year asked that he rate the Herefords before the judge did.

Merle studied them briefly and ranked them 1-2-3-4.

The judge ranked them 1-2-4-3.

The woman was impressed.

She nearly had to be revived after the judge waited a moment, pondered then reversed his decision and made it 1-2-3-4.

Another time someone asked him if he could identify a prize winning cow in a snapshot. He immediately recognized the champion Bossie Bonnie Blue Bell. It was just that he failed to tab its owner—C. E. Wilson.

But primarily he wrote science and medicine.

He won awards from the Michigan Health Council, American Osteopathic Association, Michigan Cancer Foundation Midwest Regional award on arthritis and rheumatism, and the night before he left town we threw a debauch for ourselves in his honor and some doctors gave him a citation from the Michigan Heart Association.

It must be of some value to stand high with the croakers because Merle couldn't duck the draft on his appearance.

None of the above is to suggest that Merle was lacking in humor. He took all of his tasks seriously but never himself. He ran a 90-acre farm out around Plymouth and it was when neighbors began striking oil all around it that his friend Stoddard White asked him if he might bring his son out to see a farm.

"Wait 'til we strike oil," said Oliver, "and we'll have uniformed guides."

"And these . . . what kind of islands? Where are they?" asked Hayden. No geographer he.

"The Seychelles," explained Oliver. "They're named after Seychelles, Louis XV's financial manipulator. They're in the Indian Ocean just south of the equator about 700 miles northeast of Madagascar."

"Oh," muttered Martin.

"Ella and I consider them an undiscovered Tahiti. I'm going to write a book about them among other things."

A mail boat stops there six times a year.

The Olivers left for the jumping-off point of Mombasa.

Stirs those damned dreams again, doesn't it?

It was on a Sunday afternoon at a place called Valla Habana, the cock fighting palace in Havana's native quarter, that a trainer named Conrado Suarez provided me with the incidental intelligence that is mine about this beguiling sport.

Conrado explained that the best blood once came from Spain but that now the best line was probably the chama line which had developed in Japan, although there were good lines from India, including the corniche.

Conrado was pitting a black gallo nuevo weighing three pounds one ounce against a red untried rooster that Sunday and the odds were even at the start.

The red was a flutterer, which can be a bad sign in a cock and proved so in this instance. They bet, as you know, as the fight progresses and soon the black was 2-1 and then 3-1 until soon no one would support the red at all and Conrado was considerably elated when his bird won and thus quintupled in value.

It was quite pleasant and very educational although a girl I had carted along thought it was "inhuman" and insinuated as much while trying to be polite. Conrado tried to explain that this was what the bird was bred to do and that one must do what he is bred to do, verdad. Neither got far with the other.

This becomes subject after Red Jones, the ex-umpire who now will sell you Tiger baseball and tell you pleasant falsehoods, called me in something approaching high dudgeon: "Did you see what them gendarmes did to cock fights up at Port Huron?"

What happened is that the State Police and the Port Huron

City police ambushed the Francis Morgan farm twenty miles west of the Port and consficated some seventy fighting birds.

A justice of the peace named Charles Blanchard went along to fine each of the spectators $15 and the birds were taken back to the St. Clair County Jail where the story Red was reading said that the birds would be killed and fed to the prisoners as soon as a court order for their destruction could be arranged.

I have never been to the Morgan Farm cock fights but Sonny Eliot used to frequent the establishment and after a while he came over, annoyed over the same thing that was bothering Red.

"Killing those roosters is like taking one of those thousand year bred Miura bulls from Spanish bull fighting and selling him to the Elias Bros. for Big Boy," said Sonny. "It's ridiculous."

"Can't you do something?" demanded Red. "Call up them coppers and tell 'em I'll buy chick-birds for them prisoners. But they can't kill them birds like that. Bill Sommers, my old umpire buddy, would march through snow and ice to see a good cock fight. This is terrible."

Well, now, if you can't help a man it's your bounden duty to try and make him feel better so, with a nod to the late Joe Palmer, I will quote a story about a similar occurrence down in West Virginia.

"Best chicken fight I ever saw," it goes, "was down in West Virginia. We had a fight going, and it was raided by some local police under direction of the S.P.C.A. There weren't any chickens fighting when they broke in, and, of course, the bets were all oral. So they couldn't find any grounds for holding us; they just took the birds.

"Next morning we didn't have the usual problem of getting the people out of jail; we just had to get the chickens out. So another fellow and I went down to see about it.

"It turned out the S.P.C.A. had dumped all the cocks—35 or 40 of them—into the pen.

"It was dark and they found some place to roost and went to sleep. But then the sun came up and a ray or three crept into the pen.

"The first chicken that waked up saw another cock next to him and promptly jumped on his head, and after that one thing led to another.

"When we got there there was a scene usually described as indescribable confusion. There was blood on the floor until it was slippery. About four feet over the melee, there was a tumbling mass of feathers, rising and falling like the top of a fountain. What cocks were still alive were still going at it furiously.

"It was the finest battle royal I ever saw," concluded the narrator, "and it was perfectly legal. The S.P.C.A. had staged it in the county jail."

Red and Sonny heard the story out in gleeful jubilation.

"Do you suppose something like that could happen in Port Huron?" Sonny wondered.

"Maybe we should get in our cars and drive up and see," exclaimed Jones, half out the door.

They felt better anyway which is satisfying to an itinerant healer.

"Perhaps I'd better call up and see how they're faring," seemed a saner thing to do.

Eventually a Lieutenant Willard Carleton of the Port Huron police came on the line. I explained to him what had happened in West Virginia and wondered if we had any chance for duplication.

"All the birds were kept in individual boxes," informed the lieutenant and they will be destroyed, if they haven't been already.

This information was duly relayed to the outraged cock fans.

"The whole thing is inhuman and so are you," stated this same girl from Havana who has survived time and travel with her notions still intact.

"Mebbe," said Jones. "But what them policemen did, that's inchicken."

27. wherewithal

The first auto with which I was involved was a Model T and although I was not the owner, I was one of the seventeen stockholders.

We sheared the superstructure off it so as to enable all of the vested interested to be able to cruise in it, a matter of logistics partially resolved by the running boards.

Whoever had guts enough to crank it got to drive, if he could get in in time.

It cost $50 and although I was minority shareholder I did have the honor of naming the car. Its name was "Stately."

It endured most of a long-ago summer until finally it became so uncertain that we had to abandon it. However, Stately went out in what I've considered interesting if not spectacular fashion.

We used to drive down to a place in Water-works Park called the cement docks, directly down to the river from Bewick and Hurlburt, and most of us learned to swim there.

Less athletic citizens also fished there, causing some friction between the factions, a solution being that the fishermen sort of had morning and evening rights to the docks and the swimmers held sway in the afternoons.

On Stately's last ride, there were six of us. We wore shirts and swimming trunks and hats and nothing else, the trunks and bare legs being concealed by the body of the auto.

We managed to get Stately down to within about 100 yards of the docks early one evening when all the fishermen were out. We assumed poses in Stately. One guy read a newspaper, the three in back staged a heated argument on an imaginary subject. I sat in the front with my cheeks in my hands and the guy drove.

The notion was to look as detached and unconcerned as possible.

With the stage set, Stately started for the last time and roared down its last hundred yards at a full throttled 10 or 12 miles per hour, while the fishermen turned resentfully at the racket.

They waited for us to stop.

Nobody blinked and we just rode right off into the river, swam out of the car, wrung out our shirts, retrieved our clothes and departed.

The next one belonged to me, along with a finance company.

It cost $150, was a convertible with a rumble seat and a gear shift with a red knob on it that was square and cut like one of a pair of dice.

The Model T had no gear shift, and the gear shift was a great engineering advance along with the self starter.

Early showing signs of that business acumen which was to make financial empires tremble, I put $50 down and arranged for the low payments over three years. I didn't plan on taking that long, but my new best friend, the salesman, assured that if I paid it off quicker, that was all for the best.

Three months later when I sold it, I had to pay for it first. The total price came to $360. My new best friend did not sympathize with me greatly. In fact he was rather curt when he discovered I did not wish to buy another car.

There has been a Packard, an Essex, a Terraplane, a couple of Chevies, an MG, a Corvette, even a Cadillac or two since, but driving is a thing that becomes less and less fun although the matter of the gears still fascinated me.

The Model T worked from three pedals on the floor.

Then the gear shift was a big deal.

Then came the automatic transmission and for some extra dough, you got rid of the gear shift.

I just bought another one and for some extra dough I was lucky enough to get four-speed transmission with a gear shift again.

I wish they'd make up their minds.

Oh, well, at least the salesmen and finance companies remain constant.

28. broads

There's a fellow who calls himself Dr. Doran D. Zinner who, in case you missed it, is putting a knock on kissing a girl.

Dr. Zinner got here too late for the fluoridation scene apparently, and after some research at the University of Miami, he states that tooth decay is a contagious disease and that it is transmitted about by the kiss.

Right from the beginning, I want it clear that it took ten years around here for all these crusaders to convince me that I should vote for putting fluoride in the water.

Sure, it might make the water taste lousy like it does in Philadelphia, but it would keep cavities out of the teeth.

Well . . . kissing a girl . . . buddy, it stays.

Dr. Zinner says, "For many years we thought of tooth decay as hereditary. But now we know that if an individual does not have a certain type of bacteria in his mouth he will not get caries (a professional term for cavities)."

Isn't that just like a doctor, to say caries when he's trying to carry something off?

He also says that we can eat all the candy and cake and drink all the soda pop we want if we do not have decay-causing bacteria.

I don't know what kind of girls ole Dr. Zinner consorts with, but around these corners there hasn't ever been a Baby Ruth to compare.

What kind of a deal is this?

A Faygo for a kiss.

Come to think of it seriously, though, it might make a difference in the girl, or the boy if you choose, against whether you were thirsty.

Dr. Zinner is a dentist-microbiologist who has been studying tooth decay with four colleagues for the last five years under a Public Health Service grant.

To this we dedicate our taxes.

He said the contagious nature of the bacteria was discovered first in experiments with rats and hamsters and was confirmed in experiments with human teeth.

"About 98 percent of the world population has some form of tooth decay," says Zinner, "but the majority have the slow-acting type. Still, you might get a faster-moving brand from your girl friend, wife or even a kissin' cousin."

Dr. Zinner completely contradicts a poet named James Branch Cabell, who in a book called *Jurgen* remarked:

"A kiss is now attestly a quite innocuous performance, with nothing fearful about it one way or the other."

When the agitation around the city first began about putting fluoride in the water, these feelings were mixed.

Being cursed ever so slightly by education, I was aware of a paragraph written by Justice Louis D. Brandeis in the case of Olmstead vs. United States: "Experience should teach us to be most on our guard to protect liberty when the government's purposes are beneficent. Men born to freedom are naturally alert to repel invasion of their liberty by evil-minded rulers. The greatest dangers to liberty lurk in the insidious encroachment by men of zeal, well-meaning but without understanding."

Man, when you give that a going over you wonder about fluoridation, Vietnam, the State Department, Prexy, everybody.

And in that company ole Doc Zinner, well-meaning as he may be, has got no chance.

I am impressed with this mountain of people who want to protect our teeth, although they must go to far-off places to find some of mine to protect, but the mountain is now trying to grow tall.

My prayer is that because onetime actress Carole Lombard answered a movie fan's question, "What do you think about when all those handsome leading men kiss you?" with the demure reply, "Germs!"

On the other hand, Eskimos rub noses instead of kissing.

Do you suppose there's anything to it?

The subject of wife beating or wife beatery to be more precise, came up quite naturally. On the next stool was a wife who had just been beaten.

She pointed at her nose and her eye, which was turning a little purple and announced:

"Barb did that."

Barb is her husband.

His nickname, Barb, came from prison, where he'd served a couple of years for robbery. Barb was a contraction of barbed wire.

Maybe it was the sauce but everyone immediately became interested in her and her problems.

"Maybe you like it," said the girl I live with. "There are women that do like it, being beaten, I mean. How long have you been married?"

"Two years."

"Has it happened before?"

The girl swallowed, dabbed at her damp eyes with a hankie, then nodded.

"I think you must like it," said the girl I live with. "Any man who hit me, I'd leave and never see again, the very first time it happened. If he bothered me again, I'd call the law."

It turned out the girl was from a small town in Illinois.

She had been married previously for thirteen years and had two children by her first husband. There'd been a divorce then she'd gone to Champaign to get a job and there had met Barb.

After playing house for a couple of months, they got married. A year and a half ago, they moved to Detroit.

"You must understand that he served two years in prison," she said declaring it as if Barb had received the DSC or at least the Silver Star.

"I came home from work today, and I couldn't find him," she said. "So I went out to the nearest saloon and found him there. He took me outside and began to slap me around. Not inside where any friends could see him. He's too smart for that. But outside on the street he gave it to me. Then he told me to go home. That's when I came here."

"What are you going to do now?"

"I'm trying to figure out a way to go home and get my money. I've got $150 in a galosh and, if I were sure he wasn't there, I'd go get it and go back to Illinois and the kids."

There was time, while that girl and this victim chatted rather clubbily about her troubles, for three of us, Julie, Jimmy the bartender and me, to discuss whether we'd ever hit a woman.

"I got to confess I would and have, but not often," said Jimmy.

"It would depend," I said. "If she did something that I couldn't forgive or forget and if I still wanted to stay married. I suppose I would. You'd have to do something to her. I couldn't leave her."

"I think it's indefensible what both of you just said," Julie declared. "No woman could be worth punching. It isn't normal for a man to punch a woman."

"Why don't you go to the precinct where you live and ask a couple of cops to go with you and get your money?" I asked, knowing this would make me unpopular with the department since no honest cop ever wants to get involved in a domestic quarrel.

"Would they do that?"

"Sure they would."

We had to leave shortly thereafter.

"I heard what you said about how you'd hit me if I did something wrong," accused the girl I live with.

"You might have heard me say also I couldn't leave you. That had some bearing on the case."

"What would I have to do?" she wondered.

"Think of something. If it was serious enough to make me leave you, I'd have to hit you because I couldn't leave you. Maybe if you burn the pizza heating it up after we get home."

When we got home, she called Jimmy to see what, if anything, the girl had done.

"Nothing," he said. "She's still here, but a little stiff by now. And weeping something awful."

The girl shall be called Margie for purposes of compositional convenience and is a recent graduate of the march-and-sit set, smokes marijuana for conversational purposes, and recently went to New York to live with some guy.

She has decided she is not pretty, which is an untruth, but it affects her so that she strives to make herself as unattractive as possible.

The chip on her shoulder does not need to be knocked off. It falls off at a wiggle and then she's liable to belt you.

"I hate New York. I hate the people. They don't care about you. They're rude and pushy. We wouldn't stay here but Jim's making a film. He's very good at it. Now the Army wants him. Don't you hate New York?"

She pushed her fork at some rice wrapped in grape leaves.

"They give me a whole hour for lunch."

She is a copy girl in an ad agency.

"Don't you think everybody here is awful?"

She sipped at some thick Turkish coffee.

Margie almost had an affair with a friend of mine some months ago but it didn't work out. "I can't tolerate these pseudo-intellectual convulsions of hers" was his version. "He's a square" was hers.

"It's become a difficult town," I agreed. "The crosstown traffic is terrible during the rush hours but then it's been that way for some years. If you have kids, the school problem is bad and the water shortage was only funny to us folks out in the lake country.

"But, no, I never found the people much different than other people. Some good. Some disagreeable. Nobody ever really cares about you but your mother and father and a wife or husband occasionally if you're lucky. All your critical earnestness will not change it either."

"What do you think of conscientious objectors?"

"I don't think much about them one way or the other. I would certainly say that, if a man's religion dictated him this way, that he's entitled to his beliefs. That's what the country was partially begun about."

"Jim is registering as a CO-1-A," she said somewhat belligerently. "We're not going to get married until this Army and Vietnam business gets straightened out. Why should he kill somebody in Vietnam?"

She was giving off unconnected sparks.

"Why get married at all?"

"Well, I'm not going to wait two or three years while he's away in the Army. It's an unhealthy situation. How can we get married now?"

"Beats me. I'm surprised you even thought of it. It doesn't seem important to you and maybe you shouldn't bother, unless you have a baby. Maybe the baby should not have you deciding his status in society."

"I don't care about society. Neither does Jim. I understand you went to the protest march on the Vietnamese war in Washington? What did you think?"

I ordered some coffee.

"It was all right. I guess. I always have a little trouble understanding any action that is not going to provoke a reaction. I doubt if the State Department gave a hoot about it all. Did you go? But if folks want to protest, it's all right with me."

"No, but Jim and I talked about it. We're very sincere about things. We have no business with Vietnam. How can people like war?"

"Nobody likes it, but everybody doesn't march around about it."

She was beginning to anger.

"All of you are too complacent."

"Not really. But I suspect sometimes that your objections are because this unpleasantness might inconvenience your life. Don't get sore at me."

"Just because you were in the war you think everybody else should be."

It was growing dull now. Thank goodness the hour was about up.

"No. The only thing I ever said about it to anybody which could be considered anything except antiwar was that it was a tremendously interesting personal experience, perhaps even worthwhile if it didn't maim or kill you. That's completely personal. No international implications. To cool it, riding a bobsled is an interesting experience or scuba diving. But let's not march over it. OK?"

She began gathering up that gear women manage to spread over the landscape.

"I've got to get back to the office. Thanks for the lunch. Where are you going?"

"Up to the *Times* to look up some clips in their reference department on a guy named Carl Stokes, a colored fellah who finished second in the Cleveland mayoral race. I met him a couple of nights ago. Then I'm going up to the UN building for a while."

"Going to try and stir up India and Pakistan again . . . warmonger."

She stuck out her tongue to make it impish.

"Maybe. Incidentally, your movie-making friend. Is he going to have any experience of his own to lend or will he just make films from books he's read and pot sessions with you?"

The friend that used to know her heard about the meeting.

"You and she aren't friends any more, then?" he asked.

"Zilch, my friendship I couldn't take back because I've given of it. My respect she could lose. We'll see. She looked as pretty as she lets herself look."

He thought a moment.

"That's what everybody is, I guess, what they let themselves."

29. wildlife

Ray cites his hometown as Henpeck, Kentucky, but it isn't really true.

"It's a town though, even if it hasn't got a post office. It's a real town, all right," he said.

Actually he gets his mail down the road some in Cox's Creek and he lives a piece off from Henpeck just below Buffalo Wallow Knob and down a ways from Coon Den Hollow.

He gets some square mail at University of Kentucky since he became artist-in-residence there when he decided he'd have to give up painting birds and wildcats and butterflies and trees and go back to bronc riding because "eating is an immediate thing."

When Dr. Frank Dickey, then president of Kentucky, discovered he was going back to cowboying, he was horrified. The word had spread over the campus "Ray Harm's leavin' Kentucky to go back coyboyin'" until it got to the presidential sanctum.

Dr. Dickey liked Ray's painting so much that he had assumed that such talent must make a man well-to-do at least, if not rich.

"What do you do with your paintings?" Dickey wanted to know.

"I send them to the galleries in New York," said Ray. "I'm trying to fill up the galleries. Sooner or later they'll have to sell 'em."

He'd been sending paintings into never, never for five years.

Dr. Dickey explained that he would have to fill all the gallery storerooms first, since he had no' reputation in the East, and that the storerooms grew very large in a big city.

Here he was last evening, stalking the floor in his exhibit at the Village Women's Club on East Long Lake road in Bloomfield

Hills. Mr. and Mrs. Ned Heinzerling, who run the Boy and Boot shop at the Fox and Hounds, were celebrating their first anniversary with Ray's showing.

Stalking the floor at an art exhibition, even if it's your own, doesn't compare with bronc riding, which is the way Ray made his living before he started to paint. In the eight years he was a rodeo cowboy and wild wester, he broke bones twenty-six times, slept under bridges and in ditches.

"This is better," he was saying. "You know I remember how it all was . . . really was . . . but when Dr. Dickey tells about it, he makes it sound adventurous."

The first thing you see when you enter the exhibit is a print called Eagle and Osprey, a 43-by-30-inch lithograph which for seventy-five clams, one of the Heinzerlings will press upon you and Harm will autograph.

It's a dandy and the eagle is trying to swipe a spotted weakfish from the osprey and as is sometimes the case with hijacking, both of them are going to lose the swag.

"That's what Ray wanted to call it," explained his thumper, Dave Schwartz. "'The Hijacker,' but one of his sponsors objected because the eagle is our national bird."

"Our State Department might like to have the original as a frontispiece in the hall," muttered my companion.

There were lots of people at the exhibit, providing that there is habitation above 10 Mile Road despite what you've heard. There may be Indians, and buffalo and of course there are Conestoga wagons and when trouble starts everyone runs for the stockade, but here is habitation.

I can state it for a fact.

My companion pointed out GM chieftain Lou Seaton and his wife, remarking solemnly, "I knew Mr. Seaton was a student of wildlife, but didn't know he collected paintings of it."

A lady asked Harm, "Did you ever paint a ring-tailed pheasant," and Harm didn't bat an eye as he answered, "A few ring-necks but if I ever see one of the others, I'll try."

It is difficult to discover an exhibit of wildlife paintings. Ray Harm does his in watercolor, although he claims equal facility in oil, but the former is much quicker.

The reason such exhibits are rare is twofold:

Good wildlife studies are snapped up immediately by wildlife fanciers.

The second and most important reason is that people with a genuine regard for the outdoors usually choose their lives out in it rather than bothering to reproduce it on canvas.

To do it expertly, a man should spend his boyhood among birds and animals and fish. Then he just never does anything else usually.

But Ray was the victim of a domestic squabble when he was thirteen and the court asked him to choose either his mother or father to live with.

He ran away from home instead and ended up on a ranch in Nebraska, which is where he started toward the rodeo circuit.

He is thirty-eight now and started painting when he was thirty. He could go back to the wildlife country he knew and had sorely missed, now to paint it and keep it.

The work is exquisitely fine and the hijacking one is most expensive. The smaller prints, all of them of limited number, range around $20.

Walking among the paintings . . . the pileated woodpecker . . . the yellow shafted flicker, reminded of when Sonny Eliot took Leo Derderian to do his zoo show on television recently. Leo owns a nameless saloon the trademark of which is a large bright-blue door.

As Sonny took his viewers through a zoological exhibit, he had the camera pan in on Leo standing in front of one of the glass enclosures. Without pausing or changing tone, Sonny said, "And there to the left of the screen, is a red-eyed lush from the Blue Door."

"What are you smiling at," Schwartz wanted to know.

"Oh," he said. "Ray does that too. He was giving a lecture once and mentioned a 'gimlet eyed bedthrasher' just to see if anyone would notice."

"Did they?" I asked.

"No," he responded.

There is a handsome, black-thatched young man named John Soney who is of Chippewa Indian extraction and if he had played

music for Benny Goodman you'd have overlooked Ziggy Elman:
if he played for Tommy Dorsey you might even have overlooked
Bunny Berigan's trumpet.

If he played with Miles Davis or Dave Brubeck, it might have
been the Brubeck-Soney ensemble or the Davis Duet.

John plays duck calls.

Remember the most beautiful kind of day?

The sun shone and the sky was blue.

And all of your life you've heard, every time the weather was
distasteful, well, "Wonderful weather for ducks."

This is offered as a clue to anyone who has managed to come
this far who is neither a music-lover nor fowl assassin.

These must be an appeal also to sadists or people who are parts
thereof. Now that everyone is included, we may proceed.

At quarter past four A.M. the room clerk calls to announce, as
Longfellow once remarked, "Let us then be up and doing." The
call was for 4:45 but then what's a half an hour out of anybody's
life who would not normally be strolling into one of the blind pig
cocktail joints which Police Commissioner Ray Girardin, in his
infinite wisdom, permits in the village for people who get off
work at another time besides five in the afternoon.

To other than duck nuts, permit the notion that a boat ride
over Johnson Bay before sunup is nothing.

It will not move you up half a length.

My companion was a peddler to the auto companies named
Fritz Beirmeister, who kept it entertaining.

When I missed my first duck at 8:30 he remarked:

"You shoot as if you were a member of the Audubon Society."

That was all the ducks and then the sun rose, the sky cleared
and maybe the goofy golfer I talked to was right about what a
fellow should do if he felt forced to the open air.

"At the risk of sacrilege," I suggested, "maybe we should go back
to the hotel, partake of a small Canadian ale and collide with the
sack."

To Fritz's everlasting credit, he agreed that there were no ducks.

On the way back, John Soney began to sulk.

Pride evinces itself in wonderful ways and John's father, Ford,
his uncle Elmer, his grandfather William have tended to hunters

and pseudo-hunters and though their guests might not have, the Soneys have it . . . pride.

Halfway back, John pulled in his boat and said, "I want to look."

He kicked ice off the edge of the bay and pooped and burped and tooted into his little duck flute.

A duck answered and Fritz shot it.

Perhaps there is a moral here about blind obedience, the same one I've been trying to explain to the State Department, but there you are.

After that a jet flew over, leaving its regal ethereal spume.

The sun shone so warm into the marshes that a man could sleep and I would've except that John wanted to walk a couple of miles up to a point of land. "Pay 'em and let's forget it," I told Fritz. "I made a solemn oath when I left the service that any distance longer than a half a block, it's cabsville for me."

"He's hurt," said Fritz. "He's got his pride and you're new and he wants to get you some ducks."

"I have a suggestion on what he can do with his ducks, but I'm beginning to love him, too."

"Let's go. The walk can't be more than an eternity."

So there was this pit-blind, a hole in the ground with reeds tied around it with string to cover you up.

It was drowsy warm by this time and two blacks were flying over at maybe 150 yards up and John, beady eyes riveted heavenward, began to toot his duck flute.

The two ducks are winging along at what Fritz averred must be 70 miles per hour and then they begin to turn, then began to resume their flight and then John turned them again.

"I know hunters who swear you can't call a black," said Fritz.

"He's a snake-charmer."

As you can tell, the hunting was lousy but the dialogue sparkling. The two blacks dropped down to the decoys.

You will be pleased to know that, Audubon Society or no, we got them both. It was the least you could do.

John began to feel better.

He whistled in five more.

He talks duck.

As a long-time believer that the things people have elected to do they should do well. It was stirring.

"What do you do for a living when ducks aren't?" was a question.

"I paint barns in the summertime."

It reminded me of a unicyclist I used to know.

Supply and demand is a treacherous thing.

30. gadgets

A company called Invento . . . or maybe it's not a company at all but just a cute little fellow with an awful name . . . is constantly producing handy little gadgets to enable us better to cope with the stress and stretch of modern times.

Invento produced the English Bath-Tub Tray, for example. This is an expensive apparatus that you hang in the tub where you can store your plastic boats, rubber ducks and soap bubble pipes.

Invento also made the English Electric Towel Warmer, so that when you want to towel off after a session with your tub toys, you won't get a chill.

I note the adjective "English" applied to both of these commercial appellations.

Perhaps Invento is a cute little English fellow with an awl.

At any rate, the girl I live with came home all gurgling and diabolical the other day with a new nuisance entitled the Message Minder.

This is, as you immediately divined, a machine to help you stay on top of situations. Only that I can't ever seem to remember what situation I'm supposed to stay on top of.

There was that letter I was supposed to mail. Nothing important really. Something about Internal Revenue Service. It was pretty dog-eared when she took it back. But, cripes, I hadn't lost it anyhow.

I knew a guy once who couldn't remember to come home, but that doesn't happen to me more often than once or twice a week when I get worried that something might happen and I'll miss it.

The machine is a sleek, plastic microphone, playback recorder-speaker, battery operated with an endless tape done in a shiny, lugubrious black.

Very handsome, although it looks like it might go off.

The way it works, there's a little button on the back, that goes up and down and you record instructions to yourself so that when you play it back a few hours later, you remember all the things you are supposed to do and do them.

Well, in a mechanical aptitude test I once flunked the crowbar.

Nevertheless, after a few false starts we managed to get me to where I could speak into the Minder and have the message come out without erasing the message first.

It only took about two hours.

Well, finally the machine got its first real test.

I was at home reading a book Marvin Eliot loaned me entitled, 101 *Things a Boy Can Make Out of Human Skin,* when the phone rang.

"Get the Minder," it said.

I got it.

"Put it on record," continued the phone.

"Okay."

"Now tell it," urged the phone. "Take out garbage . . . feed dogs . . . meet me at Press Club 7 o'clock . . . bring concert tickets . . . Okay? . . . I love you . . . Goodby."

I repeated it as the instructions poured on and then I played it back, feeling pretty silly when my own voice said, "Okay . . . I love you . . . goodby."

Now I know what you're thinking.

That I fouled up.

Well, you're mistaken. This isn't one of those kind of stories at all.

Everything worked out perfectly.

A betting buddy called and said he had the money from that horse and if I'd come over to the Press Club he'd pay me.

So I went over and got the money and there, unexpectedly, was the girl and she wanted to go to the concert.

Well, I didn't have any tickets but I know the guy who ushers at Meadowbrook and he let us in without any trouble and the seats are not reserved.

When we arrived at home, the dogs had become so famished they'd (there are four of them in our funny bin) tipped over the garbage pail and eaten it all up.

The only thing I did wrong.

I've forgotten where I put the Message Minder.

31. people

They were a couple you'd call attractive, thirtyish, and the twin gold bands on the third fingers were a further, if unnecessary indication of the relationship.

He looked as if, had he had a newspaper, he'd be reading it by the light of the festive decor.

"It looks to me," she was saying, "that at this time of the year you could at least try to be a little more agreeable."

He appeared pained for a moment.

"It's this time of the year that makes me feel worse than the rest of the time when I realize that another year has gotten by and it's been more of the same. Motions. We go through motions."

A couple they obviously knew stopped at their table and both their faces slipped on the artificial happy masks, and they made motions.

"Yes, thank you. And a Merry Christmas to you, too. How're the kids. Fine . . . great, we'll see if we can't make it. You drop by if you can, too. Fine. Always a pleasure seeing you."

The couple passed on and the happy masks vanished.

"That's what I mean. Neither one of us cares whether those clods have a Merry Christmas or whether Santa Claus gets stuck in the chimney, puts the fire out and freezes the whole family to death. If they come over, I wouldn't answer the door."

The girl shook her head once in quick violence as if to erase the whole scene.

"You get this way every Christmas," she said, "and I might add you're no particular bargain the rest of the year."

The owner of the establishment paused at the table and said: "How are you this evening? George, will you bring my favorite couple a happy holiday drink?"

The happy masks were on again.

"Thank you very much," chorused. "And many more of them to you, too."

The owner went away and they thanked George for the drinks when he brought them, before they put the faces away again.

"You were saying something about me being no particular bargain; well, Dick and Joy got divorced last month and kept talking about how badly they handled it. Maybe you can tell us how to do it? Do it perfectly. Do it in the grand manner."

"Oh, shut up, shut up . . . shut up . . . shut up . . ." she said.

The guy took a pull on his drink as she suddenly exclaimed "Oh, darnit" and began rummaging through her shoulder bag.

"What's the matter now?" he asked sullenly.

"Oh . . . nothing. I've been buying clothes for those kids from the church all day and I couldn't get anything for three of the families because I didn't have the sizes for the kids."

"Big deal. Little Miss Samaritan. The lady with the lamp. Miss Christmas Carol. Big deal. Well, if you haven't got the sizes, you can't buy the clothes. So forget it."

She stood up.

"I'm going to phone. Joan was going to their houses and get the sizes for me. Be back in sec . . ."

She departed. He nodded absently to a couple who passed by, finished his drink, ordered another, then checked himself and ordered one for both of them.

He shook his head and grinned to himself. Then as she returned to the table he stood up and held her chair.

"We fight every Christmas. I don't know what it is but Christmas always gets me down. It got me down when I was a kid."

"I know but I wish you weren't so brutal about it. You've got an awful cutting tongue when you get that way."

"I know, I'm sorry. Did you get the extra sizes?"

She didn't answer for a minute.

Then she said:

"Joan went around to the houses. It turned out they didn't know the sizes because they never bought anything before."

He looked at her blankly.

"Do you understand? They never bought anything before."

"Jesus," he muttered quietly, "Jesus."

She was looking at him tenderly now.

"Yes, baby, and Mary and Joseph, too."

32. the old country

A cigar store is the place where in this misspent youth there was knowledge forthcoming about baseball pools and betting on runs per team per day and per week, horse talk abounded and sometimes in the back room a billiard academy was in evidence.

But I had to go and get my cigarette lighter fixed anyway so when nonsmoker Len Barnes asked if I'd pick up a box of cigars with the Dunhill label for a guy back in his office at Michigan's *Motor News*, it seemed reasonable.

"What kind of cigars?"

"I don't smoke 'em. Just a box with the Dunhill label on it. It's a surprise. He'll get a kick out of it."

Walking into Dunhill's in London is rather like entering Tiffany's or the Chase Bank . . . tomblike. It's not a whisper they raise really but what I guess an Englishman would call well-modulated tones.

There's a fifty-year-old piece of briar or meerschaum or something on the floor and the upper level is done in paneling and burnished and whole flocks of fellows in white smocks are strolling about punctuated with tall fellows with graying sideburns wearing those white-collared shirts with the striped bodices, white cuffs and slim silvery ties.

As you wander along your way, you get a lot of hard sell and occasionally some soft sell but this is the first time I ever ran into the no sell.

One of the major-domos in the decorous stripes . . . they all look a little like Michael Wilding or C. Aubrey Smith depending on their ages . . . directed me to the cigars which were located behind glass walls on the lower level.

I've no notion of how this kind of joint affects you but my impulse is always to sidle toward the door and then if it looks like I might make it out, run like the devil.

Ah, yes, Lenny's friend's cigars. Through the glass doors and into the cigar quarters, a white-smocked young man was flicking at an imaginary mote of dust on a glass case.

Immediately he was before you pleasant, a slight smile, courteous. "May I serve you, sir?" he asked.

"I need a box a cigars for a friend of mine." He didn't turn a hair at the accent, but noticed.

"You were planning on what brand cigar?" he asked.

The only brand I'd noticed was Upmann.

"Those Upmanns would be all right. They come in one of your Dunhill boxes, don't they? It just doesn't have the name of the cigar, does it?"

"No, of course," he said. "May I beg your pardon for a moment?"

He went away and pretty soon here he was back with another one of these diplomats of the court with the two-tone shirt and the polished mien.

"Were you thinking of taking these cigars back to America with you?" he asked . . .

"Well, yes, there's this friend . . ." I began.

"He's pulling your leg, old chap," said the squire. "I don't know why they do that to friends coming over this way. These are Cuban cigars. The only decent cigars we have. You can't take them into the states, you know."

It was a little embarrassing.

"Yes, I guess I didn't know. But I don't smoke cigars so I'd forgotten it."

"So you see there would be no point in our selling you these."

"Yes. But don't you have other kinds? From other places?"

"We have fairly decent Dutch cigars and we have some very good Jamaican cigars that are very sprightly."

"Good. I'll take a dozen of either of those you mentioned."

He shrugged ever so slightly and murmured:

"It wouldn't be to your advantage really," he said. "You can get them both for half the price in New York."

I started groping for a way out now.

"But you could put them in one of your boxes . . . and . . ."

"You can get them in our boxes in New York and as I said for half the price."

"Look, I don't know when I'll ever be in New York again and I told this friend, I'd buy . . . well . . . would you sell me an empty box then?"

The two exchanged pitying glances.

Fortunately at that moment another customer happened by and in the brief respite, I fled.

I hope the new guy managed to make a purchase of something.

It was a half a block farther on when I reached in my pocket and realized I hadn't gotten my lighter fixed.

Advice costing what it does, it was no trick at all to get a couple of bucketfuls prior to this little foray on how much the French dislike Americans and what a clip joint is this City of Lights.

I discover now that I sort of resent these assertions.

In the first place, disliking Americans has become pretty fashionable around the world and the French have no patent on it.

In the second, the places where you can get clipped are just as obvious here as they are, say, on North Clark Street in Chicago or what they call The Block in Baltimore.

You get clipped in places where girls disrobe and anyone who doesn't know that by now shouldn't be given a passport either to France or Chicago or Baltimore.

Down at Cannes, along the bikini strip, there's a night club called Moulin Rouge where a British girl named Trixie Kent from Liverpool shucks her clothes each evening and then takes a bubble bath.

A couple of Americans tried to get in the tub with her one evening we went over there.

Not very chic.

And if you're interested in this display of feminine hygiene, a drink will cost you about three bucks but man, don't holler foul. It's not like Sonny Liston and Cassius Clay where you thought you might get something legitimate.

The top restaurants are expensive. Places like Tour d'Argent,

Ledoyen, Maxim's, Fouquet's, and such serve the finest food you'll ever eat. The chances are excellent that half the people in these restaurants are Frenchmen. They understand what they are getting.

The check will run to $25 or so a person.

You won't get out any better at the Four Seasons in New York or Ernie's in San Francisco or the Chop House in Detroit but you're eating awfully well, if you care about that sort of thing.

I think a factor with visiting Americans who depart weeping over their expenses is that in nearly every other country you attend, when you get through changing dollars for crowns, or kroner, or guilders or pesetas or lira, you find you've gotten the best of it.

In France, you get 4.85 francs for a dollar. All right, so what is a franc worth. I'll tell you. At a corner ice cream stand, you can buy an ice cream cone for a franc.

In other words, a tourist is used to getting things cheaper in foreign places and in France he is operating about on the same basis as he does at home . . . for hotels, taxis, meals, clothes, and everything else.

A thing I enjoy about some of the clips . . . and they are obvious ones as I've mentioned . . . is the flair with which the French perform them.

For example, take Alexandre. Alexandre's is a beauty salon where Jacqueline Kennedy, Brigitte Bardot, and some have their hair broiled.

A lady I know wrote from the states for an appointment.

I saw a woman buy another's woman's appointment and go to the shop as Mrs. Overstreet instead of Mrs. Middleburg, who she really was.

Can you imagine?

Well I might as well come right out with it.

Alexandre opened a joint for men's coiffeurs the other day and what with one thing and another a renegade friend of mine talked me into going over and getting gone over.

"What can you lose?" he insisted.

It took two hours and what I could lose turned out to be eighteen clams.

I think they cut my hair longer.

If there's a lesson here and there is someday I'll learn that you shouldn't necessarily do something just because there's no reason not to do it.

However, there was a moment during the proceedings when there was a cute little French doll in culottes giving me a manicure, while another, similarly clad, was giving me a pedicure while a third was giving me a facial massage.

Oh yes, and in my free hand I held a glass of champagne.

A clip? Well, you knew it anyway.

And as the renegade and I agreed afterward, it was a long way from the poolroom.

One of my bosses is named O'Brien and when he found out I was pausing in Dublin along the way, he was recalling a trip he once made to what must have been the auld sod to him and recounting how he laughed all the time.

There was a particular evening in a pub and he heard noises of physical dispute over the wall from the family side and stood on a table to look down and see a short and tall pair of Irishmen squared off, with the barkeep admonishing the smaller of the two.

"Don't 'it 'im, Paddy, 'e's dronk."

"Shurr," replied Paddy, "but I didn't get 'im dronk."

Pow!

I was thinking about it here in Dublin when Sean Murphy, the turf writer for a paper called *The People* and adviser to the stable affairs of Dale Shaffer, was accepting a drink.

"Shurr. I haven't had one since before the Holy Hour."

The pubs are closed for an hour each afternoon as a nod to the church.

You don't really laugh all the time, but there is an atmosphere of constant hilarity which is infectious and despite Sean's insistence that "it won't work here because this is a different place," they installed one-way streets in Dublin.

But it was peat burning in the fireplaces in the hotel and the statue of Lord Nelson still stood high on O'Connell Street then and there are no windows in the Bank of Ireland.

"There were taxes on windows, taxes to the English. So they just bricked over the windows," explained Paddy Champion, the driver, as we passed. "We call it the blind bank because you can't see what goes on inside."

"I see they haven't torn Nelson down yet."

"Taxes again," declaimed Champion heatedly. "It would cost the taxpayers of Dublin more than any Englishman was ever worth." He sucked in his breath in a great effort at control. "So there he remains."

Shaffer, who is an Irelandophile, says, "We don't think of it as backward . . . We think of all this as something constant."

Constant, certainly, are their heroes . . . in a moment there was a filling station passed named after Parnell, the patriot . . . and shortly thereafter we stood on the Curragh watching the horses work in pairs over the rolling turf.

A big bay two years old thundered by.

"Dan Donnelly," said Shaffer pridefully.

Now he had fallen for an Irish tradition I knew.

Dan Donnelly or rather I should say Sir Dan, since he was the only prize fighter ever knighted, was the finest bare knuckle fist fighter Ireland or perhaps the world ever produced. Nat Fleischer numbers him among sixty-one parties in Boxing's Hall of Fame.

There was a moment to stand and look the five uphill furlongs to the finish of the Curragh Course and be glad that you weren't a horse, at the same time understanding why a colt or mare that wins there at a two mile distance is worthy for breeding the world over.

And then we were at Donnelly's Hollow.

Understand that we are speaking of no Danny-come-lately.

Donnelly was born in 1788 and Lord Byron wrote of him at the time of his death thirty-two years later.

> "He won it in a field where arms are none
> Save those the mother gave to us. He was
> A shining star . . ."

You think the heroes die easily.

On May 12, 1965, there was a full page by writer Alan Walk in the Dublin *Evening Herald* on Donnelly.

The third sentence I thought interesting.

"He became a carpenter and until the age of twenty-six lived a normal life—working, drinking, and fighting!"

A horse trainer named Captain Kelly found Donnelly fighting in a saloon, fighting everybody, taking no sides, merely belting away until he was the last man standing.

History records that his arms were so long he could button his knee breeches without bending down. Kelly took him off to a farm, trained him and taught him and sobered him and then he licked the Irish gladiator Tom Hall at the Hollow and then a top Englishman named George Cooper, breaking his jaw with the final punch.

A tablet records these events and I walked in Donnelly's footsteps, still preserved, the ones in which he walked out of the Hollow.

He went to England and fought all comers and when the Prince Regent (later George IV) remarked, "I am glad to meet the best man in Ireland," Dan countered with, "but I'm the best in England."

We had repaired now to the nearest saloon, a place called the Hideout, and owner Jimmy Byrne was talking about the horse Dan Donnelly with Shaffer and everyone was drinking the horse well.

"And," said Byrne, "would ya loike to see Dan's arm?"

He went and got it from its glass case, what a fellow at the bar called, "Danny's pickled arm."

The story goes that after Donnelly's burial at Bully's Acre, Kilmainham, a Dublin surgeon named Hall hired a group of medical students to steal the body so he could study it.

There was rioting in the streets of Dublin over this sacrilege.

A compromise was reached:

Hall could keep the arm, the rest of the remains went back to the cemetery.

At Hall's death, the arm was sold to a traveling "peep show." A century later, it was returned to Ireland where eventually it was purchased by Byrne for the Hideout, not a mile from Donnelly's Hollow.

Like Ireland, there's some of this arm business that you take on faith.

But as Steinbeck once said, "A story is not necessarily a lie just because it didn't necessarily happen."

Last night I watched the sun go down on Galway Bay.

To walk farther on, you must have heard the song about Galway Bay or be just a simple sentimentalist. Of course, an Irisher gets a pass.

There is this song:

> "If you ever go across the sea to Ireland,
>   And especially at the closing of each day,
>   You can sit and see the sunrise over Cleta
>   And watch the sun go down on Galway Bay."

It has been many years and many promises made to many Irishers . . . professional and otherwise . . . that one day I would get to Galway and I would file a story that began with the tag line of this offering.

OK. So the sun went down.

There was a while when I thought I'd come all these thousand miles to this ridiculous town and it was going to cloud up.

What good a song with no sundown?

The girl I married in Italy ten years ago walked around the town with me. We walked and stood over the Weir Bridge and watched the whitecaps over the rocks.

There were white birds downstream and we went down to look at them. An Irish couple was walking up from them and you could ask:

"What are they?"

"Swans," they said, their hands locked in affection.

A horse cart winged by.

"Maybe we could hire one of those and ride around," said my girl.

"Those are tinkers," said the Irish guy. "Don't mess with 'em. They come to Galway every year at this time to elect their king. In the world they call them gypsies. They'll stick a knife in you."

The swans glided gently into the river.

Galway is a different Ireland.

The people walk the streets speaking Gaelic.

After leaving the swans, I went into a pub to ask if "women" ah, er "my wife" would be allowed to have a pint. There were four people at the bar who didn't look up and one bartender who didn't notice my presence.

"I said," shouting a little, "could my wife quench her thirst in here?"

No one moved. But the bartender did take about a 12-inch knife from below and plunged it into the bar. But his eyes never moved.

The language was Gaelic among them.

In the song are the lines:

"The strangers came and tried to teach us their ways,
        And scorned us just for being what we are."

No strangers were allowed.

The next morning as we drove out of Galway, we encountered a funeral.

No automobiles were involved.

Here were six sweating Gaels carrying the box down the highway. A hundred pedestrians followed. Some wore hats. Others carried them.

Paddy Champion, the driver, remarked, "He was either very popular or he had a lot of creditors."

He had slowed for the procession.

After a moment, Paddy said:

"Well, anyway, he won't care who wins the Epsom Derby this afternoon."

33. babies

"What you are then is a baby factory, eh, Connie?"

She didn't act very favorably to this comment, which was born somewhere out of a new cynicism, which is a defense mechanism of mine against any new racket that I hear of, particularly one that seemed as amoral as this one.

Connie is now nineteen years old and is pregnant for the third time in successive years. She is going to have a baby within the next couple of months. And then presumably she'll start all over again.

Both her previous babies were sold at birth on the black market for children to parents unable to have their own.

She began her business innocently, merely by becoming accidentally pregnant. She collected money for an abortion from the man she believed to be the father. She spent the money and pretty soon was too far along for an abortion.

She met a shyster lawyer, or a benevolent lawyer, or a do-gooder lawyer trying to help prospective parents, depending on how you want to characterize him, who arranged the sale of the baby to a young couple for $1000.

With the $200 she had collected from the father, that made $1200 and so a new business was, no pun intended, born.

She went to the Bahamas on an extended vacation with the money, she was impregnated again while on vacation.

When she returned to Detroit she knew a little more about her new business so she began frolicking with one of the athletic teams here in town, frolicking as busily as possible, so she had more potential fathers to place the blame on this time.

She collected from half dozen guys this time. She was obviously pregnant and the married ones in her new clan were eager to pay for an abortion.

The second baby was sold, by the same attorney, for $1500 with the father named to the prospective parents. She is a rather attractive girl and the man named was prominent in athletic circles, which accounted, according to the attorney, for the rise in price.

The attorney gets a list of names of prospective parents through one of the adoption agencies here in town. They must agree to pay all hospital bills, plus the price of the baby.

In the case of the third child, she has already realized more from the abortion fees than ever before.

"I got smart, I realized that there was no point in playing with a whole team, which is what I did before." Taking ordinary people, who don't think girls owe them something, chances for a killing in fees are better.

This time she had a young stockbroker, a used car salesman, a guy who works for the telephone company, a steel worker, a baker, all of them married, plus one single athlete, one clothing salesman, and one florist, all of these single but, "take my money and have an abortion. I don't want to get married" types.

She's collected $3600 in abortion fees alone.

The rates have gone up since she collected that first $200, a couple of years back. Now she tries for $500 each time and the stockbroker got sentimental and went for $800.

The florist rebelled and punched her in the mouth, loosening a couple of teeth. She let him alone after that.

Now if she peddles the child, for maybe $3000, which her fellow the attorney thinks is feasible, she will realize $6600 for her share of the deal. She explains it this way:

"It's easy having a baby. And even kind of fun. And the money is all tax-free."

She then said one thing, very seriously, that turned me off completely.

"I insist that the parents raise the babies as Catholics. They sign a paper agreeing to that. They wouldn't break their word, would they, after signing a paper?"

"I don't know. You're a factory, all right, but you don't give any warranties. Ask your attorney. Incidentally, what's his cut?"

She laughed in answer.

The conversation was over.

She has just had her third baby and sold it, not for $6600 she had hoped to gain from the sale, but $5500. She collected $3600 in abortion fees from all the many potential fathers. However, the $3000 she had hoped to gain from the sale to the parents did not materialize.

The parents paid her $2500 and she paid her attorney, who arranged the sale $600.

She has now met a young fellow named Aubrey and she's in love.

She met Aubrey while she was in her eighth month of pregnancy. As a matter of fact, she is so much in love, she says, that she tried to back out of delivering the child to the parents who had bid for it. She and Aubrey wanted to keep it for themselves.

However, the attorney prevailed upon her to keep her word.

And the baby, a 6½-pound boy, was delivered to the parents.

She and Aubrey are now planning on marriage and a family of their own.

Connie will be twenty next month.

There's another girl, named Rita, who is now also in her eighth month of pregnancy. She lives in one of these modern communes, where people drift in and out of the place all the time, living there for a while and then moving out.

Rita went to a friend of mine, who recently miscarried for the fifth time, and offered her baby for adoption.

My friend discussed it with her husband, who said:

"I'm a great believer in genetics and I do not want a child by a girl who couldn't even keep track of the other members of the commune," and there the matter rested.

She, too, has a new boy friend, who does not seem to mind at all that she is pregnant.

Talk about a generation gap.

I have to plead guilty to the fact that when I was in my early 20's any pregnant woman had obviously already been not only spoken for but declared for and it would never have occurred to me to become interested in her romantically.

This was true of everyone I knew.

All that has to happen now is for Rita to begin to get ideas from the world of Connie and come to me about putting her on an attorney, and I bow out of this whole business.

The thing that wrestles me about it is that I like all four of them, find them intelligent, charming and seemingly without guile whatsoever.

I now know four different pregnant girls just since I wrote about Connie. Two of them aren't sure who the father is. Two of them are sure but are going ahead with the babies and apparently have no interest in marriage.

Connie and Aubrey are two of the nicest, most pleasant people it has been my fortune to run across.

"You never really approved of the cold-blooded way I had those three children. I know. I can tell. Well, there's not going to be any abortion money or anything this time. Aubrey is going to look after me and the new baby just as soon as we get married."

"Have you set a date yet?"

"No, but it'll be pretty soon, don't you think, Aubrey?"

"Real soon," said Aubrey.

34. girls and boys

A guy who has a secretary who doesn't fall in love with him is apt to be something of a jerk, or else he has a secretary who is not in his age bracket.

Here are two of them, thrown together in business, with both of them deeming the business important, and the secretary will think of the things they do as significant.

One day there is a business triumph and she gives the credit to her boss. There's a certain dancing around the desk and then suddenly they fall into one another's arms. The next thing they're out for a drink, then out for dinner and then out together.

This is the story of bosses and secretaries, unless there's a difference between them in age or in character, which is difficult to maintain nowadays.

I offer here the tale of Tony and Marty . . . that is Martha, actually, he in his thirties, she in her twenties. He is married, no children. She is not.

Not yet anyway.

Tony and Marty work for one of the big advertising agencies.

Their relationship is complicated by the fact that he is white and she is Negro.

Not that there was any feeling between them about their race.

As a matter of fact, in the eleven months that they worked together, there has disappeared any feeling of discomfort.

If there ever was any. This is my own feeling.

Tony set out after a new account about three months ago.

Last week he landed it for his agency.

The rejoicing was rampant, and that was the day Tony and Marty melded.

"Baby . . . baby, I'm so happy for you," she said . . . they said.

They were in the agency bar with the rest of the staff celebrating.

Then they were alone and then they were finally, really . . . alone.

The next day Marty was reluctant and Tony overrode it all.

"Look, I meant it all," said Tony.

"You don't have to say that," said Marty. "It's nice of you but you don't have to say that. It was just one of those things, that's all. We were excited is another thing."

"No, Marty," said Tony. "It was the real thing. I love you, Marty. Don't talk about any of the rest of it. Give me a little time and I'll ask my wife for a divorce and then we'll get married."

"Gee, Tony, you're so extra special wonderful," answered Marty.

Since then they have been going out together every afternoon and it sounds to me as if they're in love all right.

Tony is nervous though about his job.

The head of the agency doesn't approve of any interracial marriages in the firm.

"Look, we all like Martha, Tony," says the boss. "But she was hired here to integrate the agency, not to integrate the company. Shall I fire her on your account? Maybe that's what I better do. Give her two weeks and her walking papers."

"Oh, no, Mr. ——, I'll take my severance and then give her her two weeks. Let's put this matter straight. I'm not welshing on this girl, you understand."

"I don't want to seem peremptory about this, Tony. But what I said about integrating the firm is for real. You've got to understand that."

Tony and Marty keep going out and they keep attracting attention everywhere they go. More and more all the time. It's beginning to matter a bit more to Tony each day. He's talking about starting his own agency now.

He's not quitting on Marty, anyway, for what that's worth.

I ran into Tony later while he was waiting for Marty.

"How goes it," was a simple inquiry.

"Taking up where we left off, it goes pretty well," he answered. "Marty has quit the agency which takes some of the pressure off. I've left my wife. We'll get a divorce as soon as she realizes I'm serious.

"I'm still working the big account and the boss doesn't talk to me much these days. I spoke to you last time about starting my own agency. You would put it in the paper. What it came down to was the new account wanted me *and* the agency on it. After all, that's the way I'd sold it to them.

"Their attitude is we'd better straighten out at the agency. In other words, they got a jolt right at the beginning which was bad. Some of their directors wanted another agency, and they immediately started hollering about losing me from the account.

"Therefore I'm working like crazy on the account and so is the agency. My boss doesn't say much to me about Marty. He's waiting to see what'll happen."

"How about your ex-wife and you? How's she doing?"

"Pretty good I guess, I've had a couple of luncheons with her. She doesn't really accept Marty and me yet. Marty's race bothers her a little. I think that's helped some. She's horrified about it. I think that'll help her get over me."

"Then do you think you'll be able to stay with the agency or not?" I asked.

"Maybe your boss realizes he needs you and what you do with your private life doesn't mean anything?"

"I'd like to think that were true. Except he was so God-fearing and sanctimonious about us—me and Marty—when it happened. He'll have to come down a long way from his high horse."

"Maybe he will. How're you doing with your ex on money?"

"Pretty good, I'm giving her a weekly allowance."

"Make sure it's enough. You haven't got a leg to stand on legally."

"I know that. It seems like a lot to me. I'll tell you what I'm giving her. $150 per week. And the house, of course; that's $250 per month. She's doing OK."

"Does she think so?"

"I hope so. That's a lot of bread for a gal with no kids. I've told Marty that we've got to give it to her and that's that."

At this point, Marty showed up.

She's not one of these high yellow girls where you need an Indian guide to tell whether she's a Negro or not. She is a nice chocolate color and pretty as the dickens.

"How are you?" she asked politely.

"Fine, thanks. And you? I gather you're all right from what Tony tells me."

"Just sparkling, thank you, just sparkling."

"We were talking about Tony's allowance to his ex-wife," I said. Her face clouded for an instant.

"She gets too much," she said matter-of-factly.

"You can't mean that," I said.

"I do," she said.

Right after that I left, but wondering all the time how long they could keep it up when they disagreed in this fundamental point.

They were starting to argue a little as I left.

Tony and Marty left town.

Tony brought in a new account at the agency and the next thing you knew they'd put another account executive on it with him. When he objected, his boss and he got into a real hoedown about the involvement between him and his ex-secretary, Martha, or Marty as he calls her.

"You're making a great mistake, Tony," said his boss. "Not only here at the office, but in your private life, too. I will decide who runs the accounts around here. You have decided you're an indispensable man and you're not."

"I don't like that remark about my private life. That's what it is, though . . . private."

"Look, Tony, it's time we had a little straightforward man-to-man talk about the black girl you've thrown over your wife for."

"All I want to know from you, at this point, is do I get my severance pay? I'm not quitting. You're firing me and what makes you so sure that Joe can keep the new account happy?"

The accountant was duly summoned and a check issued to Tony.

"Let me worry about the account," remarked his boss. "That's what I've been doing all my life, worrying about accounts. This won't be a new experience, thank you. And let me tell you that I think you've botched up your life terribly. I'm sorry about what I called her. But it's true. And wherever you go, you'll find out it's true. Have you noticed any cooling off among your friends since you and Marty have started twoing it? Of course you have."

"Not among my real friends, I haven't. How many of those do you get in a lifetime anyway? Two or three. Most of it's like having loyalty to an ad agency like this one. It doesn't mean a thing in the end."

Both men were white-faced at the end of the conversation.

Anyway, Tony took his check, which amounted to about $4000, and tried to make a cash settlement with his wife, at which point he was confronted by her lawyer. She is suing him for divorce on the grounds of desertion and naming Marty as correspondent.

In the confusing couple of days that followed, Tony was on the phone most of the time, looking for another job. He finally got one, for less money in Chicago.

He cut off the payments to his wife and banked the severance pay. He hired his own lawyer and the two legal adversaries are battling it out.

A judge must decide how much his wife has coming. She has no children but has been a stay-at-home housewife for the seven years they've been married. She has lived well.

Tony left for Chicago. For a thirty-two-year-old he is plenty excited, not only about his new job, which he plans to develop into something big, but about his new life, too.

Tony feels that Chicago is a bigger city and a wiser one than Detroit and that he'll be accepted there without any problems. The agency is familiar with his marital problems and feels that he's entitled to a new and clean start. They plan on giving it to him.

35. jokes

The way the subject turned onto the anatomy of a joke happened when a friend named Ken McCormick, in response to a casual, "How've you been?" answered, "OK, but I had dinner last night with a compulsive joke teller and I haven't gotten over it yet."

Chronic joke narrators will actually set my nerves jangling.

Worse than having one joke bore, and I'm sure you've had it happen to you, is the party group where one guy has to tell you the funny story he's just heard. He will barely finish when a second party will tell one. Then the third fellow has to put his story up.

They are invariably terrible stories, poorly told and remind always of what the late Malcolm Bingay said, "Pour on a little booze and all men think they're comedians."

When the round robin of amateur story tellers begins, I depart, on the theory that folks who have to have the dialogue jerry-built aren't going to inject a thought toward you ever.

The awful truth though is that I love jokes . . . funny jokes, which is the only requisite. Smutty jokes are rarely funny and seem to depend on the smut as a humorous component, which it almost never is.

"The thing that always fascinates me," said Ken, "is who keeps supplying the never-ending wellspring of jokes."

"Well most of them are the same stories with switches on them. Although did you ever notice that there are good joke years and ordinary or bad years. Vintage years, like with wine."

"Yes, or with popular songs," he added.

"The best year I remember was 1954 . . . I think it was 1954. It produced those two great stories. One of them was the one about the Martians landing in the farmyard and the chief Martian looked all around at the farmer, his wife and the animals, then walked up to the cow and said, 'Take me to your leader.'

"And the other one was about the wheeler-dealer in Tel Aviv, right after Israel was formed, explaining that the way to achieve quick success was to declare war on the United States, lose, and become the automatic recipient of lend-lease, farm surplus, etc., and the little guy in the corner asked, 'Yes, but what if we win?'

"Remember, they made a movie called *The Mouse That Roared* out of it. A real vintage year."

Over lunch he remarked, "You know how jokes spread so quickly? A guy tells a story in Los Angeles and in fifteen minutes they're telling it in New York. The stock market. They put it on the tape between quotations, or used to anyway."

"I didn't know about that, but when Western Union had the old Morse operators, all of them were horse players and if one of 'em got a tip, he'd pass it all over the country and ruin the price."

Bennett Cerf has been putting out anthologies of humor ever since *Try and Stop Me* and has recently produced one called *Laugh Day*.

He tells about vaudevillian Bobby Clark, whose waiter hovers solicitously over him with "How's the soup, sir?" And Bobby answers, "To tell the truth I'm sorry I stirred it."

After a while Ken turned and said: "You're all right about the switches and I'll tell you one you used a duplicate of not long ago, quoting Eleanor Roosevelt and you'll swear you've got it right to the end."

"Shoot."

"Well, there was this GI who arrived in Vietnam, fresh from the States and all decked out with new equipment so he resembled a recruiting poster. His commanding officer took him aside and said, 'Look, all that stuff you learned back in the States . . . forget it.'

" 'The way you fight over here you seek out a piece of jungle you think might have some Viet Cong in it. Then you shout:

"To hell with Mao Tse-tung." A Viet Cong will pop up and then you shoot him.'

"A day later he encountered the fresh GI. His equipment was tattered and bent, one arm was in a sling, he lost his helmet and there was blood caked on his face and he was limping.

" 'You didn't do what I told you,' growled the CO.

" 'Yes I did,' said the GI. 'I found a piece of jungle, like you said and I shouted like you told me. A Viet Cong jumped up, but before I could shoot him, he shouted, "To hell with LBJ."

" 'Then we stepped into the road to shake hands and a truck ran over both of us.' "

It would have been nice to have another vintage year.

36. wander

The whole point of this wander to Paris, aside from my personal enjoyment of a wander whatever the excuse, was to beat Christmas just once. Each year I get so sick of having Santa Claus shoved down my throat, the endless din of Christmas carols, all the streets strewn with holly, you know.

One day the girl I live with had a tremendous idea.

"Why don't we go to Moscow for Christmas?"

"What's that again?" I stammered.

"You know how you get so awful every year at Christmas time. Well, let's go to Moscow. Here is a noncapitalistic country, a non-Christian country if you please. I won't have to listen to you, wanting to write bah, humbug, or hanging Santa in effigy on the roof. Cripes, it's a wonder our neighbors don't band together with a 'Get out the Greenes' march. Everybody has a moratorium about something. 'Get out the Greenes' is next."

"OK so we're on our way to Moscow for Christmas."

I remarked to Les Gruber, over at the Chop House of my intentions.

"Very interesting," he said. "I can personally guarantee you a white Christmas, if without jingle bells. It gets colder than hell in Moscow. I know, I was there with the Archives of American Art one year in October. It got so cold in Kiev we all went to bed with our overcoats on."

The girl I live with mapped our itinerary and as usual, the first stop turned out to be Paris, where she promptly went shopping.

Paris is a very commercial place, as you've heard, of course.

However, except for one block of streets which a designer designed for Christmas there was practically no commercialisn attuned to Noel.

I personally sneaked out to Hermes, figuring that I better come up with a Christmas present for her. There were no Christmas displays in any of the stores, no department store Santas, no carols drumming at you.

Nowhere in Paris did we see any houses with Christmas decorations. The French apparently have never been instilled with changing the decor of a village about in the interest of Yule.

It seemed kind of a shame, too. You could really decorate the Eiffel Tower if you had a mind to.

One thing happend though.

It concerned a recent column that appeared on suicide.

At the time, I mentioned that suicides were no big deal to me. Everybody who has ever threatened me with suicide has always received the immediate rejoinder, "Be my guest." I consider that people who threaten the general populace with suicide are an invasion on the rest of our privacy. The news that some friend has done away with himself leaves me completely without feeling.

However, when we got to Paris, I called the Relais du Porquerolle, which is a famous restaurant and an old favorite of mine, renowned for its bouillabaisse, a Mediterranean fish stew, made famous in Marseilles.

I discovered that Alain Zick, the famous chef at the Relais, had committed suicide in the fall of 1967 after the Michelin Tire Co. had failed to renew the two stars they had been awarding the restaurant for the quality of this same bouillabaisse.

The restaurant had been started by the parents of the Zick brothers, who were from Marseilles. Gradually, they had inched their way up to where they got one star from Michelin, then finally two.

Then as Michelin giveth, Michelin suddenly "tooketh" away. Alain took a shotgun and ended his own life over it.

Now the Relais has closed its doors. The new joint is named La Menandiere. Its food is fair but there is no more bouillabaisse.

It occurs to me somewhat belatedly that had Dr. Bruce Danto had his suicide prevention center here in Paris, instead of Detroit, he might have caught Alain Zick before he could have pulled the trigger.

This would have made Dr. Danto feel very gratified.

Also I could have had my fish soup.

Although it was Mr. Zick's privilege.

It is always better to wait a couple of days after leaving Russia before attempting to evaluate what you have seen.

Your tendency is always a comparison with America, but is this fair when actually the new Russia is only fifty years old?

So many vague impressions clutter the mind. But is it important that the buildings are so drab, so unkempt the furniture, so yellowishly the same?

Is it important that elderly women do the snow removal? Why does the absolute deification of V. I. Lenin in an otherwise non-religious country upset one so?

Everyone seems to be working—of sorts. There are many more automobiles on the streets than when I was there ten years ago. Yet the shops still seem bereft of goods to buy.

There is obviously not a decent tailor nor suit manufacturer in the whole country. But does this really matter if the people are fed and housed and clothed after a fashion?

Emil Gilels, the famous pianist, who holds the Order of Lenin, is provided with so-called luxuries of a car and an apartment that is sufficiently large for him and his family.

Yet why does he make allusions, as he did at the airport, "This is our Kennedy Airport?" And the rest of the self-deprecating gestures that you find from him and others who have visited the States?

People accept tips more than they used to, which is a common evaluation. The only ones who do not are the young. Is this significant?

Aren't we ourselves coming to all this in reverse with our talk of guaranteed incomes, our ever-increasing welfare rolls, our medicare and our rising social security?

Are the unions doing to our country what a revolution did to Russia with constant equalization of the incomes between capital and labor?

These are all questions that constantly encroach on your

consciousness. Certain conclusions present themselves. There is not a waiter or waitress or shopgirl in Russia who could hold a job in the United States.

Where in France they say "Dinner is a slow thing because food must be lovingly prepared," in Russia they say "Dinner is infuriatingly slow because of the terrible service."

Both statements are true.

Russia, because of the guidelines upon which it oparates, is a gigantic bureaucracy, with all the efficiency that implies.

Imagine a country in which everything is run by civil service? Not a very prepossessing thought, is it?

The girl I live with, who is now more capitalistic than ever, says that she can't dig a country where there is no Kleenex, no panty hose, where the paper in the toilet is like it came off the inside of a corrugated paper box, where you can buy no aspirins, no Coca-Cola or no bubble-bath.

She put it:

"Look, at Porthaults in our country, you can buy sheets for $280 a pair. I may never purchase any, but it's nice to know I can if I choose to."

Of course, she is luxury-oriented. Still I wonder why the Russian government doesn't steal the formula of Coca-Cola and manufacture and sell it.

They would make millions, as has been proven all over the world.

Then they could claim to have invented something else.

Instead, they sell you lemonade, which is terrible.

Still, there don't seem to be any ghettos nor Appalachias in the country.

If they exist, tourists would not likely see them.

It is not, though, a country in which an American dropped suddenly, would be very happy.

One of the reasons for this is that there is nothing to dream about. Their ballet is superlative, yet their television is absymal.

Talk, talk, talk is all you get. Talk and puppet shows for the kiddies.

How they can succeed so beautifully in ballet and so ruinously on television requires some doing.

I am reminded of Gilels' wife, who is a TV addict when she

visits our country, despite her halting English. She often remains in the hotel room, glued to the TV set.

The trouble with an American in Russia is that he would assiduously have to lower his standard of living, which he would not like.

The Russians don't like it either. They are forever trying to buy your shoes or clothes from you and the kids beg you for chewing gum.

The standard of living is rising, however, and, in another fifty years, it still won't be close to ours, but it will be closer than at the moment.

Maybe, judging from what all Russians inevitably ask you— "How many cars do you have? What kind? Do you live in a house? In the city?"—what they really want is to live like Americans.

editor's note:

Doc Greene met Cassius Clay at the Olympic Games in Rome in 1960 when Clay won his medal. It had bothered Doc that Clay had been refused the right to fight in several states although the case against Clay had not been settled. As long as he was a free man Doc saw no reason why Clay should be denied the right to fight. A November 1969 column of Red Smith's triggered Doc's next move which was to see if a Frazer-Clay fight could not be arranged in Michigan. It took months to get permission for the fight in the course of which Doc was fired from the Detroit *News* for "involvement," although as long as he was with the *News* Doc had no part of the promotion or piece of the action. This piece, written for a newspaper syndicate a few days before his death, tells what happened.

As I was saying before I was so rudely interrupted, Cassius Clay is no different than dozens of non-names and luminaries whose court cases are on appeal and he should be permitted to fight somewhere.

As I see it, it's sort of what our country is all about. Until his last appeal is denied and he is jailed Cassius is entitled to pursue his profession and earn a living.

If he were a plumber he'd still be plumbing, if he ran your neighborhood delicatessen he'd still be running it, or if he were Louis Miriani he'd still be going to City Council meetings.

To quote Charles Davey, the Michigan boxing commissioner, "I have no right to act as judge and jury" in the case of Cassius, "nor has any other boxing commissioner."

It's what Red Smith called the "Vigilante" system where anyone who does not see Clay's duty the same way he does has a right to throw rocks at him.

You and I can have our opinions but it's up to those fellows in the black robes to sock it to him or not.

That isn't, though, what Davey had to say officially in the matter.

Davey told the press that the promoters, of which I was one (after the Detroit *News* summarily fired me for approaching the governor on the matter, I had not been one before that time), "put together an unacceptable package" for the promotion.

However, on Friday evening, July 17, Davey had been proud of the "package" we'd put together. The corporation had been expanded to include a group of community-representative people and most important to him, nobody was going to make a pot of gold on the fight. This was all right with Jerry Cavanagh, the former mayor and my legal representative in this, and me.

I signed a paper that afternoon guaranteeing that the first $100,000 made on the fight would accrue to future boxing promotions and that 50 percent of the total revenue would also be used for future boxing efforts in Michigan.

Shucks, with grade school arithmetic you can tell that no one fellow was going to be "rich beyond the dreams of avarice" in this one.

Davey was delighted with the package.

Davey said in the press that he would not license Clay.

In the preliminary negotiotions for the fight, Clay was not extremely interested since he had been embarrassed by numerous commissions and governors. As a result I took a license for him to fight in Michigan to New York to give him.

A photostat of that license appears here.

Clay wasn't at the meeting that day in New York so the Sports

Action, Inc. people photostated the license to show him and assuage his feelings.

Back in Detroit I returned the document to the commissioner's office. If Clay had been there he'd have it now to frame for his basement.

All of this is sort of beside the point now but on that Friday evening, July 17, Governor Milliken called Davey and told him he had changed his mind. He told him to summon his board (there are five members besides Davey) and make "damn sure every man knows my position" before he took a vote.

This was despite the fact that I have a letter from Milliken in which he concludes, "If Davey is satisfied with the fight projection, I shall not oppose the bout."

I've been trying to see him, to ask him why he changed his mind, ever since. He's awfully busy now on the campaign trail.

It's naïve to believe a politician has only his word—most of them go back on their word some time or another. Some explain why, some don't.

Somewhere along the trail, Milliken changed his mind.

I think the word I'm looking for is "expediency," the mother of the double cross.

MICHIGAN STATE ATHLETIC BOARD OF CONTROL

Professional Nº **131**

BOXER

THIS IS TO CERTIFY THAT

Muhammad Ali OF

, IS A DULY LICENSED Pro. Boxer
UNDER THE PROVISIONS OF ACT 205 OF THE PUBLIC ACTS OF 1939.

EXPIRES 6-23-71 Charles P. Davey
Charles P. CHAIRMAN Davey

Leonard T. McCarthy
Leonard T. SECRETARY McCarthy

7